P9-EME-727

A SAMPLING OF CHICAGO IN THE TWENTIETH CENTURY

# CHAOS, CREATIVITY, AND CULTURE

CHICAGO

A SAMPLING OF CHICAGO IN THE TWENTIETH CENTURY

# CHAOS, CREATIVITY, AND CULTURE

KENAN HEISE

GIBBS·SMITH
PUBLISHER

SALT LAKE CITY

First Edition

01 00 99 98  4 3 2 1

This is Peregrine Smith Book,
Published by Gibbs Smith, Publisher
P.O. Box 667
Layton, UT  84041

Designed by Scott Van Kampen
Edited by Gail Yngve

The front cover photograph is by Bill Engdahl/Hedrich-Blessing.
It is used courtesy of the Chicago Historical Society.

Printed and bound in Asia

Library of Congress Cataloging-in-Publication Data

Heise, Kenan.
Chaos, creativity, and culture: an anthology of Chicago in the
20th century / by Kenan Heise. — 1st ed.
p.  cm.
ISBN 0–87905–054–3
1. Chicago (Ill.)—History—1875 —Miscellanea. 2. Chicago
(Ill.)—Social life and customs—Miscellanea. 3. Chicago (Ill.)—
Biography—Miscellanea. I. Title
F548.5.h46  1998
977.3'11—dc21     97–42326
CIP

Some works in this anthology appeared originally in the following publications: The Floyd Dell essay on Dreiser is quoted with permission from *Floyd Dell: Essays from the Friday Literary Review*, edited by R. Craig Sautter. (December Press, 1995). The comments by Clarence A. Andrews on *The Jungle* are used with the permission of the author. The quote on *The Plan of Chicago* from *Lost Chicago*, by David Lowe is copyright © 1975 by David Lowe and is reprinted with permission of Houghton Mifflin Company. All rights reserved. *My Thirty Years War: An Autobiography*, by Margaret Anderson, (Alfred A. Knopf, 1930) is quoted here by permission. The excerpt from *So Big*, by Edna Ferber, (Doubleday, Page & Co., 1924) is used with permission from her estate. Material from *Big Bill of Chicago*, by Lloyd Wendt and Herman Kogan, (The Bobbs-Merrill Co., 1953) is quoted here by permission of Lloyd Wendt and Marilew Kogan. The material from the *Power of Black Music*, by Samuel Floyd Jr., is copyright © of Samuel Floyd Jr. and is used with permission of Oxford University Press, 1995. The Studs Lonigan excerpt is from *The Short Stories of James T. Farrell*, by James T. Farrell, (The Vanguard Press, Inc. 1934, 1935, and 1937.) *The Old Bunch*, by Meyer Levin is from (The Citadel Press, 1937). *How "Bigger" Was Born*, by Richard Wright, (Harper & Brothers, 1940); copyright renewed in 1973 by Ellen Wright. The excerpt from Ira Berkow, an author and sports columnist for the *New York Times*, is from his *Maxwell Street*, (Doubleday and Company, 1977) and is quoted with permission of the author. *Black Boy*, by Richard Wright, (Harper & Brothers, 1945); the copyright was renewed in 1973 by Ellen Wright. Reprinted by permission of Harper Collins Publishers Inc.. The pages quoted from *Mies van der Rohe: A Critical Biography* (The University of Chicago Press, 1985) and *Fantastic Images: Chicago Art Since 1945* (Follette Publishing Co. 1972) are used here with permission of the author Franz Shulze. The quotations from *The Good War*, by Studs Terkel, (Pantheon Books, 1984) is used with permission of the author. Material from *Chicago City on the Make*, by Nelson Algren, (Doubleday & Co., 1951) and *Who Lost an American?* by Nelson Algren, (The Macmillan Company, 1960, 1961, 1962, 1963) is copyright 1951, 1963 Estate of Nelson Algren and is used by permission of Donadio & Alsworth, Inc.; the pages quoted from *Chicago: The Second City*, A. J. Liebling (Alfred A. Knopf, 1952) are used with permission. *Major Campaign Speeches* and *Call to Greatness*, by Adlai Stevenson, (Random House, 1953). *Veeck As in Wreck*, by Bill Veeck with Ed Linn, (G. P. Putnam's Sons, 1962) is used with permission from Mary Frances Veeck and Ed Linn. *Something Wonderful Right Away*, by Jeffrey Sweet, (Avon Books, 1978). *A Raisin in the Sun*, by Lorraine Hansberry, (Copyright, 1951). The excerpt from the novel *A Dream of Kings* (David McKay Company, Inc., 1966) is © copyright Harry Mark Petrakis and is used with permission of the author. The poem "Bughouse Square" is from *Expresslanes Through the Inevitable City* (December Press, 1990) used with permission of the author R. Craig Sautter. "The Chicago School of Advertising," by Robert R. Burton, (*Chicago Tribune*, April 30, 1965) used with the permission of the *Tribune*. The poems "The Picasso" and "of Dewitt Williams on his way to Lincoln Cemetery" are from *Blacks*, by Gwendolyn Brooks, copyright © by Gwendolyn Brooks (Third World Press, Chicago, 1991) and are used with the author's permission. The material quoted from *Daley of Chicago* (Simon and Shuster, 1970) is used with the permission of the author Bill Gleason. The excerpt from *The Great Conspiracy Trial*, by Jason Epstein, is copyright © 1970 by Jason Epstein. Reprinted by the permission of Random House, Inc.; material from Alligator Records album cover is used courtesy of Alligator Records. The material from *The Chicago Schools: A Social and Political History*, by Mary Herrick, (Sage Publications, 1971) is used with permission. The quotation from *It All Adds Up: A Nonfiction Collection*, by Saul Bellow, (Viking, 1994) is used with permission. The two poems "The Toltec" and "Women Are Not Roses" are from *My Father Was a Toltec and Selected Poems*, by Ana Castillo, (W. W. Norton, 1995) and are used here with the permission of the author. *Roof Top Piper*, by David Hernandez, (Tia Chucha Press, a project of the Guild Complex, 1991). The poem "Amadillo Charm" is from the book of the same name, by Carlos Cumpián, (Tia Chucha Press, 1996) and is used with permission. "How Slats Lost His Marbles" is from *Slats Grobnik and Some Other Friends*, by Mike Royko, (E. P. Dutton & Co., 1973) and is used by permission of Dutton Signet, a division of Penguin Books USA, Inc.; the quoted material on Richard Nickel is excerpted from the book *They All Fall Down: Richard Nickel's Struggle to Save America's Architecture*, by Richard Cahan. Copyright © 1994 by Richard Cahan. (The Preservation Press). Excerpts from *Writing in Restaurants*, by David Mamet, (Penguin Books, 1986) and from *Aunt Ella Stories*, by Kenan Heise, (Academy Chicago, 1985) are used with permission from David Mamet. The excerpt from *Who Chicago? An Exhibition of Contemporary Imagists*, was published by (Ceolfrith Gallery, Sunderland Art Centre, 1981). The excerpt from *Blue in Chicago* is by Bette Howland (Harper & Rowe, 1978). The "Dear Readers of Chicago" letter is from *Chicago: A Special Issue of TriQuarterly* (*TriQuarterly*, 1984) It is copyrighted © Maxine Chernoff, 1984, 1986, 1997 and used with permission. Quoted material from *Burn Marks*, by Sarah Paretsky, (Delacorte Press, 1990) is copyright © 1990 by Paretsky and reprinted with permission of Bantam Books, a division of Bantam Doubleday Dell Publishing Group, Inc.; Material from the *Wild Season*, by Allan Eckert, is copyright © Alan W. Eckert, 1967, and was originally published by Little Brown & Co., Boston. It is used with permission from the author. The excerpt from *Tales from an Urban Wilderness*, by Scott Holingue, (Chicago Historical Bookworks, 1994) is used with permission. The excerpt from *Paco's Story*, by Larry Heinemann, (Farrar Straus Giroux, 1986) is used with the permission of the author. The excerpt of the Larry Heinemann article, by Jeff Lyon, and "Jim Nash Leaves His Mark on Chicago," by Greg Kot, are reprinted with the permission of the *Chicago Tribune*. A portion of the introduction to the *AIA Guide for Chicago*, by John F. Hartray Jr., Alice Sinkevitch, Editor, (Harcourt Brace & Co., 1993) is used with permission. Poetry from *hard times to hope: The Poems of Streetwise*, (StreetWise, n. d.) are used with permission. Comments from Fred Gardaphè's address to the Modern Language Association are used with permission of Gardaphè. The poem "The Story" from *the city in which i love you*, by Li-Young Lee, is copyright © 1990 of Li-Young Lee (BOA Editions Ltd. 260 East Avenue, Rochester, NY 14604, 1990) and is used with permission. The material from *Silhouette in Diamonds: The Life of Bertha Palmer*, by Ishbel Ross, (Harper & Brothers, 1960); *A Child of the Century*, by Ben Hecht, (Simon and Schuster, 1954); *The Front Page*, is by Ben Hecht and Charles MacArthur (Covici Friede, 1928). *Ernest Hemingway: A Life Story*, by Carlos Baker, (Charles Scribner's Sons, 1969); *The Sun Also Rises*, by Ernest Hemingway, (Charles Scribner's Sons, 1926); *Season with Solti*, by Barry Furlong, (The Macmillan Publishing Co., 1974); and *The Great Conspiracy Trial*, by Jason Epstein, (Random House, 1970) is quoted here by permission.

To Bob Cromie, Franz Schulze, and Gwendolyn Brooks
and to the memory of Herman Kogan and Henry Regnery, mavens
of Chicago's writers, artists, musicians, and poets

*One of the great ironies of our time is the sense of inferiority Chicagoans have about the culture of their city. The image of Chicago as a city of violence, crime, and political graft is familiar enough. But the image of Chicago as a white city, whose gleaming towers would stand beside an inland sea to create a new Athens in America—the image that captured the imagination and disciplined the spirit of Root, Sullivan, Wright, and Burnham and still touches the spirit of our best Chicago architects—is not so well known. Chicago has inspired men and women—for evil as well as good—but it has not yet inspired great, or even significant, cultural analysis. And this is very strange, for of few modern American cities can it be said, as of Chicago, that in its architecture lies the history of the struggle for the form of a new civilization, the civilization of America, which emerged after the Civil War.*

—Hugh Dalziel Duncan

# Contents

# Acknowledgments

To acknowledge that this book has been a collaborative effort is a pleasure. Such recognition for help in the creation of this book must begin with a thank you to fellow author and journalist Rick Kogan, who earlier in its formation applied a skilled and thoughtful pen to editing it.

Franz Schulze, the Betty Jan Hollender Professor of Art at Lake Forest College and the author of *Mies van der Rohe: A Critical Biography* and *Fantastic Images: Chicago Art Since 1945*, also did an excellent and encouraging piece of editing. He quashed, for instance, a lengthy attempt at an introduction with the short comment, "Let Chicago be Chicago."

The original idea for this book came from the vision of Gibbs Smith, its publisher.

Carol, spouse and friend, nudged, helped and critiqued the creation of it along its route.

The author has enjoyed help in coverage of the poetry scene from Joseph Wiley, who has been part of it for more than fifty years.

Additional help, in the matter of substance and form, came from Ben Heise, Dan Heise, Ann Coyne, Dan Lillian, John Lux, Bob Remer, Matt Rubinberg, Jason Pierce, Larry Kart, Ruth and Tom Buck, Alan Artner, Howard Reich, and Jill Schwendeman.

**Thanks to all of you.**

# Introduction

"Art is organized chaos." —Ed Paschke, a Chicago imagist

Without chaos, there is no creativity, and without creativity, there is no culture, no art. There is only imitation, and with imitation, the soul is bored—the sound of man, a grunt. Chaos, what is it? That which has no mold, substance without prefabricated form, opportunity free of preestablished rules. Chaos is words, sounds, colors, stone, wood, movement, notes that give human beings the chance to make an indigenous mark in the universe.

What is creativity? It is the process by which men and women play or often struggle with chaos and transform it into something that has taken on beauty and purpose. We call their best results art; we respect them as culture. Twentieth-century Chicago has proven an example of this happening.

1900s

CHICAGO

# 1900s: Chicago, The Emerald City

**B**etween 1900 and 1910 Chicago produced three direction-changing books in American letters: L. Frank Baum's *The Wizard of Oz,* Theodore Dreiser's *Sister Carrie,* and Upton Sinclair's *The Jungle.* Each was fresh and helped alter the course of this nation's literature. The city's style seemed chaotic, but its process was creativity, its product—the myriad manifestations of an indigenous culture.

William Dean Howells wrote an article in 1903 in the *North American Review* on "The Chicago School of Fiction." In it he said that the city's writers, such as George Ade, Hamlin Garland, and Edith Wyatt, were no longer regional writers but national figures creating a new kind of "American" writing. He also called them "not a group, but an army."

Among these national figures, in addition to the above listed, were L. Frank Baum; Theodore Dreiser; I. K. Friedman with four novels; famous lawyer Clarence Darrow, who wrote two novels, *Farmington* and his *An Eye for an Eye;* and George Horace Lorimer, whose stories, *Letters From a Self-Made Merchant to His Son,* first appeared in the *Saturday Evening Post.* Other writers included were Opie Read, Arthur Eddy, Will Payne, Ella Wheeler Wilcox, Henry Kitchell Webster, the prolific George Barr McCutcheon, Brand Whitlock, and Susan Glaspell, then a University of Chicago student.

Chicago artists from the period included the talented illustrator of the *Wonderful Wizard of Oz* books, W. W. Denslow; the highly collected illustrator Maxfield Parrish; Jules Guerin, who did the artwork for the Chicago Plan and murals for the Continental Bank Building; and Charlie Holloway, then the most prominent muralist in the country. Studying at the School of the Art

# 1900s

Institute in 1904 and 1905 was the young Georgia O'Keeffe.

From a design standpoint, it was the great era of the Chicago Arts and Crafts Society, the first such organization in the United States working to meld craftsmanship and art in working with metals, glass, wood, and ceramics. Its meetings brought together such diverse forces in the city as Frank Lloyd Wright and Hull House cofounders Jane Addams and Ellen Gates Starr.

Through John Dewey and Francis Parker, Chicago was helping to create progressive education and revolutionize how public school students are taught. Richard Sears and his successor, Julius Rosenwald, were doing the same in retailing. Wright and those working with him were meanwhile creating the Prairie Style of Architecture.

### THE WONDERFUL WIZARD OF OZ

Turn-of-the-century Chicago was Oz. It was an era when eager and innocent young people from small midwestern towns and farms were being drawn toward "The Wonder City," the heart of the heartland, Chicago. Danger and wickedness, they had been warned repeatedly, dwelt there, and the Oz story did not dispute that. It said that with a heart, courage, and a brain, a person—even one fresh off the farm—could prevail. Why? Because in this metropolis of the Midwest, magic and goodness also existed.

On April 8, 1900, L. Frank Baum had written to his brother, Harry: "Then, there is the other book, the best thing I have written, they tell me, *The Wonderful Wizard of Oz.* It is now in the press. Mr. Hill, the publisher, says he expects a sale of at least a quarter of a million copies."

Baum, a former reporter for the *Chicago Evening Post,* had teamed up with a local artist, William W. Denslow, to produce first, *Father Goose, His Book,* and then in 1900, "the other book," to which he had referred in his letter. The story was an American fairy tale, original and illus-trated with the brightest and most imaginative of drawings. In 1902, it would become a play and in 1939, one of the classic movies of all times. But, first and foremost, *The Wonderful Wizard of Oz* was and is a children's book, a central piece of American literature.

The following excerpt is the finale to the book:

"Take me home to Aunt Em!" Dorothy exclaimed, "You are certainly as good as you are beautiful! But you have not yet told me how to get back to Kansas."

"Your Silver Shoes will carry you over the desert," replied Glinda. "If you had known their power you could have gone back to your Aunt Em the very first day you came to this country."

"But then I should not have had my wonderful brains!" cried the Scarecrow. "I might have passed my whole life in the farmer's cornfield."

"And I should not have had my lovely heart," said the Tin Woodsman. "I might have stood and rusted in the forest till the end of the world."

"And I should have lived a coward forever," declared the Lion, "and no beast in all the forest would have had a good word to say to me."

"This is all true," said Dorothy, "and I am glad I was of use to these good friends. But now that each of them has had what he most desired, and each is happy in having a kingdom to rule besides, I think I should like to go back to Kansas."

"The Silver Shoes," said the Good Witch, "have wonderful powers. And one of the most curious things about them is that they can carry you to any place in the world in three steps, and each step will be made in the wink of an eye. All you have to do is to knock the heels together three times and command the shoes to carry you wherever you wish to go."

"If that is so," said the child, joyfully, "I will ask them to carry me back to Kansas at once." She threw her arms around the Lion's neck and kissed him, patting his big head tenderly. Then she kissed the Tin Woodsman, who was weeping in a way most dangerous to his joints. But she hugged the soft, stuffed body of the Scarecrow in her arms instead of kissing his painted face, and found she was crying herself at this sorrowful parting from her loving comrades.

Glinda the Good Witch stepped down from her ruby throne to give the little girl a good-bye kiss, and Dorothy thanked her for all the kindness she had shown to her friends and herself.

Dorothy now took Toto up solemnly in her arms, and having said one last good-bye she clapped the heels of her shoes together three times, saying, "Take me home to Aunt Em!" Instantly she was whirling through the air, so swiftly that all she could see or feel was the wind whistling past her ears. The Silver Shoes took but three steps, and then she stopped so suddenly that she rolled over upon the grass several times before she knew where she was.

At length, however, she sat up and looked about her. "Good gracious!" she cried. For she was sitting on the broad Kansas prairie, and just before her was the new farmhouse Uncle Henry built after the cyclone had carried away the old one. Uncle Henry was milking the cows in the barnyard, and Toto had jumped out of her arms and was running toward the barn, barking joyously.

Dorothy stood up and found she was in her stocking feet, for the Silver Shoes had fallen off in her flight through the air, and were lost forever in the desert.

### SISTER CARRIE

Theodore Dreiser's more realistic version of life than *The Wonderful Wizard of Oz* was contained in his novel, *Sister Carrie*. Dreiser's novel was published the same year (1900) as was Baum's fairy tale. This story was also about a young female arriving not in Oz but in the magnetic maelstrom of the metropolis, Chicago. It showed the young woman, Caroline "Carrie" Meeber, getting caught up in a stark city full of a different kind of opportunity. She violated conventional morality to survive and get ahead.

The book's bluntness had a profound effect on American literature. The *Newark Sunday News* said of it: "The impression is simply one of truth and therein lies at once the strength and horror of it."

A first edition of *Sister Carrie* is worth somewhat more than $1,000, because it is considered such a significant book and because copies are very scarce. It was recalled by the publisher. According to Dreiser, the publisher's wife was shocked by its seeming lack of guiding moral principles. Dreiser's biographer, W. A. Swanberg, however, wrote: "In view of the prevailing national climate, the kind of books the public were then buying, and the reaction of the critics, it seems likely that Carrie still would have been a commercial failure. The reviewers killed the book. The public simply did not want *Sister Carrie* in 1900.

# 1900s

Today, *Sister Carrie* is considered a turning point in American writing—one that lifted the moral anchor of propriety and righteousness and set it free to find a new course. The following comments on Dreiser were written in 1912 by Floyd Dell in a *Friday Literary Review* column. They are reprinted from the book *Floyd Dell: Essays from the Friday Literary Review, 1909–1913,* edited by Craig Sautter, a 1995 volume that rediscovered Dell.

The poetry of Chicago has been adequately rendered, so far, by only one writer, and in only one book. The book is, naturally enough, that one which Frank Harris declared in the *London Academy* to be "the best story, on the whole, that has yet come out of America," to wit: *Sister Carrie* by Theodore Dreiser. It is the most real, the most sincere, the most moving, of all the books with which we have dealt, or are likely to deal, in this study of Chicago in Fiction. And it is real and moving greatly by virtue of being poetic.

A good deal of the magic of a great city is that which lingers in the mind from one's first experiences in it. And the true story of adventure in Chicago begins somewhere else. Not to tell how it felt to leave the old town is to omit something of a distinct relevance to the story of Chicago. There is less of Chicago, in whole novels, ostensibly about the life of this city, than there is in the opening paragraph of *Sister Carrie:*

"When Caroline Meeber boarded the afternoon train for Chicago, her total outfit consisted of a small trunk, a cheap imitation alligator-skin satchel, a small lunch in a pepper box, and a yellow leather snap purse containing her ticket, a scrap of paper with her sister's address in Van Buren Street and four dollars in money. It was in August, 1889. She was eighteen years of age, bright, timid, and full of the illusions of ignorance and youth. Whatever touch of regret at parting characterized her thoughts, it was certainly not for advantages now being given up. A gush of tears at her mother's farewell kiss, a touch in her throat when the cars clacked by the flour mill where her father worked by the day, a pathetic sigh as the familiar green environs of the village passed in review, and the threads which bound her so lightly to girlhood and home were irretrievably broken."

\* \* \*

And then there is the coming into the city. This, like the other, has been done before in American fiction, but not in the way of Mr. Dreiser. For he writes as one who will not slur the beauty of any emotion, though it were as common as a sunset: "They were nearing Chicago. . . . To the child, the genius with imagination, or the wholly untraveled, the approach to a great city for the first time is a wonderful thing. Particularly if it be evening—that mystic period between the glare and gloom of the world when life is changing from one sphere or condition to another. Ah, the promise of the night. . . . Though all humanity be still enclosed in the shops, the thrill runs abroad. It is in the air. The dullest feel something which they may not always express or describe. It is the lifting of the burden of toil."

Carrie goes to her sister's home. "Minnie's flat, as the one-floor resident apartments were then being called, was in a part of West Van Buren street inhabited by families of laborers and clerks, men who had come, and were still coming, with the rush of population pouring in at the rate of 50,000 a year. It was on the third floor, the front windows looking down into the street, where, at night, the lights of grocery stores were shining and children were playing. To Carrie, the sound of the little bells upon the horse-cars, as they tinkled in and out of hearing, was as pleasing as it was novel. She gazed into the lighted streets when Minnie brought her into the front room, and wondered at the sounds, the movement, the murmur of the vast city which stretched for miles and miles in every direction."

\* \* \*

That passage is significant. We have writers who would be so interested in the sociological significance of the location of Minnie's flat that they would forget all about *Sister Carrie.* Others would romance about the girl until one sickened of the unreality and threw the book across the room. Others would be so preoccupied with the destiny of Sister Carrie that they would find a moral suggestion in everything they dealt with. Mr. Dreiser kept his head and used it.

\* \* \*

Mr. Dreiser has not looked to see the badness of the city, nor its goodness; he has looked to see its beauty and its ugliness, and he has seen a beauty even in its ugliness. And in doing that he has given us, there is little doubt, the Chicago of the whole Middle West—a beacon across the prairies, a place of splendor and joy and triumph, the place toward which the young faces turn and the end of the road along which the young feet yearn to tread.

—February 23, 1912

### THE JUNGLE

Great literature is set in a time and place all its own. Rarely is this more decidedly true than in *The Jungle,* an exposé novel written in 1906 by Upton Sinclair about the Chicago Union Stockyards. It is a powerful portrait of a very robust city, its people, and the forces that drive it and them. Sinclair's tale plays Chicago like a violin, gliding through both its high and low notes. Originally serialized in *The Appeal to Reason,* a Socialist Party weekly, the book excoriated the meatpackers for their treatment of workers as well as the way they butchered cattle and processed the meat.

**Photograph by
Chicago photographer
David R. Phillips**

# 1900s

When President Theodore Roosevelt read *The Jungle*, he was revolted by its passages and helped enact the law that created the Food and Drug Administration.

Sinclair's novel was dedicated not to the diners of America, however, but to its workingmen. He wanted justice for them more than the federal inspection of meat products he helped to get.

Clarence A. Andrews of the University of Iowa, an expert on the literature of Chicago, wrote of Sinclair's novel:

> *The Jungle* is a vivid book for the modern reader, and not only for its shock scenes or its depiction of the depths to which mankind may be forced through human greed. The modern reader should have no trouble at all in understanding the plight of Jurgis, who is almost destroyed by forces so vast and ambiguous that he comes to grips only with their names and minor agents. It is in the representation of this struggle—puny men fighting for survival against a vast shapeless and corrupting system—that the universality and power of *The Jungle* lies.

The following is one of the many snapshots, as it were, of everyday life in 1906 as seen by Sinclair Lewis through his characters in *The Jungle:*

> Grandmother Majauszkiene had come to America with her son at a time when so far as she knew there was only one other Lithuanian family in the district; the workers had all been Germans then—skilled cattle butchers that the packers had brought from abroad to start the business. Afterward, as cheaper labor had come, these Germans had moved away. The next were the Irish—there had been six or eight years when Packingtown had been a regular Irish city. There were a few colonies of them still here, enough to run all the unions and the police force and get all the graft; but the most of those who were working in the packing houses had gone away at the next drop in wages—after the big strike. The Bohemians had come then, and after them the Poles. People said that old man Durham himself was responsible for these immigrations; he had sworn that he would fix the people of Packingtown so that they would never again call a strike on him, and so he had sent his agents into every city and village in Europe to spread the tale of the chances of work and high wages at the stockyards. The people had come in hordes, and old Durham had squeezed them tighter and tighter, speeding them up and grinding them to pieces and sending for new ones. The Poles, who had come by tens of thousands, had been driven to the wall by the Lithuanians, and now the Lithuanians were giving way to the Slovaks. Who there was poorer and more miserable than the Slovaks, Grandmother Majauszkiene had no idea but the packers would find them, never fear.

## THE ARTS AND CRAFTS MOVEMENT IN CHICAGO: AN ARTISTIC REVOLUTION

At the turn of the century, an artistic revolution invaded the United States via Chicago. The Arts and Crafts movement originated in England and represented an intense effort to make handcrafted rather than machine-made artifacts an option for all. This revolt focused on furniture, toys, clothes, home furnishings, dishes, silverware, pottery, metal artifacts, jewelry, as well as the ornamentation and decoration of other objects people regularly use in their lives. It was known as the Arts and Crafts movement, and, by 1897, its first American chapter had been formed in Chicago.

The Chicago Arts and Crafts Society, far from being a weak tendril, flowered in the favorable soil of this creative city and provides America with hybrids of its fruits to this day.

These hybrids are seen in the interior and furniture designs of Frank Lloyd Wright, who was an active member; in the craft traditions of Hull House, where the first meetings were held; in American metal work and jewelry that both still show a Chicago and an Arts and Crafts movement influence a hundred years later; in many of the patterns of American furniture, which have often returned to the Mission and other handcrafted styles that were spin-offs of the movement; and in the ornamentation heritage of Louis J. Millet, instructor of decorative art and architecture at the Art Institute of Chicago. The latter, a close friend of Louis Sullivan, executed much of the Chicago architect's decorative work in the Auditorium, the Stock Exchange, and the Transportation Building.

Perhaps even more, the Arts and Crafts impact hit America through the Sears, Roebuck & Company and, especially, the Montgomery Ward Company catalogs that favored many of the movement's influences toward simplicity and directness, such as Mission furniture. Marshall Field & Company also carried the handcrafted jewelry, metalwork, furnishings,

THE WRIGHT STYLE

CARLA LIND

RECREATING THE SPIRIT OF FRANK LLOYD WRIGHT

and other items produced by those who were part of or were influenced by the Arts and Crafts movement in Chicago.

We see it today in the finest of jewelry and department stores as well as in the Arts and Crafts fairs that afford an outlet for the work of those who use their hands rather than machines to produce imaginative and creative items.

In a 1977 *Chicago History* magazine article, the author of *Chicago Metalsmiths*, Sharon Darling, wrote of the close association of the Arts and Crafts movement and the city of Chicago:

By the late 1890s, Chicago had become a major center of the Arts and Crafts Movement. . . . In Chicago, adherents of the movement included many instructors and students of the Art Institute, professors at the University of Chicago,

1900s

A CATALOGUE OF THE SECOND EXHIBITION OF THE CHICAGO ARTS & CRAFTS SOCIETY

# 1900s

The Rise of Chicago
as a Literary Center
from 1885 to 1920

A Sociological Essay
in American Culture

Hugh Dalziel Duncan

THE BEDMINSTER PRESS

workers in social settlements, teachers in manual training schools, reform-minded young architects, professional craftsmen, as well as hobbyists, and homemakers. . . .

## CHICAGO: A LITERARY CENTER

Hugh Dalziel Duncan, a scholar whose several books shone a halogen light on the subject of American culture, wrote two volumes on Chicago: *The Rise of Chicago as a Literary Center from 1885 to 1920* and *Culture and Democracy*. The first, done in 1948, was his doctoral thesis at the University of Chicago. The latter, published in 1965, offered a profound argument that the city's writers and architects were different because they believed culture did not have to be imitative of the past or trickle down from the upper classes, but that it could come from the people.

The Duncan quotation at the beginning of this book is from *Culture and Democracy.* The following excerpt is from his University of Chicago Ph.D. dissertation, *The Rise of Chicago as a Literary Center:*

Chicago's great development as a center of architecture, education and literature began in the last years of the 1880s. The first great form of expression was architecture. In 1900, the University of Chicago had produced what William James called a "Chicago School" of philosophy—the social thought of Dewey who came to the University in 1894. By 1910, Chicago was the creative center of American literature. Each of these contributions to American culture, and, in the case of architecture, to international culture, had its roots in the struggles by artists in the eighties and nineties to give form to words, space, and ideas, which would make possible a new kind of symbolic life.

Productivity in literature, as the following figures indicate, rose sharply after 1890. Approximately 175 books were written in Chicago from 1890 to 1900. By 1905, Chicago was second only to New York in dollar value of book and job printing. In this decade alone several thousand books were published in Chicago. Stone and Kimball; Way and Williams; Rand, McNally; and McClurg were issuing many titles, and there were many other local printers who published a few books each year. Stone and Kimball and Herbert S. Stone and Company published approximately 300 books between 1893 and 1903. Distribution facilities for printed matter were unexcelled. Chicago was now the railroad center of America, and the system worked out by Walsh for the distribution of books, periodicals, and newspapers was excellent.

The literature, architecture, and social philosophy of this period were the end of an earlier search for a definition of community life in the new urban West. The roles to be played by various social types, the Chicago "spirit," which moved her artists so deeply, were given their main outlines in these years. Chicagoans realized they had to define themselves to themselves as well as to others. The Chicago Fair of 1893 was to be a world's fair, and Chicagoans prepared to stage themselves in international, as well as national and local terms. The first impression left by a survey of the many novels written during this period is their concern with the scene. Even the romantic novels of Mrs. Catherwood deal with urban values. As if to dispel any doubt among Chicagoans that she was concerned with the function of literature in society, she entered the debate between Field and Garland in which Field championed "romance," Garland "veritism" or "realism." She does not defend "romance" in terms of its acceptability (the familiar recourse to

"It's what the public wants") but in terms of its ennobling effect. She condemned Chicago culture and Chicago elites because they were concerned with money and material things rather than with aristocratic ideals of disinterested action, honor, dignity and the life of the mind and spirit.

Other Chicago writers, and by far the greater number, were concerned directly with Chicago. Chicagoans wanted to read about Chicago. And it was not long (1903, when Howells' article on the "Chicago School of Fiction" appeared) until Americans were told that Chicago writers like Ade were no longer regional "Chicago" writers, but national figures who were creating a new kind of "American" writing. The appetite for Chicago material was enormous. It was understood in every city news room that any story about the city, providing it had local color, could be included in the daily edition. The elites of the city, or at least those who made any pretensions to literary culture, were able to laugh at themselves in their portrayal by Field as heavy-handed packers (with "brine-soaked" hands) thumbing through old books in McClurg's, falling asleep at Theodore Thomas' concerts, and other sufferings attendant upon the rigor of "making culture hum." Certainly the novels of Fuller, Chatfield-Taylor, and Will Payne were highly critical of the Chicago plutocracy.

## SCHOOL REFORM, 1900

The creating of a genuine culture begins in freedom and education. It requires the opportunity to express oneself and of possessing the tools with which to do so. Two Chicago educators at the turn of the century, Francis W. Parker and John Dewey, dramatically looked to the common schools to provide this for children and, therefore, for society.

Primary education at this point in American history had been described in another American city (New York) as a "hard, unsympathetic, mechanical drudgery . . . into which the light of science has not entered. Its characteristic features lie in the severity of its discipline, a discipline of enforced silence, immortality, and mental passivity."

In Chicago, Parker in the 1890s had headed the Cook County (Chicago) Normal School, which was producing the city's teachers, while Dewey was founding and directing (from 1896 to 1904) the University of Chicago Laboratory School. Both were experimenting with education and were pushing for informality in the classroom. Their ideas would establish the basic tenets of progressive education.

### John Dewey

Dewey felt that the goal of education is the growth of the child in all aspects of his or her being. He was to put in more than fifty years on behalf of school children. He thoroughly shared Parker's ideas about democracy and education, once stating:

> The educational regimen thus consists of authorities at the upper end handing down to the receivers at the lower end what they must accept. This is not education but indoctrination, propaganda. It is a type of "education" fit for the foundations of a totalitarian society and, for the same reason, fit to subvert, pervert, and destroy the foundations of a democratic society.

The following is from his book, *School and Society: The School and Social Progress*:

> We are apt to look at the school from an individualistic standpoint, as something between teacher and pupil, or between teacher and parent. That which interests us most is naturally the progress made by the individual child of our acquain-

*The School and Society by John Dewey*

## 1900s

# 1900s

tance, his normal physical development, his advance in ability to read, write, and figure, his growth in the knowledge of geography and history, improvement in manners, habits of promptness, order, and industry—it is from such standards as these that we judge the work of the school. And rightly so. Yet the range of the outlook needs to be enlarged. What the best and wisest parent wants for his own child, that must the community want for all of its children. Any other ideal for our schools is narrow and unlovely acted upon, it destroys our democracy. All that society has accomplished for itself is put, through the agency of the school, at the disposal of its future members. All its better thoughts of itself it hopes to realize through the new possibilities thus opened to its future self. Here individualism and socialism are at one. Only by being true to the full growth of all the individuals who make it up, can society by any chance be true to itself. And in the self-direction thus given, nothing counts as much as the school, for, as Horace Mann said, "Where anything is growing, one farmer is worth a thousand reformers."

**Francis Parker**

Parker urgently defended the common school in Chicago at a time when the entire educational system in the city seemed in total chaos. The number of pupils in the city's public schools had more than tripled between 1885 and 1896, rising from 79, 276 to 312, 825, and the number of teachers had increased in that same time from 1,296 to 4,668. A report by a commission headed by University of Chicago President William R. Harper in the early 1900s called Chicago's schools worse than those in the lowest wards of Manhattan. Downstate Illinois legislators meanwhile were refusing to increase funding for the city's schools because they believed it would be throwing the money away on the children of aliens and foreigners. Still, Parker deeply believed in the common school as the only salvation for a democratic society. The following is from his book, *Talks on Pedagogics:*

The aristocratic idea of charity is still a potent influence in education. Our school system began as charity schools—charity schools such as the Volksschule of Germany. Many wealthy people who have the traditional or *parvenu* feeling of class distinction look today upon the common-school system as a charity and hold that there should be one education for rich children and another for the poor; that the children of the rich should not mingle with and be contaminated by the children of the poor. I have had much to do with both classes, and I wish to say here that in my contact with the poorest children I have found as much of intrinsic morality and vigorous mental power in them as in rich children. This false idea of contamination is born of the past, a reappearance of the old-time aristocratic idea of separation and isolation. In a good school, with excellent teachers and the right surroundings, there is no more danger of contamination than is to be found in the ordinary home and class environment of children.

When, in American society, classes become permanent and the children of these classes are educated in separate schools, the doom of the republic is sealed. There can be no separated classes in a republic; the lifeblood of a republic must stream from the ground up; there can be no stratified society.

No child, no citizen of a republic, can be educated into citizenship outside of the common school; the common school is not a charity; it is the inalienable right of every child, and common education is the imperative duty of every community. On a lower plane we may look at universal intelligence as the one means for the preservation of the republic; society, in order to preserve itself, must develop the highest character in every child.

The charity idea obtains largely among manufacturers and people who depend upon laborers and servants. I once talked with a gentleman upon a religious subject; he seemed to be imbued, or thought he was, with the spirit of Christ; he was a nail manufacturer. When I spoke to him about the education of his employees, suggesting that they should have better opportunities for personal improvement, he said: "But that would spoil them as laborers. I must have employees; there must be a class of workers." This Christian gentleman was entirely willing to suppress human souls in the interest of nails.

## CHICAGO'S CHAOS

"Chicago is the place to make you appreciate at every turn the opportunity which chaos affords."
—John Dewey

A factor that consistently stands as a landmark throughout Chicago's history is chaos. Dramatically represented by the photograph on page 12 of Dearborn and Randolph in the first decade of the twentieth century, it is an element that has frequently put smirks on the faces of the city's critics while enabling Chicago and its people to demonstrate their ingenuity and creativity.

Author Julian Street, visiting the city, wrote of the metropolis of the Midwest: "Chicago is stupefying. It knows no rules, and I know none by which to judge it. It stands apart from all the cities in the world, isolated by its own individuality, an Olympian freak, a fable, an allegory, an incomprehensible phenomenon, a prodigious paradox in which youth and

**Chicago's "splendid chaos" Queen and guttersnipe of cities, cynosure and cesspool of the world: Not if I had a hundred tongues, everyone shouting a different language in a different key, could I do justice to her splendid chaos. The most beautiful and the most squalid, girdled with a twofold zone of parks and slums; where the keen air from lake and prairie is ever in the nostrils and the stench of foul smoke is never out of the throat; the great port a thousand miles from the sea; the great mart which gathers up with one hand the corn and the cattle of the West and deals out with the other the merchandise of the East; widely and generously planned, where it is not safe to walk at night; the chosen seat of cutthroat commerce and munificent patronage of art; the most American of American cities and yet the most mongrel; the second American city of the globe, the fifth German city, the third Swedish, the second Polish, the first and only veritable Babel of the age. Where in all the world can words be found for this miracle of paradox and incongruity.**

**—G. W. Stevens**

maturity, brute strength and soaring spirit, are harmoniously confused."

## DANIEL BURNHAM AND THE 1909 CHICAGO PLAN

A city, especially one like Chicago, ultimately chooses its own culture, its own style. Rarely is this choice more clearly defined than it was in 1909 when the midwestern metropolis was offered the *Chicago Plan*, by Daniel Burnham and Edward Bennett. Sponsored by the Commercial Club, this major effort at uniform planning for the core of the city promised to lead it out of its chaos, make it beautiful, and glorify the lakefront. To sell it, a book with beautifully colored illustrations, *The Wacker Manual*, became a textbook in all the city's public schools. The plan called for very broad connecting boulevards, museums, and theaters in Grant Park, a series of islands just off the shore, and a lakefront civic center. It would make Chicago the Paris of

## 1900s

COPYRIGHT, 1909, BY COMMERCIAL CLUB OF CHICAGO

CXII. CHICAGO. PROPOSED BOULEVARD TO CONNECT THE NORTH AND SOUTH SIDES OF THE RIVER; VIEW LOOKING NORTH FROM WASHINGTON STREET.

The boulevard is raised to allow free flow of east-and-west teaming traffic under it, and both Michigan Avenue and Beaubien Court are raised to the boulevard level. The raised portion throughout its entire length, from Randolph Street to Indiana Street, extends from building line to building line. It is approached from the cross streets by inclined roadways or ramps; these may be changed to the east side or omitted.

Painted for the Commercial Club by Jules Guerin.

Randolph Street

A map from the Chicago Plan, showing the civic center on Lake Michigan, the improved waterways and lakeshore, the complete system of streets and arteries, and the forest preserve system.

the New World, a place noted not for its hustle and bustle but for its leisurely strolls amid halls of culture and refinement.

In the end, Chicago rejected most of the package, seeing it as something better serving a French or German city rather than the needs or style of the rambunctious port on the midwestern prairie. The city put it aside just as it had classical architecture and a formal writing style. Those who shared Burnham's definition of a European model of beauty have never fully understood why, and as Herman Kogan and Lloyd Wendt wrote more than a half of a century later, "Chicago still is debating the merits of a civic center and other as yet unrealized aspects of the plan."

The following comments on the *Chicago Plan* are from one of the most thoughtful books yet written on the city—*Lost Chicago*, by David Lowe:

If giantism was Burnham's first sin, his second was an insensitivity to the importance of people to a city. Once again this was the failure of perception. Burnham longed to emulate the grand boulevards that Haussmann had cut through the old city of Paris. But Burnham did not understand that above their first floor shops most of the buildings lining Haussmann's boulevards contained apartments, and behind them was densely populated medieval Paris. In the evenings, on holidays, the people of Paris became boulevardiers, using the broad thoroughfares as urban parks, to window shop, to chat, to stroll, or from the table of a cafe to enjoy the greatest city pleasure of all, watching the passing show. In contrast, when Burnham turned to the creation of his boulevards he envisioned them lined almost exclusively with commercial and city structures. Indeed his plan helped empty the Loop of people.

Make no little plans; they have no magic to stir men's blood and probably themselves will not be realized. Make big plans; aim high in hope and work, remembering that a noble, logical diagram once recorded will never die, but long after we are gone will be a living thing, asserting itself with ever-growing insistency. Remember that our sons and grandsons are going to do things that would stagger us. Let your watchword be order and your beacon, beauty.

**Attributed to Daniel Burnham**

1910s

CHICAGO

# 1910s: The Most Civilized Place in America

enry L. Mencken, the pundit of Baltimore and the nation's literary maven in 1917, called Chicago "the most civilized city in America." In Chicago, he wrote, "originality still appears to be put above conformity. . . . There is," he added, "a mysterious something that makes for individuality, personality and charm. In Chicago, a spirit broods upon the face of the water. Find a writer who is indubitably an American in every pulse-beat, snort and adenoid, an American who has something new and peculiarly American to say and who says it in an unmistakably American way and nine times out of ten you will find that he has some sort of connection with the gargantuan and inordinate abattoir by Lake Michigan. . . ."

Edgar Rice Burroughs was creating Tarzan here. Others writing in or about the city at the time included Sherwood Anderson, Ring Lardner, Theodore Dreiser, Willa Cather, John Dos Passos, Floyd Dell, Myrtle Reed, Arthur Davison Ficke, Hamlin Garland, Frank Norris, Henry B. Fuller, and Francis Hackett as well as two University of Chicago professors and writers, Robert Morss Lovett and Robert Herrick.

By 1912, Harriet Monroe had started *Poetry: A Magazine of Verse* with the help of Chicago poets, artists, editors, and backers.

In 1913, Willa Cather wrote a memorable novel, *The Song of the Lark,* about a young woman, impoverished but talented, taking voice training in Chicago. The same year, sculptor Loredo Taft created his *Fountain of the Great Lakes* and was attempting to train and develop a new school of American sculpture in Chicago.

Other city artists from this era included painter Frederick Clay Bartlett as well as renowned illustrators Ralph Fletcher Seymour and John T. McCutcheon.

Margaret Anderson began publishing *The Little Review* in 1914. Its self-

**Mary Garden**

# 1910s

proclaimed goal was to be "fresh and constructive, and intelligent from the artist's point of view" and offer "untrammeled liberty," something it did when she published the banned *Ulysses,* by James Joyce.

In addition in 1914, the women of Hull House were inspiring a community theater movement that would explode in New York and across the country, while the *Chicago Defender,* a national newspaper for African Americans became known as a local voice for a developing Chicago's black culture.

By 1918, Chicago writer Ernest Poole had won the first Pulitzer Prize ever awarded for fiction for the novel, *His Family,* rounding out another impressive decade in Chicago history.

## MARY GARDEN AS SALOME

No account of Chicago and its cultural history should ignore the performance of opera star Mary Garden as Salome in *Libretto,* the opera based on Oscar Wilde's play of the same name. The event took place November 25, 1910. Writing for *Chicago History Magazine* in the spring of 1972, Richard Fletcher described it as sending "a skyrocket flashing across Chicago's operatic horizon, illuminating everything it passed."

New York and Philadelphia police and the morally pure had attempted to have the performance curtailed but had not succeeded.

The Chicago-raised, Paris-trained opera singer later expressed how she saw the role of the biblical dancer who performed to get Herod to behead John the Baptist: "I was presenting a pagan pervert."

Chicago Police Chief Leroy T. Stewart saw it no less prosaically, commenting on the performance: "Miss Garden wallowed around like a cat in a bed of catnip."

Chicago society and opera had a powerful figure ultimately calling the shots. She was Edith McCormick Rockefeller, the daughter of John D. She had the final say on everything to do with opera in Chicago. She unilaterally canceled the fourth performance of Salome after having watched the first. According to Mary Garden in her autobiography, the only reason given by Edith and then repeated was: "I said to myself, 'Edith, your vibrations are all wrong.'"

Mary Garden took the show to Milwaukee, where the chief of police there said that the "Dance of the Seven Veils" had reminded him ". . . irresistibly of a thuringer sausage dancing on a hot griddle."

## *TARZAN OF THE APES*

With his flights of imagination, Edgar Rice Burroughs certainly demonstrated H. L. Mencken's statement that in Chicago, "originality is still put above conformity." Burroughs, a native of Chicago and a resident for many years of Oak Park, created Tarzan, the Ant Men, Opar, the City of Gold, and the high priestess La. He took Tarzan to the Forbidden City and the core of the earth. The author, however, never visited Africa where his Tarzan novels were set and of course never set eyes on the surface of Mars where his science-fiction stories were staged. He also wrote a Chicago novel, *The Mucker* (1921), about a young man falsely accused of murder, but it is not why we remember Burroughs. The first Tarzan story appeared in 1912 and the novel, *Tarzan of the Apes,* in 1914. It was the first of thirty Tarzan books. They have been translated into fifty-six languages and their main character has become popular through movies, comic books, and radio shows. If the writing at times fell short of classical literature standards, four generations of readers have nevertheless appreciated the originality, creativity, and imagination of Burroughs.

The following is from *The Return of Tarzan:*

At sunset they buried William Cecil Clayton beside the jungle graves of his uncle and his aunt, the former Lord and Lady Greystoke. And it was at Tarzan's request that three volleys were fired over the last resting place of "a brave man, who met his death bravely."

Professor Porter, who in his younger days had been ordained a minister, conducted the simple services for the dead. About the grave, with bowed heads, stood as strange a company of mourners as the sun ever looked down upon. There were French officers and sailors, two English lords, Americans, and a score of savage African braves.

Following the funeral Tarzan asked Captain Dufranne to delay the sailing of the cruiser a couple of days while he went inland a few miles to fetch his "belongings," and the officer gladly granted the favor.

Late the next afternoon Tarzan

and his Waziri returned with the first load of "belongings," and when the party saw the ancient ingots of virgin gold they swarmed upon the ape man with a thousand questions; but he was smilingly obdurate to their appeals—he declined to give them the slightest clue as to the source of his immense treasure. "There are a thousand that I left behind," he explained, "for every one that I brought away, and when these are spent I may wish to return for more."

The next day he returned to camp with the balance of his ingots, and when they were stored on board the cruiser Captain Dufranne said he felt like the commander of an old-time Spanish galleon returning from the treasure cities of the Aztecs. "I don't know what minute my crew will cut my throat, and take over the ship," he added.

The next morning, as they were preparing to embark upon the cruiser, Tarzan ventured a suggestion to Jane Porter.

"Wild beasts are supposed to be devoid of sentiment," he said, "but nevertheless I should like to be married in the cabin where I was born, beside the graves of my mother and my father, and surrounded by the savage jungle that always has been my home."

"Would it be quite regular, dear?" she asked. "For if it would I know of no other place in which I should rather be married to my forest god than beneath the shade of his primeval forest."

And when they spoke of it to the others they were assured that it would be quite regular, and a most splendid termination of a remarkable romance. So the entire party assembled within the little cabin and about the door to witness the second ceremony that Professor Porter was to solemnize within three days.

D'Arnot was to be best man,

A Hull House production of *Alice in Wonderland*

and Hazel Strong bridesmaid, until Tennington upset all the arrangements by another of his marvelous "ideas."

"If Mrs. Strong is agreeable," he said, taking the bridesmaid's hand in his, "Hazel and I think it would be ripping to make it a double wedding."

The next day they sailed, and as the cruiser steamed slowly out to sea a tall man, immaculate in white flannel, and a graceful girl leaned against her rail to watch the receding shore line upon which danced twenty naked, black warriors of the Waziri, waving their war spears above their savage heads, and shouting farewells to their departing king.

"I should hate to think that I am looking upon the jungle for the last time, dear," he said, "were it not that I know that I am going to a new world of happiness with you forever," and, bending down, Tarzan of the Apes kissed his mate upon her lips.

## BORN IN CHICAGO: THE AMERICAN LITTLE THEATER MOVEMENT

The American Little Theater Movement began in Chicago almost ninety years ago, an event theatrical historians consider a turning point in American drama. On that day, theater became not just a spectator, but also a participatory art, allowing hundreds of thousands of performers to take the stage or literally to build one. Within a decade of this

*Chaos, Creativity, and Culture*

birth, it was said, the number of stages on which amateurs performed within a ten-mile radius of Broadway increased from two to five hundred. The effects are still with us, especially in Chicago where, with seating for numbers ranging from twenty to two hundred, numerous small theaters proliferate.

The credit for this birth is usually given to Maurice and Ellen Browne after they gathered together a crew and cast of amateurs in November 1912 to stage *The Trojan Women*. The place was in a small theater created on the fourth floor of the Fine Arts Building still standing on Michigan Avenue.

The spiritual mother of this performance was Lady Augusta Gregory, a sixty-year-old playwright with the Abbey Players who were visiting Chicago from Ireland. She told the Brownes:

By all means, start your own theater; but make it in your own image. Don't engage professional players; they have been spoiled for your purpose. Engage and train, as we of the Abbey have done, amateurs: shop girls, school teachers, counter jumpers, cut-throat thieves rather than professionals and prepare to have your heart broken.

Playwright George Bernard Shaw later recalled the opening of the Little Theater, saying: "The work twenty years ago on a flour floor back in Chicago—that is what matters."

Maurice Browne received the title, "Father of the American Little Theater." Browne, on his part, would deny the honor, pointing rather to the director of Hull House Players in Chicago.

Hull House, founded in 1889 by Jane Addams and Ellen Gates Starr, was a fresh, strong breeze in Chicago. It was a formidable force because its women, rather than looking patronizingly down on the poor, worked alongside them and opened up avenues for their energy, creativity, and talents to express themselves. The Hull House Theater, such

an avenue, was founded in the 1890s and revitalized a decade later by Laura Dainty Pelham.

In his autobiography, Browne wrote: "The Hull House Players gave plays of distinction with skill, sincerity and understanding. Mrs. Pelham, not I, was the true founder of The American Little Theater Movement."

The following article written about the Hull House Players by Elsie Weil appeared in the September 1913 issue of *Theatre Magazine:*

The Hull-House Players are not amateurs. They act with a finish and artistic precision which, as one Chicago critic said, inflicts on them the penalty as well as the privilege of being considered professionals. They are not college students entering into dramatics as a sort of lark; they are not people of comparative leisure resorting to amateur acting to fill up part of their playtime. Rather they are hard-working young folks, who have plenty of troubles and worries, some of them with families to look after, and yet who come to their acting as to something that will freshen up the wilted aspect of life for them after the daily grind. Everyone must have some interest outside of the "bread alone" struggle to keep wholesome and happy. With some it is athletics, books, traveling or cards. With these young people it is their acting, and they are satisfied to have it take up most of their spare time. They have two rehearsals a week, and just before a new production, all-day rehearsals on Sundays. Their connection with the company not only provides all their amusement, but a stimulating intellectual life for them as well. They have high ideals of life and society and prefer to present those plays that deal with the serious moral and social problems of the day, such as those of Shaw, Galsworthy and Pinero.

# 1910s

Harriet Monroe started *Poetry: A Magazine of Verse* in 1912. It continues to prosper and to be innovative. In its early years, the brash little magazine published verses by T. S. Eliot, Amy Lowell, Ezra Pound, Sara Teasdale, Nicholas Vachel Lindsay, Joyce Kilmer, and a then unknown Chicago poet, Carl Sandburg. It represented both quality and excitement. Since then, it has helped introduce America and its poets to each other through more than four generations. The following are from its first year's pages:

## To Whistler, American

(On the loan exhibit of his paintings at the Tate Gallery.)

You also, our first great,
Had tried all ways;
Tested and pried and worked in many fashions,
And this much gives me heart to play the game.

Here is a part that's slight, and part gone wrong,
And much of little moment, and some few
Perfect as Durer!

"In the Studio" and these two portraits, if I had my choice!
And then these sketches in the mood of Greece?

You had your searches, your uncertainties,
And this is good to know—for us, I mean,
Who bear the brunt of our America
And try to wrench her impulse into art.

You were not always sure, not always set
To hiding night or tuning "symphonies;"
Had not one style from birth, but tried and pried
And stretched and tampered with the media.

You and Abe Lincoln from that mass of dolts
Show us there's chance at least of winning through.

—Ezra Pound

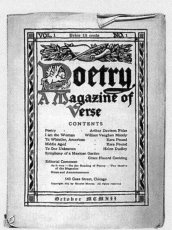

Nicholas Vachel Lindsay was an early discovery by the editor of *Poetry Magazine*. His poem, "General William Booth Enters into Heaven," about the death of the founder of the Salvation Army, was published in the fourth issue of the magazine and established him as one of the most original of American poets. The following represents the first two verses of the poem:

# General William Booth Enters into Heaven

(To be sung to the tune of "The Blood of the Lamb" with indicated instruments.)

Booth led boldly with his big brass drum.
    *Are you washed in the blood of the Lamb?*
The saints smiled gravely, and they said, "He's come."
    *Are you washed in the blood of the Lamb?*    (Bass drums)
Walking lepers followed, rank on rank,
Lurching bravos from the ditches dank,
Drabs from the alleyways and drug-fiends pale—
Minds still passion-ridden, souls powerful frail!
Vermin-eaten saints with moldy breath,
Unwashed legions with the ways of death—
    *Are you washed in the blood of the Lamb?*

Every slum has sent its half-a-score
The round world over—Booth had groaned for more.
Every banner that the wide world flies
Bloomed with glory and transcendent dyes.
Big-voiced lasses made their banjos bang!
Tranced, fanatical, they shrieked and sang,     (Banjo)
    *Are you washed in the blood of the Lamb?*
Hallelujah! It was queer to see
Bull-necked convicts with that land make free!
Loons with bazoos blowing blare, blare, blare—
On, on, upward through the golden air.
    *Are you washed in the blood of the Lamb?*

# 1910s

The vigorous words of Carl Sandburg's poetry are still often used to describe Chicago even though they no longer quite fit the much-changed metropolis. : "Chicago" was printed in the magazine in 1914 and probably became his best-known poem and the lead poem in his 1916 collection, *Chicago Poems:*

CHICAGO POEMS
CARL SANDBURG

# Chicago

    Hog Butcher for the World,
    Tool Maker, Stacker of Wheat,
    Player with Railroads and the Nation's Freight Handler;
    Stormy, husky, brawling,
    City of the Big Shoulders:

They tell me you are wicked, and I believe them; for I have seen
    your painted women under the gas lamps luring the farm boys.
And they tell me you are crooked, and I answer: Yes, it is true
    I have seen the gunman kill and go free to kill again.
And they tell me you are brutal, and my reply is: On the faces of
    women and children I have seen the marks of wanton hunger.
And having answered so I turn once more to those who sneer at
    this my city, and I give them back the sneer and say to them:
Come and show me another city with lifted head singing so proud
    to be alive and coarse and strong and cunning.
Flinging magnetic curses amid the toil of piling job on job, here is
    a tall bold slugger set vivid against the little soft cities;
Fierce as a dog with tongue lapping for action, cunning as a savage
    pitted against the wilderness,
            Bareheaded,
            Shoveling,
            Wrecking,
            Planning,
            Building, breaking, rebuilding,
Under the smoke, dust all over his mouth, laughing with white teeth,
Under the terrible burden of destiny laughing as a young man laughs,
Laughing even as an ignorant fighter laughs who has never lost a battle,
Bragging and laughing that under his wrist is the pulse, and under
    his ribs the heart of the people,
            Laughing!
Laughing the stormy, husky, brawling laughter of Youth, half-
    naked, sweating, proud to be Hog Butcher, Tool Maker, Stacker
of Wheat, Player with Railroads and Freight Handler to the Nation.

The verses of labor's battle hymn, "Solidarity Forever," were written by Ralph Chaplin in Chicago on January 17, 1915. He and a friend first sang the song on the way to a hunger march that started from Hull House. The protest was subsequently broken up by the police with billy clubs and shots fired over the marchers' heads.

# Solidarity Forever

When the Union's inspiration through the workers'
    blood shall run.
There can be no power greater anywhere
    beneath the sun;
Yet what force on earth is weaker than the feeble
    strength of one?
But the Union makes us strong.

[Chorus]:
Solidarity forever,
Solidarity forever,
Solidarity forever,
For the Union makes us strong.

Is there aught we hold in common with the greedy parasite
Who would lash us into serfdom and would crush us with his might?
Is there anything left to us but to organize and fight?
For the Union makes us strong. [chorus]

It is we who plowed the prairies; built the cities where
    they trade;
Dug the mines and built the workshops; endless miles of
    railroad laid.
Now we stand outcast and starving, 'midst the wonders
    we have made;
But the Union makes us strong. [chorus]

All the world that's owned by idle drones is ours and
    ours alone.
We have laid the wide foundations; built it skyward
    stone by stone.
It is ours, not to slave in, but to master and to own,
While the Union makes us strong. [chorus]

They have taken untold millions that they never toiled to earn,
But without our brain and muscle not a single wheel can turn.
We can break their haughty power; gain our freedom
    when we learn
That the Union makes us strong. [chorus]

In our hands is placed a power greater than their hoarded gold;
Greater than the might of armies, magnified a thousand fold.
We can bring to birth a new world from the ashes of the old.
For the Union makes us strong. [chorus]

Chaplin was a Wobbly, or member of the Industrial Workers of the World, an organization founded in Chicago in 1905 that wanted to organize workers into one big union. The militant preamble to the constitution of the Chicago-based I.W.W. read in part:

# I.W.W. Preamble

The working class and the employing class have nothing in common. There can be no peace so long as hunger and want are found among millions of working people and the few who make up the employing class have all the good things of life.

Between these two classes a struggle must go on until the workers of the world organize as a class, take possession of the earth and the machinery of production, and abolish the wage system.

We find that the centering of the management of industries into fewer and fewer hands makes the trade unions unable to cope with the ever growing power of the employing class. The trade unions foster a state of affairs, which allows one set of workers to be pitted against another set of workers in the same industry, thereby helping defeat one another in wage wars. Moreover, the trade unions aid the employing class to mislead the workers into the belief that the working class have interests in common with their employers.

These conditions can be changed and the interest of the working class upheld only by an organization joined in such a way that all its members in any one industry, or in all industries, if necessary, cease work whenever a strike or lockout is on in any department thereof, thus making an injury to one an injury to all.

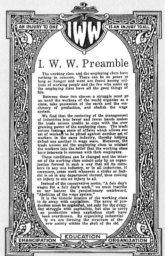

Instead of the conservative motto, "A fair day's wages for a fair day's work," we must inscribe on our banner the evolutionary watchword, "Abolition of the wage system."

It is the historic mission of the working class to do away with capitalism. The army of production must be organized not only for the everyday struggle with capitalists, but also to carry on production when capitalism shall have been overthrown. By organizing industrially we are forming the structure of the new society within the shell of the old.

## "CHICAGO, THE MOST CIVILIZED CITY IN AMERICA"

On Sunday, October 28, 1917, Henry L. Mencken startled *Chicago Tribune* readers with an essay that called their town "the most civilized city in America." Culturally, he said, it was "alive from snout to tail" and stood as "the most thoroughly American of cities." The article had first appeared in *Smart Set Magazine,* which he edited. In 1920, a version of the essay would appear in the *London Nation.*

Although the piece has often been quoted, it has likely appeared nowhere else in its entirety since then. Here is the complete 1917 article:

American in every chitling and sparerib, and it is alive from snout to tail.

The most civilized city in America? Chicago, of course! And per corollary the most thoroughly American, at least among the big ones. A culture is bogus unless it is honest, which means unless it is truly national—the naive and untinctured expression of a national mind and soul.

That of Boston is as bogus as a set of false teeth. The Bostonian is simply a fourth-rate colonial snob. Even in his preposterous speech, he tries to conceal the damnable fact that he was hatched a Yankee. Take him at his best and he is still ashamed of his nationality. Run a Manchester commercial gent through Harvard and you would have a Back Bay intellectual.

The trouble with New York is that it has no nationality at all. It is simply a free port—a place where the raw materials of civilization are received, sorted out, and sent further on.

In the arts it is a mere wholesaler. It prints two-thirds of the books in the country—and can't show a single author worth printing. It has the world's largest warehouse of artists—and never produces a picture worth hanging. Its social pushers pour out millions for music—and even Boston has a better orchestra.

Philadelphia? A Sunday school with a family entrance up the alley. An old maid with the *Decameron* under her pillow. A Devil's Island for both artists and gentlemen. A first-rate book or symphony coming out of Philadelphia would astonish the world almost as much as an ostrich coming out of a hen's egg.

San Francisco? Dead, done, extinct, kaput, murdered by the New Thought and an act of God.

Pittsburgh, Baltimore, St. Louis, New Orleans, Washington, Cleveland, Detroit, Newark? Mon Doo! My word, my word!

But in Chicago, there is the mysterious something. In Chicago, a spirit broods upon the face of the water. Find me a writer who is undoubtedly an American and who has something new to say, and who says it with an air, and nine times out of ten I will show that he has some sort of connection with the abattoir by the lake—that he was bred there, or got his start there, or passed through there during the days when he was tender.

Run down the list for yourself. Chicago turned out Henry B. Fuller, the first American novelist to get away from the mooney old

# 1910s

spinsters from New England and depict the actual human beings of America. It turned out Frank Norris, the first to make that new sort of novel a big, living thing. It turned out Theodore Dreiser, who brought it to full beam and dignity. And it turned out four-fifths of the lesser fellows—Herrick, Patterson, Anderson, and their like—who worked it out on lower planes.

What has the East produced to match the work of these men? On the one hand, it has produced a lot of cheap trade goods of the Robert W. Chambers type—sentimental thrillers for sedentary fat women. And on the other hand it has turned out a lot of pretentious fluff of the Howells type—empty blather about alleged human beings whose chief character is that they are not mammals.

You know George Moore's jest—that Henry James went to Paris and read Flaubert, and Howells remained at home and read Henry James? Well, what is the work of an average eastern novelist but a laborious reboiling of the bones of Howells?

Turn from the novel to other manifestations of literary frenzy. Who is the chosen merry Andrew of New York, the favorite town wag, the maker of the local jokes? Franklin P. Adams, a Chicagoan.

Who, among all American humorists, has been the most popular since Mark Twain (himself born within the circle of Chicago and a Westerner all his days)? Finley Peter Dunne, a Chicagoan.

And who, of the national jesters, is the most American, the closest to the soil, the shrewdest and most penetrating in his dealings with national issues and national types? George Ade of Chicago.

All these men started in Chicago; all of them show Chicago habits of mind, all of them reek of Chicago in every line they write.

One hears a vast hullabaloo in New York about the Little Theaters. They become a fashionable diversion, and hence more booby traps. The first and best Little Theater in America was set up in Chicago. It ran for years before New York ever heard of it. When New York heard of it at last, New York made fun of it.

And now every alley in New York has a Little Theater, and all the ideas tried out in Chicago years ago are set before the oafs of Broadway as great novelties, and the New York critics hail them as revolutionary, and the pockets of many a wandering tripe seller of Forty-second Street are agreeably stuffed.

Art? Progress? The theater of the future? The future of your grandmother! The theater of four or five years before last. There was more real music in the old Tomaskircho at Leipzig, says James Huneker, than in all your modern opera houses and concert halls put together. There was more serious purpose and honest striving and sound understanding in Maurice Browne's little playhouse in Chicago than in all the Demi-Tasse theaters and Half-Portion theaters and Macdougal's Alley theaters between Fourth Street and the Harlem River.

Another matter that kicks up a vast bother among the newly intellectual is the new poetry movement.

Go to Boston and you will find various ambient composers of verse libre pointed out on the street with the same awe that New Yorkers used to show in pointing out Diamond Jim Brady and Bim the Button Man. Go down into Greenwich Village and you will find others publicly exhibiting themselves at $2 a peep at nightly balls in Webster Hall.

But out in Chicago you will still find the first magazine ever devoted to this new verse, and either the actual corpse or the plain tracks of four fifths of its best professors, from Nicholas Vachel Lindsay to Carl Sandburg, and from Harriet Monroe to Edgar Lee Masters.

In brief, all American literary movements that have youth in them, and a fresh point of view, and the authentic bounce and verve of the country and the true character and philosophy of its people—all these came out of Chicago.

It was Chicago, and not New York, that launched the Chap Book saturnalia of the nineties—the first of her endless efforts to break down formalism in the national letters and let in the national spirit. It was Chicago that produced the "Little Review." It was Chicago that turned out Ring Lardner, the first American author to write in the American language.

There was a time when San Francisco seemed likely to take the first place. Mark Twain and Bret Harte were given their starts out there; such fellows as Frank Norris and Jack London felt the spell of the town; there was in it a certain tolerant and expansive spirit that indubitably had a charm for men of ideas.

But the earthquake finished San Francisco. The old romance was blown up over night and on the ruins the Philistines planted their dullness. Today San Francisco is simply a third-rate American town—a town full of vice crusaders and other such prehensile messiahs, but as empty of artists as Hoboken.

But Chicago, so far at least, has escaped any such flattening. The sharp winds from the lake seem to be a perpetual antidote to that Puritan mugginess of soul, which wars with civilization in all American cities. In Chicago, originality still appears to be put above conformity. The idea out there is not to do what others do, but to do something they can't do. This idea is the foundation of all artistic endeavor. The artist is either an anarchist, or he is not worth a hoot. One may either train for the Union League Club or one may train for Parnassus; one cannot train for both.

The trouble with New York intellectually, is just here. The curse of the town lies in the fact that it seems to foster the spirit of the pusher and bounder—that puts much higher values upon conformity, acceptance, intellectual respectability, than it puts on actual ideas.

The typical New Yorker is forever trying to get into something, to be recognized in this or that circle, to be accepted grudgingly by someone he envies—usually some cad. He lives in the place, not where ideas are hatched, but where the rewards are distributed—and any system of distributing definite awards is bound to encourage the usual, the acknowledged, the tried and found harmless.

This deadening spirit shows itself not only in the ludicrous horde of social climbers who infest the town, wildly trying to buy their way into a codfish aristocracy through opera houses, picture galleries, and various pecksniffian philanthropies, but also in actual artists.

A writer, let us say, begins in Chicago. His aim out there is to do something new, to express himself fully, to pump his writing full of the breath of life. Then he comes to New York—and immediately he begins to write as if his main object were to get a favorable notice in the *Nation* or even the *New York Times*. In other words, he takes the veil. Once a producer of ideas, he is now merely a producer of platitudes.

And so in painting, in playwriting, in music, even in architecture. The only architectural novelty that America has ever achieved, the skyscraper, was born in Chicago—the fact almost goes without saying. In New York its first daring has been flattened out; it is now merely imitative and hideous. New York has conventionalized it; as it conventionalizes all things.

The New York spirit is a spirit of timidity, of regularity, of safe mediocrity. New York esteems, not what is vital and original, but what is approved. The typical New Yorker, whether artist or mere trader, is always looking over his shoulder furtively, in fear that he may have done something that is not nice and so brought down upon himself some inexplicable and preposterous penalty. He is afraid of himself. He is afraid, above all, of being an American. He is an imitator of imitators—a fourth-rate European, twice diluted.

This is not the spirit of the artist, it is not the spirit of the creator and innovator in any field. The true artist is Beethoven, pursuing his undeviating course through thick and thin, expressing his ego utterly, pouring out his inmost soul, unutterably contemptuous of his inferiors and their opinions. The true artist is

Cezanne, wholly the man and wholly the Frenchman. It is the function of art to make visible and overwhelming the precise things that the timid mob man, his nose in his rut, can never see.

I give you Chicago. It is not London-and-Harvard. It is not Paris-and-buttermilk. It is American in every chitling and sparerib, and it is alive from snout to tail.

### THE *CHICAGO DEFENDER*

In the era before and during World War I, the *Chicago Defender*, an African American newspaper, had both local and national editions. It was a cohesive driving force not only in the city where it had been founded by Robert S. Abbott in 1905 but also throughout the South. There, copies were often delivered surreptitiously. It is still published as a daily in Chicago.

In 1918, the paper editorialized to its Southern readership: "I beg of you, my brethren, to leave the blighted land. You are free men. . . . Your neck has been in a yoke. . . . To die from the bite of frost is far more glorious than that of the mob."

The *Defender* attacked the Ku Klux Klan and lynchings, and promised a better life to the descendants of slaves if they took the chance and left their near-bondage.

It was in the pages of the *Defender* during the years just before World War I that Americans first read of the new

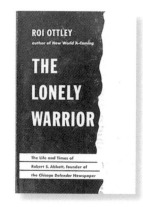

music, then spelled "jass." In a 1915 article entitled "Patronize Businesses Along the Stroll," it gave what one commentator called "an unmitigated moral blessing to the community, night-club investments and the music they represented." The Stroll was the bright-light nightclub district on South State Street.

The *Chicago Defender* attempted to show African Americans, both those isolated as tenant farmers in the South and others among the poorest of the poor in the North, that they had something in common—a shared culture (especially music) and a stand-up newspaper in Chicago.

## HENRY B. FULLER AND MARGARET ANDERSON

As early as in the days before World War I, Henry B. Fuller explored in his novel, *Bertram Cope's Year,* a vague but certain theme of young men caring about other men. The story was set on the campus of Northwestern University.

Along the same lines, Margaret Anderson's posthumously published *Forbidden Fires* was a fictionalized account of her romance with French actress-singer Georgette Leblanc. Her 1930 book, *My Thirty Years War,* was dedicated to Leblanc.

These two noteworthy Chicago writers were among the first Americans to write openly about gay and lesbian themes, blazing the trail for the Gay Rights movement in America.

**Henry B. Fuller**

### Henry B. Fuller

Fuller was the city's first native-born writer of stature. Having produced two outstanding novels before the turn of the century, *The Cliff-Dwellers* and *With the Procession,* he was not to be as successful with subsequent books, including *Bertram Cope's Year.*

As a person, he has been described as emotionally reticent and was so in his writings, which is not to say he did not have strong feelings. He, like authors Mark Twain and Finley Peter Dunne, was deeply committed to trying to stop American military aggression in the Philippines. Their efforts would be paralleled in the 1960s by members of the anti–Vietnam War movement. His biographer, John Pilkington Jr., refers to Fuller's "despondency over the role of American democracy in the Philippines."

Of the marketplace failure of Fuller's effort at working with a gay theme, Pilkington wrote:

> After finishing *Bertram Cope's Year* in May, 1918, Fuller negotiated with several New York firms for its publication; but, probably because of its subject, he could not reach agreement with any of them. Eventually, his friend, Ralph

Seymour, who printed *Poetry: A Magazine of Verse,* brought out the novel as a favor to Fuller. When it appeared in October, 1919, very few copies were sold; and it was generally ignored in the periodical press. Sometime later, Fuller collected the unbound sheets from Seymour and destroyed them.

### Margaret Anderson

Margaret Anderson was appreciated, according to an observer, "for her vitality, her beauty and her voluble enthusiasms." She founded the *Little Review* in 1914 and promised in it "untrammeled liberty." She kept her promise when, for the first time in America, she copublished James Joyce's *Ulysses,* a deed for which she was convicted and fined.

The following are the opening lines from her book, *My Thirty Years War:*

My greatest enemy is reality. I have fought it successfully for thirty years.

What have I been so unreal about? I have never been able to accept the two great laws of humanity—that you're always being suppressed if you're inspired and always being pushed into the corner if you're exceptional. I won't be cornered and I won't stay suppressed. This book is a record of these refusals.

It isn't that I'm aggressive. But life is antagonistic. You spend a few years fighting your family because they want you to be what you don't want to be—mine wanted me to be Aimee McPherson. You make friends who love your ideas and lose them because they don't know what an idea is. You fight the mob because it wants to make you or break you. You fall in love, and you soon find out what that is—giving to one human being the opportunity to invade and misunderstand you that you wouldn't dream of giving to the mob.

So then you fight the individual. And finally you find your stride . . . and from then on everything goes just as badly as ever. So then you fight the whole system again from the beginning.

### RING LARDNER

Ring Lardner, an excellent sports columnist, was an even better short-story writer. His column, known as "In the Wake of the News," ran in the *Chicago Tribune* from 1913 to 1919. Lardner's short stories began appearing in the *Saturday Evening Post* in 1914. These took

**Ring Lardner**

the form of letters back home from fictitious rookie pitcher, Jack Keefe. By classic standards, the word "bad" could be used in labeling the language, grammar, and spelling in every page, and in almost every sentence in them. It was not, however, a style that was wrong or bad but rather the idiom of the people that Lardner used. With it he wove charming and very funny stories, serving them up as literature on a platter of wonderfully "incorrect" English. The following is the first letter in the initial collection of his stories, *You Know Me Al:*

Chapter I
A Busher's Letters Home
Terre Haute, Indiana,
September 6.

FRIEND AL: Well, Al old pal I suppose you seen in the paper where I been sold to the White Sox. Believe me Al it comes as a surprise to me and I bet it did to all you good old pals down home. You could of knocked me over with a feather when the old man come up to me and says Jack I've sold you to the Chicago Americans.

I didn't have no idea that anything like that was coming off. For five minutes I was just dumb and couldn't say a word.

He says We aren't getting what you are worth but I want you to go up to that big league and show those birds that there is a Central League on the map. He says go and pitch the ball you been pitching down here and there won't be nothing to it. He says all you need is the nerve and Walsh or no one else won't have nothing on you.

So I says I would do the best I could and I thanked him for the treatment I got in Terre Haute. They always was good to me here and though I did more than my share I always felt that my work was appreciated. We are finishing second and I done most of it. I

can't help but be proud of my first year's record in professional baseball and you know I am not boasting when I say that Al.

Well Al it will seem funny to be up there in the big show when I never was really in a big city before. But I guess I seen enough of life not to be scared of the high buildings eh Al?

I will just give them what I got and if they don't like it they can send me back to the old Central and I will be perfectly satisfied.

I didn't know anybody was looking me over, but one of the boys told me that Jack Doyle the White Sox scout was down here looking at me when Grand Rapids was here. I beat them twice in that series. You know Grand Rapids never had a chance with me when I was right. I shut them out in the first game and they got one run in the second on account of Flynn misjudging that fly ball. Anyway Doyle liked my work and he wired Comiskey to buy me. Comiskey come back with an offer and they excepted it. I don't know how much they got but anyway I am sold to the big league and believe me Al I will make good.

Well Al I will be home in a few days and we will have some of the good old times. Regards to all the boys and tell them I am still their pal and not all swelled up over this big league business.

Your pal, Jack

### SHERWOOD ANDERSON

In his book, *Midwest Portraits,* Harry Hansen described novelist and poet Sherwood Anderson as a "dreamer, philosopher, corn-fed mystic, a man who gathered unto himself all the torment of life." Anderson, the author of *Winesburg, Ohio* and *Windy McPherson's Son,* worked during the day and wrote at night. He completed four novels before ever seeing one in print. Floyd

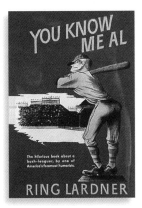

# 1910s

Dell called him "the city's great unpublished author." His efforts "to make it," his ambition and drive, were so strong that they led to a nervous breakdown followed by amnesia. Despite all the barriers he had to meet, his advice to writers was to stay true to themselves, not to imitate the success of others or produce what publishers wanted.

His comments use different metaphors than do the words of Louis Sullivan and other Chicago writers, but they seem to say the same thing: Don't imitate, but rather trust in your own originality and integrity.

Here are two of Anderson's exhortations expressing this:

> Truth and honesty is what we need most. We must break away from the standards set by the money-making magazines and book publishers in Europe and America, to older, sweeter standards of the writing craft itself. In proclaiming this we are not announcing a new doctrine; actually it is as old as the world; it is merely the voice of the new man come into the new world, proclaiming his right to speak out of the body and soul of youth, rather than through the bodies and souls of master craftsmen who are gone. It holds the promise of a perpetual sweet birth of the world. But be sure you recognize the new—there will be thousands of voices crying out that they carry the real message—do not be misled by them, for "temples have been wrecked before only to be rebuilt." Be ready to accept hardship for the sake of your craft in America.

\*\*\*

> So whenever the writer finds himself baffled in drawing a character or in judging one drawn by another, let him turn thus in upon himself, trusting with childlike simplicity and honesty the truth that lives in his own mind. Indeed

one of the great rewards of living with small children is to watch their faith in themselves and to try to emulate them in this art. This practice has been such a help and delight to me.

## BERTHA HONORÉ PALMER EMBRACES THE IMPRESSIONISTS

Of art, Bertha Honoré Palmer, the grandest dame of the grande dames of Chicago society, once said:

> What is art? I cannot argue with Loredo Taft, who is a pundit, but in my limited conception it is the work of some genius graced with extraordinary proclivities not given to ordinary mortals. Speaking of art . . . my husband can spit over a freight car.

Argue, she did, however, with Andrew Carnegie and other patronizing art patrons for criticizing the "picture buyers" who encouraged the impressionists. To Carnegie, they were "Frenchy," "unholy," and "blurred." Bertha Palmer hesitated not a whit to buy them, as told in the following excerpt from her biography, *Silhouette in Diamonds,* by Ishbel Ross:

> If all else about Mrs. Bertha Palmer were forgotten, she would still be remembered as the person who introduced impressionist art to the United States in a convincing way. From the 1880s on she was a bold collector who displayed her paintings with pride and dared the traditionalists to spurn them. A tour of the gallery that her husband added to their mansion became one of the more esoteric rites of Chicago's social life at the turn of the century.
>
> Her collection covered three periods—the romantics, the Barbizon school, and the impressionists. But she stopped short of the cubists and abstractionists and

*Chaos, Creativity, and Culture*

**44**

never owned a Cezanne, Gauguin, Matisse, or Picasso. By the time they flourished, her husband was dead and she was overstocked with pictures. She had moved on to medieval furnishings and oriental porcelains and jade. But she had definitely affected the prevailing taste in art.

Daniel Catton Rich, director in turn of the Art Institute of Chicago and of the Worcester Art Museum, views her as a true pace setter in American art. He believes that if she had rounded up old masters, such as Sir Joseph Duveen, she would have drawn her own following in that field. But Mrs. Palmer found it adventurous and chic to back the impressionists. They made fashionable interior decoration as well as being experimental art.

"In collecting you always have to have a leader and she was prescient enough to realize that they would catch on," Mr. Rich comments. "She made the impressionists a style and helped the independents to move ahead. She was definitely creative and never a copyist in any field. She had an open mind and an alert eye for new trends and her interest in art was genuine. In collecting impressionist, Chinese, and Renaissance art she was a great eclectic in policy. She made few mistakes in her selections, from her Millets, Corots, and Daubignys of the Barbizon school, to a romantic like Delacroix, and on to her impressionists."

Only a few of her friends could accept her frieze of Monets at first but today the Art Institute of Chicago glories in her paintings by Sisley, Pissarro, Delacroix, Corot, Degas, Renoir, and Monet that it acquired in 1922 through the terms of Mrs. Palmer's will.

**Bertha Honoré Palmer**

1920s

CHICAGO

122—Fountain of Time, Washington Park, Chicago

# 1920s: Gangsters, Jazz, Sculpture, and the University of Chicago

I n the 1920s, Chicago is well remembered for Al Capone and for its almost equally corrupt mayor, Big Bill Thompson. But it was also home to jazz musician Louis Armstrong; architect Louis Sullivan; opera diva Mary Garden; Nobel Prize winner Ernest

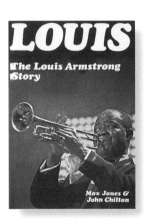

Hemingway (a native of Oak Park and a short time of the Near North Side); artist Stan Szukalski; the *Chicago Literary Times*; the irreverent artistic Dill Pickle Club; storyteller, poet, and playwright Ben Hecht; and University of Chicago's young president, Robert Maynard Hutchins.

Among the town's poets were Carl Sandburg, Harriet Monroe, Lew Seratt, Edgar Lee Masters, Nicholas Vachel Lindsay (though often in Chicago, actually only a visitor from Springfield), Eunice Tietjens, Maxwell Bodenheim, Harriet Converse Moody, and the so-called "Column Poets," whose works appeared in daily newspaper columns such as the *Chicago Tribune*'s "Line-O-Type."

Other writers of the decade included Lester Cohen, H. Chatfield-Taylor, the *Tribune*'s Bert Leston Taylor, and Burton Rascoe, the *Examiner's* Charlie MacArthur, as well as the *Chicago Daily News* writers Carl Sandburg, Ben Hecht, Bob Casey, Harry Hansen, Lloyd Lewis, and Henry Justin Smith.

Women writers with connections to Chicago were writing novels and winning the Pulitzer Prize. These writers included Willa Cather (1923), Edna Ferber (1925), and Margaret Ayer Barnes (1931), as well as a fourth, Chicagoan Janet Ayer Fairbanks, the runner-up in 1926.

# 1920s

The Chicago of the 1920s, according to Alson J. Smith, author of *Chicago's Left Bank,* was also enjoying the "Golden Age of Chicago Art." Its artists, besides Taft and Szukalski, included Rudolph Weisenborn, who headed the city's radical No-Jury Society (No-Jury Means Freedom); primitive painter T. A. Hoyer (a former professional acrobat); block printer Wallace Smith who illustrated many of Ben Hecht's books; block-print artist, Todros Geller; Gauguin-style painter Jerome Blum; the capricious and rebellious Joseph Allworthy; and Carl Hallsthammer, a superb wood sculptor.

African American and white Chicagoans were impacting the jazz scene. The latter included reedmen Mezz Mezzrow, who later wrote *Really the Blues,* and Bix Beiderbecke, as well as a group of very talented musicians from the Far West Side known as "the Austin High Gang." The former were well represented by Louis Armstrong, Joseph "King" Oliver, and, for a time, Jelly Roll Morton.

## LOUIS ARMSTRONG

Louis "Satchmo" Armstrong—who learned the coronet in the Waifs Band in New Orleans while he was doing a stretch in the Colored Waifs Home for Boys there—was invited to come to Chicago in August 1922 and play with his former mentor, Papa Joe "King" Oliver. The latter, who had earlier moved north, was leading a group called King Oliver and His Creole Jazz Band.

Armstrong's autobiography, *Satchmo: My Life in New Orleans,* ends with the following account of his first night playing with Oliver in the Lincoln Gardens on Chicago's South Side:

When we cracked down on the first note that night at the Lincoln Gardens I knew that things would go well for me. When Papa Joe began to blow that horn of his it felt right like old times. The first

number went over so well that we had to take an encore. It was then that Joe and I developed a little system for the duet breaks. We did not have to write them down. I was so wrapped up in him and lived so closely to his music that I could follow his lead in a split second. No one could understand how we did it, but it was easy for us and we kept it up the whole evening.

I did not take a solo until the evening was almost over. I did not try to go ahead of Papa Joe because I felt that any glory that came to me must go to him. He could blow enough horn for both of us. I was playing second to his lead, and I never dreamed of trying to steal the show or any of that silly rot.

Every number on opening night was a "gassuh." A special hit was a piece called "Eccentric" in which Joe took a lot of breaks. First he would take a four bar break, then the band would play. Then he would take another four bar break. Finally at the very last chorus Joe and Bill Johnson would do a sort of musical act. Joe would make his horn sound like a baby crying, and Bill Johnson would interrupt on that high note as though to say, "Don't cry, little baby." Finally this musical horseplay broke up in a wild squabble between nurse and child, and the number would bring down the house with laughter and applause.

After the floor show was over we went into some dance tunes, and the crowd yelled, "Let the youngster blow!" That meant me. Joe was wonderful and he gladly let me play my rendition of the blues. That was heaven.

Papa Joe was so elated that he played half an hour over time. The boys from downtown stayed until the last note was played and they came backstage and talked to us while we packed our instruments.

They congratulated Joe on his music and for sending to New Orleans to get me. I was so happy I did not know what to do.

I had hit the big time. I was up North with the greats. I was playing with my idol, the King, Joe Oliver. My boyhood dream had come true at last.

## THE TRIBUNE TOWER COMPETITION: MODERNISM AND "THE BUILDING THAT WAS NOT BUILT"

On its seventy-fifth anniversary, June 10, 1922, the *Chicago Tribune* announced an international architectural competition for designing its new structure. The rules designated the height but stated few other requirements other than that it be "the world's most beautiful office building."

Frederick W. Revels, director of the Department of Architecture at Syracuse University, a major critic in the field, stated that the Tribune Tower Competition was the most significant event in architectural history since professionalizing architecture.

If it were, it was not because the critics all agreed that the goal had been reached of creating *Tribune* publisher Colonel McCormick's "most beautiful" commercial structure in the universe. Rather it was indirectly that the competition led to a new commercial architectural format in Chicago and around the world.

More than 300 architects, including a third from other countries, submitted 263 entries. The timing was important. World War I was behind them, and European firms especially were looking to the future and to American architects such as Frank Lloyd Wright and Louis Sullivan and consequently, to a new modernism, devoid of the classical influences of Athens and Rome. The competition afforded a global cross-pollination of ideas as well as an extraordinary forum of publicity for the ideas that flowed from the various entries, especially those of second-place finisher, Eliel Saarinen.

Here, in a passage from the 1939

Plate Number 1

WPA *Illinois: A Descriptive and Historical Guide,* writers from the Great Depression era's Works Progress Administration assessed the impact of the Tribune Tower Competition:

In 1922 a Gothic design by Raymond Hood and John Mead Howells of New York won the $50,000 first prize in the worldwide competition by the *Chicago Tribune* for its new building. Here, were it not for a strange quirk, the satisfactory solution of height was indicated; the shaft of the building was frankly vertical, and the Gothic detail and crown struck no

1920s

incongruity and yet retained the note of traditionalism. The quirk was the second-prize design, the "building that was never built." The work of Eliel Saarinen of Finland, it followed no style but took Sullivan's creed and stated it more boldly than he had ever dreamed. It discarded the cornice, stripped the ornament away, and frankly exposed its structural plan, relying solely on set-back masses and strong vertical lines. Tile basic elements in the design were soon widely imitated, and the Gothic and Classic styles were completely discarded thereafter for skyscrapers.

Before long, office building architects began to work with even simpler surfaces and bold sculptural masses dictated by the set-back provisions of the zoning laws and the necessity of supplying light to as many offices as possible. Two firms led in designing a series of soaring, clean-limbed towers in this new style. One was Holabird and Root, beginning with 333 Michigan Avenue and ending with the Board of Trade and Palmolive buildings. The other was Graham Anderson, Probst, and White with the Field Building, Merchandise Mart, and Civic Opera.

## ERNEST HEMINGWAY

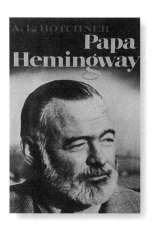

Novelist Ernest Hemingway, a native of suburban Oak Park, won the Nobel Prize for literature in 1954. He had blossomed as a novelist in Paris during the mid-1920s. Living among such expatriates as poet essayist Gertrude Stein, novelist F. Scott Fitzgerald, poet Ezra Pound, and fellow Chicago authors Sherwood Anderson and John Dos Passos, he wrote his first novel, *The Sun Also Rises*, between 1924 and 1926. It is a story of the wandering through Europe of a group of friends, young people of the kind whom Stein had spoken to as "a lost generation."

In Hemingway's story, the precious medals that men had been awarded for bravery during the war less than a decade earlier have become a joke to the young travelers in Europe. Sojourning in Spain, they find the bloody encounters of man versus bull, an antidote to the boredom heightened by their earlier precipice living during the war.

The following two 1920s accounts contrast with each other.

The first, from Carlos Baker's biography, *Ernest Hemingway: A Life,* describes the Hemingways' own style of living on the Near North Side of Chicago in 1921:

He [Ernest] was having trouble getting a job. An Oak Parker named Tubby Williams hired him on a piecework basis to write advertising copy for Firestone Tires, and he collaborated halfheartedly with his high school classmate, Morrie Musselman, who was trying to write a comedy for the stage. Bill Home came to his rescue in November by inviting him to share a third-floor room on North State Street. Home paid the rent and they ate around the corner at a Greek lunchroom called Kitsos, which employed a colored cook and offered steak and potatoes for sixty cents. On Sundays they often went out to Oak Park to stoke up on Dr. Hemingway's homemade chicken pies. Ernest boasted to his friends that he was "grinding out stuff" each day for the *Toronto Star Weekly.* In fact, however, Cranston printed only a handful of his articles between the end of October and the turn of the year.

In December he answered a want ad in the *Chicago Tribune.* An editor named Richard Loper needed a man to write for the *Cooperative Commonwealth,* a slick-paper monthly magazine put out by the Cooperative Society of America. The starting salary was forty dollars a week and Ernest grabbed at the chance. The

December number contained twenty pages of advertising and eighty of reading matter, much of it dashed off by Ernest himself. He wrote his mother that he was going to use his first salary check to buy some clothes, both over and under, and that he was trying to follow her instructions by being "very busy, very good, and very tired."

Christmas had sneaked up on him, with no time left for shopping. His presents for his sisters would have to be "paper seeds in small denominations." He wished all the family a Merry Christmas, but not a Happy New Year. Any new year, said he, morosely, was just one more lurch nearer the grave.

Such was far from the life his characters experience in the following account of a bullfight from *The Sun Also Rises:*

The bull-fight on the second day was much better than on the first. Brett sat between Mike and me at the barrera, and Bill and Cohn went up above. Romero was the whole show. I do not think Brett saw any other bull-fighter. No one else did either, except the hard-shelled technicians. It was all Romero. There were two other matadors, but they did not count. I sat beside Brett and explained to Brett what it was all about. I told her about watching the bull, not the horse, when the bulls charged the picadors, and got her to watching the picador place the point of his pic so that she saw what it was all about, so that it became more something that was going on with a definite end, and less of a spectacle with unexplained horrors. I had her watch how Romero took the bull away from a fallen horse with his cape, and how he held him with the cape and turned him, smoothly and suavely, never wasting the bull.

She saw how Romero avoided every brusque movement and saved his bulls for the last when he wanted them, not winded and discomposed but smoothly worn down. She saw how close Romero always worked to the bull, and I pointed out to her the tricks the other bull-fighters used to make it look as though they were working closely. She saw why she liked Romero's cape work and why she did not like the others.

Romero never made any contortions, always it was straight and pure and natural in line. The others twisted themselves like corkscrews, their elbows raised, and leaned against the flanks of the bull after his horns had passed, to give a faked look of danger. Afterward, all that was faked turned bad and gave an unpleasant feeling. Romero's bull-fighting gave real emotion, because he kept the absolute purity of line in his movements and always quietly and calmly let the horns pass him close each time. He did not have to emphasize their closeness. Brett saw how something that was beautiful done close to the bull was ridiculous if it were done a little way off. I told her how since the death of Joselito all the bull-fighters had been developing a technic that simulated this appearance of danger in order to give a fake emotional feeling, while the bull-fighter was really safe. Romero had the old thing, the holding of his purity of line through the maximum of exposure, while he dominated the bull by making him realize he was unattainable, while he prepared him for the killing.

"I've never seen him do an awkward thing," Brett said.

"You won't until he gets frightened," I said.

"He'll never be frightened," Mike said. "He knows too damned much."

# 1920s

"He knew everything when he started. The others can't ever learn what he was born with."

"And God, what looks," Brett said.

"I believe, you know, that she's falling in love with this bullfighter chap," Mike said.

"I wouldn't be surprised."

"Be a good chap, Jake. Don't tell her anything more about him. Tell her how they beat their old mothers."

"Tell me what drunks they are."

"Frightful," Mike said. "Drunk all day and spend all their time beating their poor old mothers."

"He looks that way," Brett said.

"Doesn't he?" I said.

They had hitched the mules to the dead bull and then the whips cracked, the men ran, and the mules, straining forward, their legs pushing, broke into a gallop, and the bull, one horn up, his head on its side, swept a swath smoothly across the sand and out the red gate.

## CHICAGO'S WOMEN WRITERS

Almost any list of the Chicago area's literary figures you find will probably be dominated by men. Yet, Chicago can boast of far more female writers who made worthwhile literary contributions than such listings indicate.

—The city's first novelist was Juliette Kinzie, author of *Wau-Bun*.

—Edith Franklin Wyatt, a member of the Chicago School of Fiction, was highly praised by American pundit William Dean Howells for not having "gone back out of her own or out of her own city to gather material for her stories and sketches."

—Three women who wrote novels and who lived for at least a time in Chicago won Pulitzer Prizes within a nine-year span. A fourth in that same period (1923–1932) was announced as second. Ironically, those nine years were the same ones in which Al Capone dominated the news about Chicago in the *New York Times*

and other papers around the country.

—Willa Cather was awarded the Pulitzer in 1923 for *One of Ours*. In 1915, she had written the wonderful Chicago novel *The Song of the Lark* about a young opera student in the city, Thea Kronborg. In 1935, she produced another Chicago-setting novel, *Lucy Gayheart*.

—Edna Ferber won a Pulitzer in 1925 for *So Big* about Dutch immigrants in Chicago and suburban South Holland.

—After Sinclair Lewis had refused the prize in 1926 for *Arrowsmith*, Chicagoan Janet Ayer Fairbanks was officially announced as having been "second."

—Her sister, Margaret Ayer Barnes, also a Chicagoan, was presented the prize for her *Years of Grace* in 1931.

Among the other names that also belong on any list of prominent women writers from the Chicago area are Clara Louise Burnham, Frances Willard, Myrtle Reed, Caroline Kirkland, Harriet Monroe, Margaret Anderson, Emily Kimbrough, Era Bell Thompson, Gwendolyn Brooks, Lorraine Hansberry, M. S. Craig (who also wrote under the name Mary Francis Shura), Jean Auel, Susan Sussman, Maxine Chernoff, Edith Freund, Ana Castillo, June Brindel, and Sara Paretsky.

The following is excerpted from Edna Ferber's *So Big:*

Chicago was his meat. It was booming, prosperous. Jeff Hankins's red plush and mirrored gambling house, and Mike Mc-Donald's, too, both on Clark Street, knew him daily. He played in good luck and bad, but he managed somehow to see to it that there was always the money to pay for the Fister schooling. His was the ideal poker face: bland, emotionless, immobile. When he was flush they ate at the Palmer House, dining off chicken or quail and thick rich soup and the apple pie for which the hostelry was famous.

**Willa Cather**

Waiters hovered solicitously about Simeon Peake, though he rarely addressed them and never looked at them. Selina was happy. She knew only such young shop girls she met at Miss Fister's school. Of men, other than her father, she knew as little as a nun—less. For those cloistered creatures must, if only in the conning of their Bible, learn much of the moods and passions that sway the male. The Songs of Solomon alone are a glorious sex education. But the Bible was not included in Selina's haphazard reading, and the Gideonite was not then a force in the hotel world.

Willa Cather, better known today for her southwestern novels *Death Comes for the Archbishop* and *Shadows on the Rock,* was

**Edna Ferber**

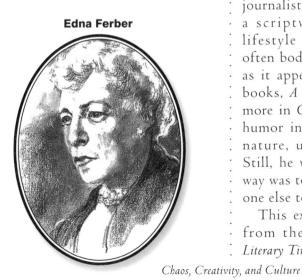

a very prolific writer also recognized for her midwestern and Chicago novels and short stories. This passage is from Willa Cather's 1935 novel, *Lucy Gayheart.* The story parallels her earlier *The Song of the Lark,* in which the heroine had also comes to Chicago. to study music. Both works demonstrate Cather's feel for the characters, the situation, and the city:

The next afternoon Lucy was walking slowly over toward Michigan Avenue. She had never loved the city so much; the city which gave one the freedom to spend one's youth as one pleased, to have one's secret, to choose one's master and serve him in one's own way. Yesterday's rain had left a bitter, springlike smell in the air; the vehemence that beat against her in the street and hummed above her had something a little wistful in it tonight, like a plaintive hand-organ tune. All the lovely things in the shop windows, the furs and jewels, roses and orchids, seemed to belong to her as she passed them. Not to have wrapped up and sent home, certainly; where would she put them? But they were hers to live among.

### BEN HECHT

Ben Hecht, a talented writer and a true literary character, was a Chicago journalist, a poet, an author, and later a scriptwriter in Hollywood. His lifestyle and writing were bold and often bodacious. Chicago in the 1920s as it appeared in his autobiographical books, *A Child of the Century* and even more in *Gaily, Gaily,* was quintessential humor in the form of offbeat human nature, underlined by exaggeration. Still, he was a terrific storyteller. His way was to avoid taking himself or anyone else too seriously.

This example of Hecht's writing is from the first issue of the *Chicago Literary Times,* March 1, 1923, published

*Chaos, Creativity, and Culture*

**Ben Hecht**

# 1920s

per out of their ears. Sandburg's tom-tom sounds through the new tar-smelling subdivisions. Szukalski thrusts his walking stick into the eye-sockets of LaSalle Street, Hecht explodes an epithet under the Old Ladies Home. Beating his bosom, Anderson sinks to his baggy knees gurgling mystically to God. The cubistical Bodenheim ululates on the horizon. Ehu! Ehu! The Pleiocene fogs are lifting.

This second selection is a postscript from the play, *The Front Page,* by Hecht and his friend and fellow reporter, Charlie MacArthur. Who else ever wrote an epilogue that was apologetic and took everything back?

Epilogue

This epilogue is one of apology. When we applied ourselves to write a newspaper play we had in mind a piece of work which would reflect our intellectual disdain of and superiority to the Newspaper.

What we finally turned out, as the reader may verify if he will, is a romantic and rather doting tale of our old friends—the reporters of Chicago.

It developed in writing this play that our contempt for the institution of the Press was a bogus attitude; that we looked back on the Local Room where we had spent half our lives as a veritable fairyland—and that we were both full of a nostalgia for the bouncing days of our servitude.

The same uncontrollable sentimentality operated in our treatment of Chicago which, as much as any of our characters, is the hero of our play.

The iniquities, double dealings, chicaneries and immoralities which as ex-Chicagoans we knew so well returned to us in a mist called the Good Old Days, and our delight in

by Hecht and Max Bodenheim. Note that both men mention themselves in the third person in this page one piece:

Chicago, the jazz baby—the reeking, cinder-ridden, joyous Baptist stronghold; Chicago, the chewing gum center of the world, the bleating, slant-headed rendezvous of half-witted newspapers, sociopaths and pants makers—in the name of the Seven Holy and Imperishable Arts, Chicago salutes you.

Civilization overtakes us. The Philoolulu bird lies on its back with its feet in the air—extinct. The Muses, coughing and spitting, reach their arms blindly towards the steel mills and the stockyards.

The cognoscenti pull the flypa-

our memories would not be denied.

As a result *The Front Page*, despite its oaths and realisms, is a Valentine thrown to the past, a Ballad (to us) full of Heim Weh and Love.

So it remains for more stern and uncompromising intellects than ours to write of the true Significance of the Press. Therefore our apology to such bombinators, radicals, Utopians and Schoengeisten who might read this work expecting intellectual mayhem.

In writing it we found we were not so much dramatists or intellectuals as two reporters in exile.

—The Authors.

## CLARENCE DARROW

Chicago lawyer Clarence Darrow is best remembered for his words in the courtroom, specifically those in his closing argument at the Loeb/Leopold trial. He was also the author of an autobiography, the two novels *An Eye for an Eye* and *Farmington,* the book of literary essays *A Persian Pearl,* as well as discourses and debates on a wide variety of subjects that included the negative position on the question, Is life worth living?

Writers, including playwright David Mamet, have studied Darrow's ability to express himself as a pristine example of how to communicate through the simple direct speech for which Chicago and the Midwest are known.

Here is a short excerpt from his closing argument in the trial of Richard Loeb and Nathan Leopold. Following his strategic instructions, the two had admitted they had killed little Bobby Franks to prove to themselves that they could get away with the perfect crime. Darrow's job was to convince the judge to sentence them not to death but rather, as he did, to life plus ninety-nine years. To defense lawyers, Darrow's closing argument is the touchstone for the presentation of using mitigating circumstances to check a compulsion for the death sentence in American courts.

The following Leopold/Loeb trial speech is from *Clarence Darrow on Capital Punishment,* reprinted in 1991 by Chicago Historical Bookworks:

The easy thing and the popular thing to do is to hang my clients. I know it. Men and women who do not think will applaud. The cruel and thoughtless will approve. It will be easy today; but in Chicago, and reaching out over the length and breadth of the land, more and more fathers and mothers, the humane, the kind and the hopeful, who are gaining an understanding and asking questions not only about these poor boys, but about their own— these will join in no acclaim at the death of my clients. These would ask that the shedding of blood be

**Clarence Darrow**

stopped, and that the normal feelings of man resume their sway. And as the days and the months and the years go on, they will ask it more and more. But, your Honor, what they shall ask may not count. I know the easy way. I know your Honor stands between the future and the past. I know the future is with me, and what I stand for here; not merely for the lives of these two unfortunate lads, but for all boys and all girls; for all of the young, and as far as possible, for all of the old. I am pleading for life, understanding, charity, kindness, and the infinite mercy that considers all. I am pleading that we overcome cruelty with kindness and hatred with love. I know the future is on my side. Your Honor stands between the past and the future. You may hang these boys; you may hang them by the neck until they are dead. But in doing it you will turn your face toward the past. In doing it you are making it harder for every other boy who in ignorance and darkness must grope his way through the mazes, which only childhood knows. In doing it you will make it harder for unborn children. You may save them and make it easier for every child that some time may stand where these boys stand. You will make it easier for every human being with an aspiration and a vision and a hope and a fate. I am pleading for the future; I am pleading for a time when hatred and cruelty will not control the hearts of men. When we can learn by reason and judgment and understanding and faith that all life is worth saving, and that mercy is the highest attribute of man.

## LOREDO TAFT

Chicago sculptor Loredo Taft had a profound and exciting notion. He felt art was a part of the essence of humankind, not incidental or an adornment to make a city, a park, or a cemetery somehow beautiful. One reads this in his writings but, more importantly, senses it in his works that are scattered about Chicago. These include a statue of a seated woman with children, now in the Belden Triangle; two monuments named *The Crusader* and *Eternal Silence,* in Graceland Cemetery; the *Fountain of the Great Lakes,* placed outside the Art Institute of Chicago; and, most of all, his *Fountain of Time* in Washington Park. The viewer feels something special in his works, a message of hope even when they speak of death or of us (rather than time) passing. Taft's sculptures are separate from the city's most heartfelt voice because they are classical and renaissance in execution. But within that context, they share Chicago's voice of freedom and originality in a limited way, not of copying the past but rather of listening to the voice of self-expression for guidance.

**The Fountain of Time**

*Chaos, Creativity, and Culture*

## LOUIS SULLIVAN AND THE CHICAGO REVOLUTION IN ARCHITECTURE.

Louis Sullivan, generally recognized to be the father of modern architecture, died in poverty April 14, 1924. He did not live to see his ideas or Chicago architecture receive the world's acclaim they are given today. In his book, *Culture and Democracy,* Hugh Duncan wrote of this: "What was then [the 1920s] thought to be a style—and not a very important style, at that—is now accepted as the world architecture. We no longer send our architects to Paris or Rome; now Europeans come to America, and specifically to Chicago."

Just three days before Sullivan's

**Louis Sullivan**

**Door of the Transportation Building at the World's Columbian Exposition in Chicago, designed by Louis Sullivan and considered by some the beginning of modern architecture**

# 1920s

death, Frank Lloyd Wright and other friends of Sullivan's rushed him the first off-the-press copy of his book, *The Autobiography of an Idea.* Its pages would subsequently help him and the Chicago School of Architecture establish a reputation not only for innovation but also for revolution in building design. Today, Sullivan is respected almost as much for his teachings and writings as for his architectural work.

Here, in the extraordinary book published at the time of his death, Sullivan warns about the abuse of architecture:

The work on the World's Columbian Exposition completed, the gates thrown open 1 May, 1893, the crowds flowed in from every quarter, continued to flow throughout a fair-weather summer and a serenely beautiful October. Then came the end. The gates were closed.

These crowds were astonished. They beheld what was for them an amazing revelation of the architectural art, of which previously they in comparison had known nothing. To them it was a veritable Apocalypse, a message inspired from on high. Upon it their imagination shaped new ideals. They went away, spreading again over the land, returning to their homes, each one of them carrying in the soul the shadow of the white cloud, each of them permeated by the most subtle and slow-acting of poisons; an imperceptible miasm within the white shadow of a higher culture. A vast multitude, exposed, unprepared, they had not had time nor occasion to become immune to forms of sophistication not their own, to a higher and more dexterously insidious plausibility. Thus they departed joyously, carriers of contagion, unaware that what they had beheld and believed to be truth was to prove, in historic fact, an appalling calamity. For what they saw was not at all what they

believed they saw, but an imposition of the spurious upon their eyesight, a naked exhibitionism of charlatanry in the higher feudal and domineering culture, conjoined with expert salesmanship of the materials of decay.

\*\*\*

The damage wrought by the World's Fair will last for half a century from its date, if not longer. It has penetrated deep into the constitution of the American mind, effecting there lesions significant of dementia.

## HERMAN KOGAN AND LLOYD WENDT ON "BIG BILL" THOMPSON

On rare occasions, two writers can combine and become one and still be both eloquent and powerful. In Chicago, this happened with two journalists, Herman Kogan and Lloyd Wendt, who produced five books together. They captured Chicago in each of these volumes on the city's history and characters, especially in the following passages from *Big Bill of Chicago,* their book about the city's preposterous mayor:

**Mayor William Hale "Big Bill" Thompson**

*Chaos, Creativity, and Culture*

Once upon a time there really was a Big Bill Thompson. And he was the tumultuous mayor of the city of Chicago in wild and incredible years.

In the beginning he was a fearless hero, by chance a champion of reform, and he strutted and shouted his way into the city's heart. Chicago was young then, as great cities go, and complex and contradictory. Flirting behind a china teacup or an ivory fan or the door of a Levee panel house, Chicago asked only to be pleased. Big Bill knew the arts of pleasure, and his raw voice called for fun while his hired minstrels and professional praise-shouters sang his fame as a builder of golden dreams.

While he carried on his romance with the city and had his way with her, it became clear to many that he was loud and boisterous but neither hero nor reformer. Chicago, they said, was a dissolute harridan who deserved to be fooled. And there were defenders who spoke up for Big Bill's and Chicago's good names. The din of the cries echoed far. Removed in distance and time, many marveled that one city could arouse so much evil report, that one man could evoke such fervent loyalties and unquenchable hatreds.

Some said of him: "God made just one William Hale Thompson and forgot the mold. Truth, courage, consecration, ideas of right, ideas of justice—all are in him. Call him a Napoleon, call him Abraham Lincoln—when history is written, they will write high in the blue sky above all of them the name of William Hale Thompson!"

And others: "He has given the city an international reputation for moronic buffoonery, barbaric crime, triumphant hoodlumism, unchecked graft, and a dejected citizenship. He nearly ruined the property and completely destroyed the pride of the city. He made Chicago a byword of the collapse of American civilization."

Who was Big Bill Thompson—a master politician, a firm patriot, a defender of American ideals, a friend to the oppressed, a supreme showman, a great sportsman, a prince of good fellows, a humanitarian who yearned only to do miracles for the city he ruled?

Or was Big Bill Thompson ". . . indolent, ignorant of public issues, inefficient and incompetent as an administrator, incapable of making a respectable argument, reckless in his campaign methods and electioneering oratory, inclined to think evil of those who are not in agreement or sympathy with him, and congenitally demagogical."

Or was Thompson a charlatan and a genius, a knave and a saint, a rogue and a knight, a builder and a despoiler, a mountebank and a gentleman, a P. T. Barnum and a George Washington, a churl and a gallant, a petulant child and a canny thinker? "Bill Thompson's the man for me!" sang some, and others answered, "He has the carcass of a rhinoceros and the brain of a baboon!" Some cried, "Big Bill's heart is as big as all outdoors!" And others replied, "The people have grown tired of this blubbering jungle hippopotamus!"

When this romance started, Chicago was a city of opportunity, no place for the weak, the docile or the squeamish. Its workers slaughtered more pork and beef, loaded more grain, made more soap, tanned more hides, poured more steel, built more plows and railroad cars than any other place in the land. Most of these workers had not journeyed to the city to create a

# 1920s

political utopia. They came to make homes and to make money. They created what was needed for the vast commerce that grew up in the wilderness they had opened: houses and bridges and streets, factories, hotels and skyscrapers. They dispatched buyers and sellers, promoters and schemers. They sent out mail-order catalogs and to produce them they set up massive printing plants. When their tasks were done, they were weary, most of them, and they left the chores of politics and politicking to those who hungered for power and prestige.

Big Bill came riding home from the West at a time when the city seemed ripe for the kind of man he was. In his affair with Chicago, he was sometimes tender, sometimes rapacious. Those who loved him praised even his faults. Those who hated him denied even his virtues. But no one could say that Big Bill gave sparingly of his ardor. Nor was his romance with the city of Chicago ever dull.

## STANISLAS SZUKALSKI, ARTIST

Ben Hecht, in his autobiographical *A Child of the Century,* wrote of a young Polish immigrant artist:

For twenty years my friend Stanislas Szukalski experienced disasters which would have killed off a dozen businessmen. Sickness, hunger and poverty yipped everlastingly at his heels. Defeat stood constantly at his doorway like a sheriff with a subpoena. And during his struggle he heard only the catcalls of critics and the voices of derision.

But the Polish American artist's appeal to his friend's artistic soul was without equivocation as Hecht later wrote:

**An Imaginary King, by Stanislas Szukalski**

We entered a dim lighted barren room that looked big enough to house a regiment. And a regiment seemed to be in it, lined against its shadowy walls. They were Szukalski's statues in plaster, bronze and clay.

I had never seen any statues like them, nor have I yet after 39 years. They were like a new and violent people who had invaded the earth. They seemed to be without skins, and their sinews writhed like imprisoned serpents. Torment and grandeur were in them, a mysterious shout seemed to hang over their heads. It was the shout of Prometheus from his rock. Lucifer and Christ were there and the wrath of God. Hypocrisy, valor, despair and rapture gestured commandingly in the shadows. There were figures that cringed with withered hands held out for alms, and heroes who seemed strangled by their own strength. Secrets animated all the statues.

Szukalski came to Chicago as a young man in 1913, the son of a Polish blacksmith who had been run over in a car accident. The Art Institute of Chicago gave him a show during World War I but removed one of his paintings because the trustees felt it offensive to the British. Szukalski protested by smashing the glass in the frames of his other paintings and knocking his sculptures off their pedestals.

He lived in the 57th Street colony of artists and writers, where he earned the reputation as its enfant terrible.

Later, Szukalski returned to his native Poland, where he was feted as the country's greatest artist with a national museum erected for his works. According to Hecht, the Nazi Luftwaffe destroyed the museum and the artist escaped Poland with his life, coming back to the United States and giving up his art.

## PALACES FOR THE PEOPLE

There's a chance that someone visiting Chicago in the 1920s or early 1930s would arrive asking about Al Capone but leave talking about the city's movie palaces. The Chicagoland area had forty-five, each of which could seat 1,000 or more moviegoers. Of these, fourteen had more than 3,000 seats in them. The biggest was the Uptown with a capacity of 4,307. It was the largest in the world.

Size, however, was outdone by grandeur. They were marked by ornate crafting—high-vaulted, intricately designed ceilings and sweeping stairways. The Tivoli, a South Side neighborhood theater at 63rd Street and Cottage Grove Avenue, had a lobby made of solid marble and modeled after the chapel that Jules Hardouin designed for King Louis XIV at Versailles.

Chicago's palaces were not for royalty nor for millionaires but for working-class men and women, children, old people, factory workers, and teenage lovers—for dreamers who never made it big and never would. The architecture was baroque, art deco, Spanish, or French. Always, the palaces were opulent but generally stopped short of being vulgar.

The statuary was also spectacular, especially to moviegoers who worked long hours in the city factories, catalog houses, packing plants, and offices. It could be symbolic as in Loredo Taft's statues of *Eternal Woman* at the Paradise at Crawford Avenue near Washington Street.

THE THEATRE HISTORICAL SOCIETY
CONCLAVE · 1977
CHICAGO

*Chaos, Creativity, and Culture*

61

Robert Maynard Hutchins

George Rapp, who, along with brother Cornelius, designed many of Chicago movie palaces, once said:

Watch the eyes of a child as it enters the portals of our great theaters and treads the pathway into fairyland. Watch the bright light in the eyes of the shop girl who hurries noiselessly over carpets and sighs with satisfaction as she walks amid furnishings that once delighted the hearts of queens. See the toil-worn father whose dreams have never come true, and look inside his heart as he finds strength and rest within the theater. There you have the answer why motion picture theaters are so palatial.

**The following is from the 1935 *Chicago Daily News Almanac*:**

**Of a total of 358 motion-picture theaters in the city the leading houses are given according to seating capacity as shown on the records of the county assessor:**

| Theater/Seats | | |
|---|---|---|
| Uptown 4,307 | Regal 2,810 | LaGrange** 2,000 |
| Tivoli 3,984 | Avalon 2,800 | Portage Park 1,960 |
| Chicago 3,940 | Sheridan 2,800 | Riviera 1,948 |
| Marbro 3,939 | State-Lake 2,756 | Grove 1,856 |
| Oriental 3,900 | New Palace 2,533 | State 1,850 |
| Paradise 3,700 | Pickwick* 2,500 | Jeffery 1,804 |
| Granada 3,442 | Capitol 2,499 | Symphony 1,706 |
| Belmont 3,257 | Stratford 2,490 | United Artists 1,700 |
| Belpark 3,231 | Terminal 2,443 | Roosevelt 1,591 |
| Senate 3,127 | Tiffin 2,299 | Maryland 1,540 |
| Century 3,087 | McVicker's 2,284 | Teatro del Lago*** 1,000 |
| Norshore 3,018 | Gateway 2,092 | |
| Tower 3,014 | Highland 2,086 | * In Park Ridge. |
| Piccadilly 2,892 | Nortown 2,046 | ** In LaGrange. |
| Harding 2,861 | Roseland-State 2,030 | *** In no man's land, |
| | Pantheon 2,028 | now part of Wilmette. |

## ROBERT MAYNARD HUTCHINS AND THE UNIVERSITY OF CHICAGO

The University of Chicago announced April 26, 1929, that its new president—one who was younger than many of its students and almost all of its professors—would be thirty-year-old Robert Maynard Hutchins, who had been dean of Yale University Law School. Of that day, his biographer, Harry S. Ashmore, would later write:

Upon his precipitate elevation to the rank of university president, Robert Hutchins took stock of his own learning and recognized that he had arrived at the age of thirty with some knowledge of the Bible, of Shakespeare, of Faust, of one dialogue of Plato and of the opinions of many semi-literate and a few literate judges, and that was about all.

Hutchins' radical theory was to help students become people who change their environment rather than facilely adapt to it.

*Chaos, Creativity, and Culture*

1930s

CHICAGO

# 1930s: New Sounds in Music, the Chicago African American Flowering, Studs Lonigan, and a World's Fair

Here is what was happening with music in Chicago in the 1930s:

—Gospel music was born;

—The blues and jazz became urbanized and each developed a new Chicago style;

—Country and western music was broadcast into people's homes across the United States for the first time through the radio broadcasts of the *WLS National Barn Dance;*

—Carl Sandburg, performing as a folksinger and touting his newly published *American Songbag,* became a direct link to the folk music revival of the 1950s and 1960s and specifically to the founding of the Old Town School of Folk Music in the city;

—Benny Goodman invented and defined swing;

—The Chicago Symphony Orchestra received recognition, far more than any major orchestra, for performing and encouraging the work of American composers;

The 1930s also heralded a new African American energy and self-esteem that exploded into a dramatic cultural flowering in the city.

The world's fair "A Century of Progress" introduced America to new ways of thinking about architecture, science, education, and transportation as well as fan dancers. It exhibited America's products, styles, and paintings, including a new American symbol, *American Gothic.* Melvina Hoffman was sculpting the Field Museum's Hall of Man.

Among the Chicago writers of the 1930s was James T. Farrell who created Studs Lonigan—a unique, American literary character—and a trilogy of novels.

During this era, both African

# 1930s

American and Jewish theater flourished in Chicago.

The writers, artists, and actors of the Works Progress Administration in Chicago included Studs Terkel (actor and Pulitzer Prize winner), Willard Motley (interviewer and novelist), Jack Conroy (author and editor), Nelson Algren (novelist and essayist), Saul Bellow (novelist), Richard Wright (novelist), Curtis MacDougall (author), Sam Ross (novelist), Frank Yerby (novelist), and Margaret Walker (poet).

## MARY BORDEN ON CHICAGO AND AL CAPONE

The following excerpt is from a 1931 *Harper's Magazine* article, "Chicago Revisited," written by Mary Borden. During World War I, she had served as director of a mobile hospital in France where she met and married a British officer. After moving to England, she became a successful novelist there. Her niece Ellen Borden Stevenson married Adlai Stevenson, the Democratic candidate for the presidency in the 1950s. Later, after Ellen divorced Adlai, she would prove herself a special friend of Chicago writers and artists.

The following is from the magazine piece written when Mary Borden returned to Chicago in 1930 after a twelve-year absence.

## "THE SOUP KITCHEN OF A GANGSTER"

I did not see Al Capone, in spite of the fact that when I told them in Paris and London and New York I was going back to Chicago, my native city, they had all immediately said that I should. It was the inevitable response, though the tone varied. Sometimes scornfully, sometimes slyly, maliciously, sometimes enviously they said, "Oh! You'll see Al Capone." I didn't. I saw only his soup kitchen. But it was through no fault of my own, for I am a sufficiently typical daughter of my great, roaring, bumptious town to feel that it needs from me no apology;

that as long as all American cities are going in for gangs and rackets, and all the American world, including congressmen, senators, wet and dry judges, policemen and parsons, are buying whisky, it need not be particularly ashamed of having produced the Ace of Bootleggers, Al the Scarface.

No. I saw the soup kitchen because it was there for all to see with "Free Soup, Coffee, and Doughnuts for the Unemployed" printed in large letters over its grimy doorway, and I didn't see Al Capone because he was invisible. Wanted by the police on the charge of being a public enemy, he was not, when I arrived, granting audiences to sightseers. Al is discreet if Chicago is not. He is more difficult of access than the Pope. But not from shame does he hide. No one is ashamed of anything in Chicago; everything is moving too quickly; everyone is too specialized, and it is all too much fun. Each one, whether crook or politician or expert gunman, architect or banker or broker, is too good of his kind to be conscious of anything less positive and less exhilarating than his own power. The city itself is like that, too big, too busy, too powerful, and in too much of a hurry to have any negative emotions. There's a lot of room in Chicago. There's the whole prairie to spread over in three directions, but there's no room for doubt or hesitancy. Everything about the big, blustering place is positive and superlative. I should as soon think of apologizing for Henry VIII or Lorenzo de Medici.

Chicago the notorious, the talk of the world, laughs at its critics. To quote from Carl Sandburg: "laughing the stormy, husky, brawling laughter of youth; half naked; sweating, proud pork butcher; tool maker, stacker of wheat, player with railroads and freight handler to the nation." Go there, as I did. Get out of your train and drive up Michigan Avenue. I defy you not to respond to the excitement in the air, not to feel the drumming pulse of the great dynamo beating in your own veins, not to throw your hat to the sky and shout. . . .

Chicago is gorgeous and it is awful. . . . The bread line outside Al Capone's soup kitchen stretched down one of these bleak, windswept streets past Police Headquarters. I had been there, turning the leaves of what they call the Death Book, most dreadful of all souvenir albums in the world. And there was undoubtedly a connection between the two lots of men, those who stood shivering outside the soup kitchen and those who, enclosed in the covers of the police album, lay sprawled on the bare boards of matchbox rooms or crouched in the corners of taxis with their heads bashed in. For Al Capone is an ambidextrous giant, who kills with one hand and feeds with the other.

## THE BIRTH OF GOSPEL MUSIC

Gospel music was born in Chicago in the early 1930s. Some writers argue that it was in 1930 at the National Baptist Jubilee, which was held in the city. Specifically, they say, it was when Willie Mae Fisher sang Thomas Dorsey's song, "If You See My Savior, Tell Him You Saw Me." Other historians of black music, including Samuel A. Floyd, the author of *The Power of Black Music,* point to the publication in 1932 of Dorsey's "Precious Lord, Take My Hand." The composer-musician had previously worked as pianist for the ribald "Mother of the Blues," Ma Rainey. In "Precious Lord," he brought together the blues with elements of "shout" music and the spiritual that had long been part of southern black church services. It was a historic synthesis of two strains of music.

The same year as Dorsey wrote his breakthrough hymn, he founded the Ebenezer Baptist Church Choir on the South Side of Chicago. He later established the equally famous Pilgrim Baptist Church Choir. These started it but other choirs throughout the city and then across the country embraced gospel-blues, or the "Dorsey Song" style.

The 1940s and 1950s became "the golden age of gospel music" as the African American church circuit resounded with the inspired singing of Mahalia Jackson, Robert Anderson, and ever larger choirs of gospel singers. They helped create a music tradition that has become profoundly respected even by

**Gospel singer Robert Anderson**

1930s

# 1930s

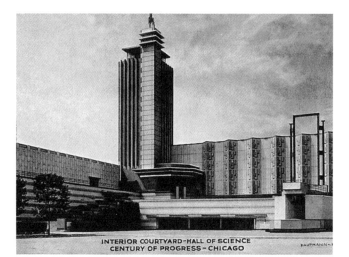

INTERIOR COURTYARD-HALL OF SCIENCE
CENTURY OF PROGRESS - CHICAGO

those untouched by its exultant message of joy and salvation coming from a personal savior, "a precious Lord."

In *The Power of Black Music*, Samuel A. Floyd Jr. wrote of the impact of Dorsey's breakthrough hymn:

> "Precious Lord" received a "resounding affirmation" in its premiere performance by Theodore Frye (with Dorsey at the piano) at Ebenezer Baptist Church in 1932. Taken around to other churches by the duo, it apparently received equally rousing welcomes; those receptions led ultimately "to the rise of gospel blues as an established song form in old-line churches." With this slow gospel song, Dorsey expanded on Tindley's practice of leaving gaps and spaces for "ring" play and added innovations of his own. Most of Dorsey's songs are composed of sixteen measure sections and make use of blues inflec-

tions, favoring flatted thirds and sevenths and off-beat melodic accents, and "Precious Lord" is not an exception. The simple but unique melody line, accompanied by harmony that is advanced for the genre, is a gospel singer's delight; and the poetry and setting of the lyrics are superb.

## THE 1933 AND 1934 CHICAGO WORLD'S FAIRS

Chicago in 1933 and again in 1934 had extraordinarily successful world's fairs known as the "A Century of Progress" Exhibition to commemorate the 100th anniversary of the incorporation of Chicago as a village. By the second fair, the more formal title was much less used. Held in the depth of the Great Depression, the two fairs somehow came together, with a million ways to get people to spend a few cents for entrance, souvenirs, postcards, rides, food, commercial exhibits, or views into the future. It also had fan dancer Sally Rand, a lot of hustling, music, art exhibits, ethnic restaurants, the latest automobiles, new inventions such as air-conditioning and a replica of the 1803 government outpost here, Fort Dearborn. It was a beguiling hodgepodge of lifestyles and culture, much more so than had been the 1893 World's Columbian Exposition, which had attempted to imitate European culture.

The WPA 1939 *Illinois: A Descriptive and Historical Guide* commented: "the basic principles of functionalism were but half understood."

The Great Depression of 1929 put a stop to skyscraper building, but it saw another great Chicago fair—"A Century of Progress" Exposition of 1933–34. The need for economy dictated a light temporary form of construction and prevented lavishness in design. Intense colors were used instead, which produced an impressive effect until they weathered to pastel shades.

The architecture of this exposition was an attempt to crystallize the tendencies in modern design, but it was evident, as Frank Lloyd Wright was quick to point out, that to the designers "the modern" was just another style, and that the basic principles of functionalism were but half understood. He admitted, however, that the visitors might be impressed by the refreshing value of simplicity. This possibility and the experiments with new materials and methods of construction may prove to have been the main achievements of the fair architecturally.

*American Gothic,* **by Grant Wood**

## AMERICAN GOTHIC

During the 1933 "A Century of Progress" Exhibition, visitors both from the country's farms and cities alike were amused and more than a little delighted by a new painting on exhibit at the Art Institute of Chicago. This was not what art was supposed to do, was it? The work was titled *American Gothic* and it had been painted in 1930 by a former Art Institute student, Grant Wood. The figures who posed for it were his sister and a dentist friend. Meant as a satire of the styles of such German and Flemish painters as Holbein, Durer, and van Eyck, the painting was adopted by America as a nostalgic symbol of this country's past and by Chicago as one of its great art treasures.

## THE BLACK CULTURAL FLOWERING OF CHICAGO, 1935–1950

The Negro Renaissance in Harlem between 1917 and 1935 has increasingly become recognized as an across-the-board cultural flowering in music, art, poetry, and fiction that arose from Harlem homes, churches, nightclubs, and music halls.

Today, writers such as Robert Bone, James Grossman, and Samuel Floyd Jr. have started pointing to another blossoming, one that occurred in black Chicago and that lasted roughly from 1935 to 1950. It was a stunning era and place for the development of the black music that was to become the nation's. In Chicago during the 1920s and 1930s, distinct Chicago-style jazz

## 1930s

# 1930s

THE ART OF
**ARCHIBALD J.
MOTLEY, JR.**

BY
JONTYLE
THERESA
ROBINSON
AND
WENDY
GREENHOUSE

and blues were developed, gospel music was born, and boogie-woogie became urbanized.

Chicago during those years produced such nationally recognized African American writers as Richard Wright, Gwendolyn Brooks, Era Bell Thompson, Horace Cayton, and Willard Motley.

Archie Motley, Willard's uncle, left Chicago an extraordinary record of this era. It was one he did through his oil paintings, using a style that was as distinct as were the writing and the music by other Chicago blacks of that period.

In *The Power of Black Music,* Samuel Floyd Jr. elaborated and detailed what had happened in the Windy City during those harsh but fruitful years. The following excerpts give a few very abbreviated highlights from a section devoted to his description and analysis of the Black Chicago Renaissance.

Robert Bone (1986) has posited the notion of a Chicago Renaissance that spanned the years 1935 to 1950 and that featured ideals and practices that parallel those of the Harlem movement. Bone's hypothesis is persuasive when one compares the main features of the Harlem flowering with the black cultural activity that took place in Chicago. As the Harlem Renaissance had been made possible by patronage, so the activity of black artists and intellectuals in Chicago was supported by public and private funding, primarily from the Works Progress Administration, as well as from some of the sources that had sponsored Harlem's literary activity of the 1920s (the Julius Rosenwald Fund, the Wanamaker family, the Harmon Foundation, and Casper Holstein). As A'Lelia Walker's Dark Tower had served as the primary gathering place for black intellectuals in Harlem, Horace Cayton's and Estelle Bond's Chicago homes served a similar purpose in the Chicago flowering. As the Harlem Renaissance had the white Carl Van Vechten and the black intellectual Alain Locke as liaisons with white supporters of the movement, Chicago's nonblack supporters were encouraged and attracted primarily by Edwin Embree, the white administrator of the Julius Rosenwald Fund. As in Harlem, the Chicago Renaissance was based on the premise that African Americans would "measure up" to the artistic, intellectual, cultural, and economic standards of the white world and eventually become part of a race-free society. The Harlem Renaissance had been driven in part by the racial politics of W. E. B. Du Bois, and the activity in Chicago was stimulated to some extent by the revolutionary politics of Richard Wright, as reflected in his novels *Native Son* (1940) and *Black Boy* (1945). The Harlem Renaissance had been fueled by the African American folk experience, but sustained by an integrationist outlook; so was the activity in Chicago. The attitudes toward music that prevailed among middle-class blacks in Chicago in the 1930s were identical to those of the Harlem Renaissance intellectuals:

some accepted the spiritual as incomparable black folk music, to be used as the foundation for "high art," but rejected the blues and only tolerated jazz, considering the former as socially unredeeming and the latter as decadent; others viewed all vernacular black music as aesthetically valuable, if not socially acceptable. In Chicago, as in Harlem, the music of the rent-party, theater, and cabaret worlds was separate from, yet ironically supportive of, some of the New Negro ideals.

According to Grossman (1989), "Chicago in the early years was filled with aromas of southern cooking . . . ; the sounds of New Orleans Jazz and Mississippi blues; [southern] styles of worship; [southern] patterns of speech," all of which fit into "an interactive process" in which these cultural activities and values modified and were modified by new ideas, values, and habits within the context of northern discrimination, economic insecurity, and an urban life-style that was new to recent migrants. This interactive process created among Chicago's African Americans an impulse toward an ardent self-affirmation that found its most public expression in the city's community of musicians, writers, and visual artists. In the music, it was probably manifest as early as the second decade of the twentieth century, when the blues and jazz began to make an impact on Chicago and when, in 1919, the National Association of Negro Musicians was founded there to effect "progress, to discover and foster talent, to mold taste, to promote fellowship, and to advocate racial expression." But in spite of significant early activity by such figures as Kemper Harreld, Maude Roberts George, and Estelle Bonds, this great impulse for self-affirmation apparently did not flourish

on a large and impressive scale until the 1930s.

On June 15, 1933, the Chicago Symphony Orchestra presented an evening of "Negro Music and Musicians," featuring Roland Hayes in a performance of Coleridge-Taylor's "Onaway, Awake, Beloved" from *Hiawatha's Wedding Feast*, pianist Margaret Bonds in a performance of white composer John Alden Carpenter's *Concertina*, and the premiere of Florence Price's *Symphony in E Minor*. Because of the unprecedented magnitude of this event, it should be taken as the landmark event for the musical aspect of the Chicago Renaissance, preceding by more than eighteen months the year of commencement fixed by [Robert] Bone. This concert had been preceded by two major accomplishments by black composers in Chicago: Florence Price's completion of her *Symphony in E Minor* (1932) and William Dawson's completion of his *Negro Folk Symphony* (1934).

## CHRISTOPHER MORLEY

In 1935, noted American writer Christopher Morley wrote a book that he subtitled *A Love Letter for Chicago*. The title was *Old Loopy*. It was written with poetic verve and eloquence, evoking the affection many had for the city. In it Morley recalled Hollywood columnist Louella Parsons saying, "There are two kinds of people in this country. There are the ones who love Chicago and the ones who think it is unmitigated hell. I love it. If the world has been my oyster, Chicago has been my cocktail sauce."

The following is also from *Old Loopy:*

It is not my wish nor ability to offer a philosophic essay on Chicago. I simply want to tell her I love her. She is one of the few big towns that can be loved as an integer; a subtle unity holds her together, makes her apprehensible. It

is partly her essentially provincial spirit; the deep inferiority complex which is so valuable to the artist, goading him to excess, both achievement and despair; and it is partly some underlying vein of rank vitality. The wild onion for which she was named (most Chicagoans have forgotten this) is an accurate symbol. An exquisite garlic of paradox is still discernible in her doings. Garlic is a magnificent savor if leniently used. She appeals to something untamed, young and central in the romantic heart. Most sentimental of towns, she weeps over her defaulting financiers and loads the coffins of gunmen with tons of flowers.

\*\*\*

She is unruly at heart; more than a little goofy; she will be the last to be tamed by the slow frost of correctness. The persecutions of cruel climate and economic zigzag are likely to keep her temperament at extremes. I don't recognize the descriptions sometimes given her of "the hog-butcher of the world, the city of big shoulders." In my chance glimpses she has always seemed completely feminine: willful, witty, strung with myriad nerves.

\*\*\*

Everything about her has always contradicted the foretold and expected. She spikes the small beer of living with the pure alcohol of the impossible.

### STUDS LONIGAN, THE OLD BUNCH, AND NATIVE SON: THREE PARALLEL CHICAGO NOVELS

#### James T. Farrell

In the early 1930s, University of Chicago student James T. Farrell had the good fortune to be in the class of James Weber Linn, who was a professor of English, a highly regarded novelist in his own right and, incidentally, the nephew and biographer of Jane Addams. Farrell wrote a short story for the class,

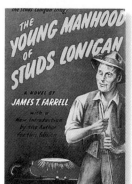

a tragic tale about a young South Side Irishman by the name of Studs Lonigan. It was published in the magazine, *This Quarter.* Linn encouraged his student to expand the story. Farrell did so, into a trilogy of books, and a major literary career was launched.

A vibrant debate ensued after the three books hit the bookstores. Were they art, sociology, or photographic realism? Today, the trilogy is acknowledged as both literature and the strong voice of Chicago in the 1930s.

Here is an excerpt from that career-launching short story as Farrell wrote it:

It was raining outside; rain pouring like bullets from countless machine guns; rain spattering on the wet earth and paving in endless silver crystals. Studs' grave out at Mount Olivet will be soaked and soppy, and fresh with the wet, clean odors of watered earth and flowers. And the members of Studs' family will be looking out of the windows of their apartment on the South Side, thinking of the cold, damp grave and the gloomy, muddy cemetery, and of their Studs lying at rest in peaceful acceptance of that wormy conclusion which is the common fate.

At Studs' wake last Monday evening everybody was mournful, sad that such a fine young fellow of twenty-six should go off so suddenly with double pneumonia; blown out of this world like a ripped leaf in a hurricane. They sighed and the women and girls cried, and everybody said that it was too bad. But they were consoled because he'd had the priest and had received Extreme Unction before he died, instead of going off like Sport Murphy who was killed in a saloon brawl. Poor Sport! He was a good fellow, and tough as hell. Poor Studs!

The undertaker (it was probably old man O'Reedy who used to be usher in the old parish church) laid Studs out handsomely. He was outfitted in a somber black suit and a white silk tie. His hands were folded over his stomach, clasping a pair of black rosary beads. At his head, pressed against the satin bedding, was a spiritual bouquet, set in line with Studs' large nose. He looked handsome, and there were no lines of suffering on his planed face. But the spiritual bouquet (further assurance that his soul would arrive safely in Heaven) was a dirty trick. So was the administration of the last sacraments. For Studs will be miserable in Heaven, more miserable than he was on those Sunday nights when he would hang around the old poolroom at Fifty-eighth and the elevated station, waiting for something to happen. He will find the land of perpetual happiness and goodness dull and boresome, and he'll be resentful. There will be nothing to do in Heaven but to wait in timeless eternity. There will be no cat houses, speakeasies, whores (unless they are reformed), and gambling joints; and neither will there be a shortage of plasterers. He will loaf up and down gold-paved streets where there is not even the suggestion of a poolroom, thinking of Paulie Haggerty, Sport Murphy, Arnold Sheehan and Hink Weber, who are possibly in Hell together because there was no priest around to play a dirty trick on them.

**Meyer Levin**

What Farrell did for the Irish around Grand Boulevard and 55th Street on the South Side, novelist Meyer Levin performed for the West Side Jews who lived near Douglas Park. In his 1937 book, *The Old Bunch,* he chronicled a memorable list of images, characters, and stories that would be there in the book for generations to come. In her review, *Chicago Tribune* literary critic Fanny Butcher compared the two works:

*The Studs Lonigan Trilogy* is primarily the saga of man (one man) in relation to his environment. *The Old Bunch* is the saga of an environment.

The members of the old bunch grow from adolescence to maturity in its pages, but they are as incidental to the unrolling of the panorama of Chicago from 1921 to the end of the Century of Progress as are the notes in a concert program, which illumine and interpret, but do not themselves make the music.

The following is from Levin's book:

Turning again onto Independence Boulevard was like walking up the last side of a rectangle bounding that world. Almost everybody lived inside that rectangle. Well, Sam Eisen lived down on Troy Street, and the Meisels over on Sixteenth; but the half mile square that he had bounded was somehow warmer, full of life, it was the body containing the guts of the neighborhood though there might be limbs spreading outward.

Across the parkway that ran in the middle of the boulevard, making it such a swell street, Harry could see some of the girls gathered on the stairs of the Moscowitz house. He blushed, even though they were at such a distance.

It was funny how on some streets one side seemed dead, the other alive. Take in business. Rudy Stone had told him that Mrs. Kagen's drug store was a dying proposition because it was on the wrong side of Roosevelt Road. Rents on the other side were twice as high, but worth it. The Central Park was on the busy side.

But further along the boulevard, when he saw Joe Freedman getting into the Buick, he waved and crossed over. They circled around

# 1930s

to Garfield Park and back, Harry listening to the motor. The valve tappets were making a racket again.

"I'll come over Sunday morning and tighten them up," he offered. He got out and lifted the hood of the engine; he could just make out the valves popping. If there had been a little more daylight left he would have started to work right away. Joe was a lousy driver and was killing the car. Between him and his sister Aline what chance did a car have? But you could hardly blame Aline as girls are always hard on a car.

"She had it out yesterday," Joe complained. "Every time she has it out she comes back with something on the blink."

Aline emerged. She was wearing a bright red little skirt, like all the girls were wearing. It had white buttons. Through her georgette waist he could see the straps of her chemise. "Well, what's the matter now? Hello, Harry," she said, and he could feel her standing near him. He wanted to offer to drive her wherever she was going, but after all it wasn't his car.

She was just going over to Rose Heller's but Aline was so lazy she had to take the car even if it was around the corner to the grocery. She admitted it: "What's the use of walking if you have a car?"

As she clashed gears, the fellows looked at each other, wincing.

### Richard Wright

Set in the 1930s on the South Side of Chicago, Richard Wright's *Native Son* has become an undisputed classic of American literature, selling millions of copies. It focused on one man (Bigger Thomas), as had *Studs Lonigan*, but also on the environment (the locked ghetto of the South Side of Chicago), as did *The Old Bunch*. A *New York Times* reviewer said of it: "*Native Son* declares Richard Wright's importance, not merely as the best Negro writer, but as an American author as distinctive as any of those writing today."

In "How 'Bigger' Was Born," an article that Wright wrote for *The Saturday Review of Literature* in 1940, he tells of how he had known many Bigger Thomases in the South and later in Chicago. One of the experiences that had propelled him to write his novel was working at a South Side boys' club, where he was paid "to distract Bigger with ping pong, checkers, swimming, marbles, and baseball in order that he might not roam the streets and harm the valuable white property which adjoined the Black Belt."

Wright's descriptions, both in the piece and in his novel, speak today as they have for more than fifty years of so many men routinely imprisoned, shot on the street, or condemned to death (to the plaudits of politicians and many American people) for being a Bigger Thomas. The following is from Wright's article:

The Bigger Thomases were the only Negroes I know of who constantly violated the Jim Crow laws of the South and got away with it, at least for a sweet brief spell. Eventually, the whites who restricted their lives made them pay a terrible price. They were shot, hanged, maimed, lynched, and generally hounded until they were either dead or their spirits broken.
***
Bigger was not nationalist enough to feel the need of religion or the folk culture of his people. What made Bigger's social consciousness most complex was the fact that he was hovering unwanted between two worlds—between powerful America and his own stunted place in life—and I took upon myself the task of trying to make the reader feel this No Man's Land. The most that I could say of Bigger was that he felt the need for a whole life and acted out of that need; that was all.

*Chaos, Creativity, and Culture*

## DRAMA ON THE RADIO

The serious on-air dramas of early radio and their less-respected little sisters, the soap operas, were born in Chicago in the 1930s. They were created with imagination, originality, and authenticity, especially at first. Many of their writers and actors, such as E. G. Marshall and Chicago's own Orson Welles, were among the tops in the nation.

The original radio soap operas were about middle-class America. In the fifteen minutes of radio time allotted each serialized installment, stories unraveled of ordinary people living in those hard times—some with a measure of affluence—and dealing with one human problem after another.

The female leads of radio soaps, unlike those on many of today's television soaps, did not represent rich women or flashy professionals with almost everything but character. Rather, the pioneer soap-opera women were portrayed as strong individuals who knew better than the men how to survive, crossing the emotional and financial peaks and valleys of life.

Even though the script writers were usually the hired pens of Chicago advertising agencies, the stories in both drama and soap opera were closer to the morality plays of the Middle Ages than the drama of Broadway or Hollywood. It was the Great Depression, and these radio dramas were free entertainment. They took people away from their daily lives, sweeping them into another world, allowing them to use their imaginations. They sold soap and other home-use products.

Soap opera fans displayed extraordinary loyalty, and, as a result, more than a few actors registered considerable

1930s

**Benny Goodman**

# 1930s

longevity on the air. In 1933, Ma Perkins of Chicago's *Virginia Payne* began playing "Ma." She performed in that role for twenty-seven years—7,065 shows.

The following is taken from *Chicago: The Glamour Years: 1919 to 1941*, by Thomas and Virginia Aylesworth:

Chicago was a leader in radio. The original reason that Chicago stepped to the fore in early radio was that New York radio stuck with plays written for the stage and Hollywood was wedded to the screen script. Chicago, however, had always been an innovator, and experimentation was the order of the day. Thus a new art form was invented in the Windy City—the dramatic play written for radio. Radio drama as we know it actually began in studios in the Merchandise Mart in the middle 1930s. The program was *First Nighter*, a weekly half-hour drama supposedly set in a small theater off Times Square.

Chicago radio writers also invented the soap opera, short fifteen-minute playlets with plots that go on forever. They were broadcast daily from Chicago; it seemed as if there were hundreds of them going out over the Columbia

Broadcasting System and National Broadcasting Company stations (at the time NBC consisted of two networks, the Red and the Blue; later, the Red Network became the American Broadcasting Company). Notable soaps included *Stella Dallas, Ma Perkins, Vic and Sade* (a now forgotten, delightfully humorous soap, which, in its heyday, was heard four times a day and used two different scripts for the broadcasts), *Our Gal Sunday, Myrt and Marge, Lorenzo Jones, Helen Trent*, and countless others.

## BENNY GOODMAN: THE KING OF SWING

Swing music was born in Chicago in the 1930s, according to Benny Goodman, popularly acclaimed as "the King of Swing." He reigned during the subsequent decades as that sound floated over the airways and across ballroom floors around the world.

When he was thirteen years old, Goodman had started playing with bands on the Great Lakes excursion boats. His early style imitated Leon Rappolo of the New Orleans Rhythm Kings as well as King Oliver and Louis Armstrong. He amalgamated their music with that of the classics as he looked for a style that would pull many diverse elements together. Precise and highly disciplined, he found the sound of swing, a music that took off from the late 1920s arrangements of black musicians such as Earl Hines. Goodman brought this sound to national attention during his band's engagement from November 1935 to May 1936 at the Chicago Congress Hotel.

Here, in excerpts from his book, *Maxwell Street*, Ira Berkow tells the story of Goodman, whose origins were on Maxwell Street in Chicago and whose early training was at Hull House nearby.

By twelve, Benny was doing well in the Hull House band, which played Sousa march music and wore snappy red uniforms. At home, his brother Charlie got hold of a phonograph with a horn. Charlie brought home records. One record he brought was by Ted Lewis, "who we figured was a pretty hot clarinet player." Goodman listened to it so much that he was soon able to imitate Lewis remarkably well. Charlie had heard about a "Jazz Night," at the Balaban and Katz Central Park Theater, every Thursday. It was comparable to an amateur night.

One night Charlie persuaded the manager to allow his brother Benny, in Buster Brown collar with bow tie, to play clarinet. Benny did so well that a couple of weeks later, when one of the acts didn't show up, the manager in desperation sent for Goodman to fill in. "I was on the street playing 'shinny,' but I grabbed the clarinet and hustled around to the theater," Benny recalled.

Goodman did an impersonation of Ted Lewis, with battered old top hat. He was paid five dollars for this first professional engagement. Then Goodman began to take classical lessons with a renowned teacher, Franz Schoepp, who once taught at the Chicago Musical College. Benny began playing for money. Still a kid in knee pants, he caught on in the famous Bix Beiderbecke riverboat band that made excursions to and from Chicago and Michigan City, Indiana, on Lake Michigan.

He had joined the American Musicians' Union and began playing more and more jobs. He was learning a new style playing with bands such as (Bix) Beiderbecke's. Besides that, he found it necessary to buy a tuxedo to be properly dressed for nightclub dates. It was the first formal suit ever owned by anyone in the Goodman family. By the time Benny had begun attending Harrison High School, he had become the family's principal breadwinner. His father had died.

At sixteen, Goodman had earned a great enough reputation that Ben Pollack, leader of a rising band of the day, sent Benny a wire from California to come out and join him. Pollack signed Goodman to a salary of one hundred dollars a week. Eighty dollars a week more than the highest salary his father ever earned. While still a teenager, he would also play with the famous Red Nichols band. He returned to Chicago, eventually, and played in some of the top nightclubs and dance halls. Recordings and radio dates followed. By 1934 he had decided to form his own band, one that would play primarily dance music "in a free style" in a way most musicians wanted to play and weren't allowed to on the ordinary job. He had his pick, virtually, of numerous good musicians.

"The point was that no white band had yet gotten together a good rhythm section that would kick out, or jump, or rock, or swing (all these expressions being ways musicians describe the vitality that comes from music played at just the right tempo with a lot of rhythmic snap), using arrangements that fit in with this idea, which would give the men a chance to play solos and express the music in their own individual way," said Goodman.

Goodman believed that if the musicians really enjoyed what they were playing, then the public would, too.

### BLACK BOY

In *Black Boy*, Richard Wright gave readers an autobiographical take on his childhood in the South and his planned move to Chicago.

David Mamet, in a different context, spoke of midwestern writers' penchant to tell stories about growing up. The playwright's insightful comments in an introduction to *Aunt Ella Stories*, a volume of stories about growing up during the depression, can aptly be applied to Wright's *Black Boy:*

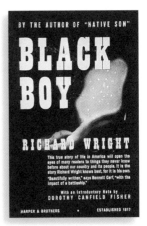

# 1930s

It's always seemed to me that every region has its one story and that all the writers there tell it.

All Los Angeles novels are about a Dark Secret—they are about deracination and abandonment and the key to a mystery.

Finally, they are adolescence and the secrets, which inform them all, are Death and Sex.

The New York novel is about Young Manhood. It is about getting on in a cold world. And the Midwestern American story—the one that all of us Chicagoans and our neighbors always tell—is about the first discovery of the multiplicity and beauty of the universe—that story is about what it is like to be a boy.

The following is from the last chapter of *Black Boy:*

The accidental visit of Aunt Maggie to Memphis formed a practical basis for my planning to go north. Aunt Maggie's husband, the "uncle" who fled from Arkansas in the dead of night, had deserted her; and now she was casting about for a living. My mother, Aunt Maggie, my brother, and I held long conferences, speculating on the prospects of jobs and the cost of apartments in Chicago. And every time we conferred, we defeated ourselves. It was impossible for all four of us to go at once; we did not have enough money.

Finally sheer wish and hope prevailed over common sense and facts. We discovered that if we waited until we were prepared to go, we would never leave, we would never amass enough money to see us through. We would have to gamble. We finally decided that Aunt Maggie and I would go first, even though it was winter, and prepare a place for my mother and brother. Why wait until next week

or next month? If we were going, why not go at once?

Next loomed the problem of leaving my job cleanly, smoothly, without arguments or scenes. How could I present the fact of leaving to my boss? Yes, I would pose as an innocent boy; I would tell him that my aunt was telling me and my paralyzed mother to go to Chicago. That would create in his mind the impression that I was not asserting my will; it would block any expression of dislike on his part for my act. I knew that southern whites hated the idea of Negroes leaving to live in places where the racial atmosphere was different.

It worked as I had planned. When I broke the news of my leaving two days before I left—I was afraid to tell it sooner for fear that I would create hostility on the part of the whites with whom I worked—the boss leaned back in his swivel chair and gave me the longest and most considerate look he had ever given me.

"Chicago," he repeated softly.

"Yes, sir."

"Boy, you won't like it up there," he said.

"Well, I have to go where my family is, sir," I said.

The other white office workers paused in their tasks and listened. I grew self-conscious, tense.

"It's cold up there," he said.

"Yes, sir. They say it is," I said, keeping my voice in a neutral tone.

He became conscious that I was watching him and he looked away, laughing uneasily to cover his concern and dislike.

"Now, boy," he said banteringly, "don't you go up there and fall into that lake."

"Oh, no, sir," I said, smiling as though there existed the possibility of my falling accidentally into Lake Michigan.

He was serious again, staring at me. I looked at the floor.

"You think you'll do any better up there?" he asked.

"I don't know, sir."

"You seem to've been getting along all right down here," he said.

"Oh, yes, sir. If it wasn't for my mother's going, I'd stay right here and work," I lied as earnestly as possible.

"Well, why not stay? You can send her money," he suggested.

He had trapped me. I knew that staying now would never do. I could not have controlled my relations with the whites if I had remained after having told them that I wanted to go north.

"Well, I want to be with my mother," I said.

"You want to be with your mother," he repeated idly. "Well, Richard, we enjoyed having you with us."

"And I enjoyed working here," I lied.

There was silence; I stood awkwardly, then moved to the door. There was still silence; white faces were looking strangely at me. I went upstairs, feeling like a criminal. The word soon spread through the factory and the white men looked at me with new eyes. They came to me.

"So you're going north, huh?"

"Yes, sir. My family's taking me with 'em."

"The North's no good for your people, boy."

"I'll try to get along, sir."

"Don't believe all the stories you hear about the North."

"No, sir. I don't."

"You'll come back here where your friends are."

"Well, sir. I don't know."

"How're you going to act up there?"

"Just as I act down here, sir."

"Would you speak to a white girl up there?"

"Oh, no, sir. I'll act there just like I act here."

"Aw, no, you won't. You'll change. Niggers change when they go north."

I wanted to tell him that I was going north precisely to change, but I did not.

"I'll be the same," I said, trying to indicate that I had no imagination whatever.

As I talked I felt that I was acting out a dream. I did not want to lie, yet I had to lie to conceal what I felt. A white censor was standing over me and, like dreams forming a curtain for the safety of sleep, so did my lies form a screen of safety for my living moments.

"Boy, I bet you've been reading too many of them damn books."

"Oh, no, sir."

I made my last errand to the post office, put my bag away, washed my hands, and pulled on my cap. I shot a quick glance about the factory; most of the men were working late. One or two looked up. Air. Falk, to whom I had returned my library card, gave me a quick, secret smile. I walked to the elevator and rode down with Shorty.

"You lucky bastard," he said bitterly.

"Why do you say that?"

"You saved your goddamn money and now you're gone."

"My problems are just starting," I said.

"You'll never have any problems as hard as the ones you had here," he said.

"I hope not," I said. "But life is tricky."

"Sometimes I get so goddamn mad I want to kill everybody," he spat in a rage.

"You can leave," I said.

"I'll never leave this goddamn South," he railed. "I'm always saying I am, but I won't . . . I'm lazy. I like to sleep too goddamn much. I'll die here. Or maybe they'll kill me."

I stepped from the elevator into the street, half expecting someone to call me back and tell me that it was all a dream, that I was not leaving.

This was the culture from which I sprang. This was the terror from which I fled.

## LUDWIG MIES VAN DER ROHE AND LASZLO MOHOLY-NAGY

The United States in the 1930s gained many of the intellectuals and creative geniuses living in Germany as they fled the oppressive Nazi state. Among those settling in Chicago were architect Ludwig Mies van der Rohe and designer Laszlo Moholy-Nagy. Along with Walter Gropius, the two had been a part of the Bauhaus, a school of architecture and design in Germany that blended arts and crafts and emphasized training students equally in both. The school's underlying philosophy focused on directness, simplicity, and a practicality not unlike Sullivan's "Form follows function." Mies was invited to Chicago to head the School of Architecture at the Armour Institute (now the Illinois Institute of Technology.) Moholy-Nagy came to form a school of design—a new Bauhaus.

EDITED BY RICHARD KOSTELANETZ
Documentary Monographs in Modern Art

## Mies van der Rohe

Having left Nazi Germany, Mies van der Rohe arrived in Chicago in August 1938. The great Bauhaus architect, who had mastered the one-room building, uttered and repeated his axiom, "Less is more."

His direct unadorned style of design used glass as no one before him had. It became extraordinarily successful and popular, creating a new utilitarian look to the skylines built throughout the world. In the following passages, his biographer Franz Schulze wrote of the challenge to his style and works that arose in his last years—the 1960s:

Seventeen years—nearly one full generation—separate the death of Ludwig Mies van der Rohe from the observance of his centenary in 1986. During his later maturity he was widely regarded as one of the twentieth century's several most important architects, whose only peers were Frank Lloyd Wright and Le Corbusier. Critics frequently contended that, the excellence of his work aside, he influenced building more than any other designer of his day. He was the most rigorous of rationalists in a time little blessed with rationality, a stern disciplinarian who insisted that those styles which had grown out of other epochs had no place in this one. Instead, Mies argued, modern building must be the concrete realization of the modern spirit, which in architecture is most evident in the technology of steel and glass. The lucidly rectilinear forms he created seemed to his contemporaries so ineluctable in their logic that the building art itself must be, as he said it was, a reasonable process leading to an unassailable truth. Nostalgia for the ideals of the past was a false end, mere self-expression an equally inadmissible means.

The time to take issue with such an understanding of things coincided more or less with Mies's death; thus in the late 1960s and early 1970s his philosophy was repeatedly attacked as simplistic and even inhumane, just as modernism in the arts fell under the suspicion that it had failed to remake the world while neglecting to appreciate the richness of history and its residual meaning to contemporary minds. While Mies was not the only modernist architect accused of such error, because of his stature he became a lightning rod that attracted most of the thunderbolts of the so-called postmodernist revolution.

Yet he rose well above most of the storm-tossed modernist landscape, and when the elements subsided at the turn of the 1980s, he was still there, occupying as high an elevation as any structure in sight. Rationalists and romantics alike, structuralists and pictorialists, took his work as the prime standard by which they measured their own endeavors either in emulation or rejection of him.

### Laszlo Moholy-Nagy

Moholy-Nagy was a man hungry for ideas, a searcher for solutions and an experimenter. This did not always please his fellow Bauhaus professor, Mies van der Rohe, who already had his answers in a style that advocated less of everything but glass.

The Hungarian-born designer entered a United States in which the advertising industry had discovered that design, when varied and interesting, can help sell products. Consumers have a voracious hunger for the new, the colorful, and the imaginative.

Moholy-Nagy, on his part, was the man for them. He was strongly influenced by constructivism, an approach to design that had Russian roots. The constructivists believed that good art, archi-

tecture, and design should construct the environment, not adorn it. The Bauhaus' young design professor agreed most heartily. He said, "Constructivism is pure substance. It is not confined to the picture frame and the pedestal. It expands into industry and architecture, into objects and relationships. Constructivism is the socialism of wisdom."

Moholy-Nagy founded the New Bauhaus in 1937 in the old Marshall Field mansion at 1905 South Prairie Avenue. It didn't take, and he started his own School of Design in 1939. Along with his own work, the design school prospered, changing the course of design. Among the many ideas he contributed were the use of functional typography and the creation of photomontages. His influence went far beyond the creation of ads or works of art. They included film, furniture, dishwashers, and draperies. He died of leukemia in 1946 and the School of Design was integrated into the Illinois Institute of Technology in 1952.

1930s

1940s

CHICAGO

# 1940s: World War II, Art, Poetry, Television, and a Chicago School of Painting

During World War II, Chicago became an arsenal for democracy as an unprecedented number of Americans arrived to fill jobs, while others discovered the city by stopping long enough to make train connections. The town had far more to offer than just the lakefront, skyscrapers, and nightlife they saw. It had a multitude of opportunities. Some servicemen and -women on their way to war determined to return to the city once peace came. Chicago offered hope, the kind portrayed in Richard Wright's *Black Boy,* just as the 1930s truly had the tragic edge portrayed in Wright's *Native Son.* An equally vital picture, one of perseverance, came through in Era Bell Thompson's *American Daughter* about a young black woman's arrival in the city.

Also in the forties, the young artist Bill Mauldin, who had been living at the Lawson YMCA, was drafted and began sketching World War II dogface antiheroes, Willie and Joe.

The city witnessed the first nuclear reaction December 2, 1942, and at the same time the Chicago School of Television offered *Stud's Place; Kookla, Fran, and Ollie;* and *Dave Garroway,* as well as a new and innovative approach to live, on-the-air theater.

Chicago writers, writing in the 1940s, included Frank Brown, fresh young Pulitzer Prize-winning poet Gwendolyn Brooks, National Book Award winner Nelson Algren, nature writer Leonard Dubkin, novelist Peter DeVries, novelist Marion Strobel, author Mary Jane Ward (*The Snake Pit*), mystery novelist Craig Rice, and future Nobel Prize novelist Saul Bellow.

In the mid-1940s, blues legend Muddy Waters (McKinley Morgenfield) followed the well-trod path from the Mississippi Delta to Chicago. Pioneering

# 1940s

the bottleneck blues on his electric guitar, he developed the amplified sound that earned him the title "The King of Chicago Blues."

Artists associated with the School of the Art Institute created a new school of art identified with the city that, according to art critic Franz Schulze, "explored the surreal and the fanciful—fantastic."

Chicagoan Ivan Albright was manifesting the innovation and grotesqueness that critics and the people had come to identify and often respect in his work. He and his brother Zsissly collaborated on the famous pictures used in the classic 1944 movie *The Picture of Dorian Gray*.

## WORLD WAR II AND STUDS TERKEL

The nation knows Studs Terkel as the articulate man who compiled some strong readable books of interviews on a variety of subjects. These have included works on Chicago, work, race, the American dream, older citizens, and himself. His book on World War II,

entitled *The Good War*, won the Pulitzer Prize in 1985. Chicago also knows him as a pixieish, plaid-vested, storyteller whose careers have spanned the 1930s and the Works Progress Administration Writers Project, which he was part of as an actor. In the 1940s, they saw when he was a pioneer television host with *Studs' Place* and subsequently a raconteur and jazz aficionado on his WFMT radio interview show. For the city, he is an amiable man with a social conscience. He knows how to tell a story, play jazz, have fun, and do the right thing. The following interviews with Bill Mauldin and Herman Kogan are from *The Good War*.

### Bill Mauldin

The image one has of American wars before World War II is that they were fought by officers, especially generals, with the help of a faceless mass of ordinary soldiers, with a hero popping up every now and then. A young cartoonist and European Theater infantryman, fresh out of the Art Institute of

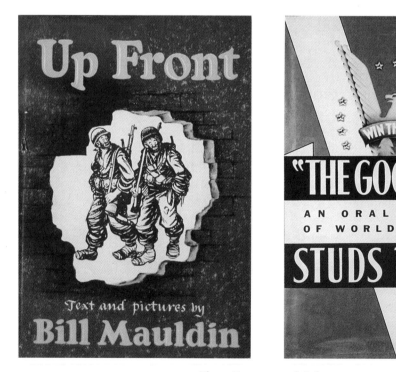

*Chaos, Creativity, and Culture*

Chicago, helped dispel that myth. His Willie and Joe were grubby members of the unwashed military proletariat. They were privates and they quickly became American icons, not by doing heroic deeds or killing large numbers of the enemy, but by surviving the dangers of battle and the rigors of the time in between. [Mauldin subsequently won two Pulitzer Prizes (1945 and 1959) for editorial cartooning.]

## Willie and Joe

TERKEL: For millions of American newspaper readers during World War Two, this one panel cartoon, "Up Front," offered the indelible portrait of the infantryman: craggy faced, unshaven, disheveled, sardonic. His two protagonists, Willie and Joe, became eponyms for the American dogface. He was an eighteen-year-old GI when he first drew them.

Today, at sixty-one, bearded, he has the appearance of a fin de siecle Parisian artist. He works out of his home in Santa Fe.

MAULDIN: Eighteen? Gad, that was forty-three years ago. Yeah.

I was in Chicago, going to art school, in 1939 when the war started in Europe. I was living in the Lawson YMCA . . .

I joined the National Guard. It was a truck company. My friends convinced me it was a good way to stay out of the infantry. (Laughs.) It was such a miserable outfit, I transferred to the infantry. That was almost eighteen months before Pearl Harbor. We weren't in it yet.

Willie and Joe were really drawn on guys I knew in this infantry company. It was a rifle company from McAlester, Oklahoma. There were Indians in it and a lot of laconic good ol' boys. These two guys were based on these Oklahomans I knew.

People like that really make ideal infantry soldiers. Laconic, they don't take anything too seriously. They're not happy doing what they're doing, but they're not totally fish out of water, either. They know how to walk in the mud and how to shoot. It's a southwestern sort of trait, really. Don't take any crap off anybody.

I never once heard an infantry soldier who'd been in combat refer to Germans as Nazis. Or North Vietnamese or North Koreans as reds, or commie rats, or any of that stuff. There were a lot of ethnic slurs: slopes, gooks, and things like that. I heard about krauts, squareheads. People who fight these wars could care less about ideology. Me, too.

I'm not sure they were exclusively American. I think that kind of attitude goes with infantrymen of any army in any war. There was a general consensus that they should put Montgomery and Patton and Rommel in the same ring and take off the gloves and let 'em go at it. Patton made it clear he loved war. So did Montgomery. The only nice guy of that trio was Rommel. (Laughs.)

I think Willie and Joe would have voted for Roosevelt cynically, sardonically, with a lot of reservations. He really wasn't their cup of tea. They would have considered Roosevelt too much of a bleeding heart. They couldn't bring themselves to be Republicans. Someone like Harry Truman would be more their cup of tea. (Laughs.) I'm really expressing my own feelings. I dug Truman. I still do. It really shows you what my limitations are. (Laughs.)

Willie and Joe are my creatures. Or am I their creature? They are not social reformers. They're much more reactive. They're not social scientists and I'm not a social scientist. We're moral people who do not belong to the moral majority. (Laughs.) One of my principles is, Thou shalt not bully. The only answer is to muscle the bully. I'm very combative that way.

## HERMAN KOGAN

Herman Kogan, an author mentioned in connection with his cowriting of *Big Bill of Chicago* and one of the mavens to whom this book is dedicated, was foremost a journalist. He was one of several editors of his generation who held a Phi Beta Kappa key. Ernie Tucker, city editor of Chicago's *American,* was another. They represented the kind of journalists who helped transform reporting in Chicago from the *Front Page* journalism of the 1920s and 1930s into the profession that earned respect and awards for its independence and responsibility by the late 1960s and 1970s. The fact that many key reporters had taken time out to cover World War II and later the Korean War, doing so with great sensitivity, also helped raise the level of the whole profession in Chicago.

The following is from Kogan's interview in Terkel's *The Good War:*

KOGAN: In 1943, I wound up in the Marine Corps. It was the last place I ever thought I'd be. When I was twelve years old, all the kids in my neighborhood had joined the Boy Scouts. My parents refused to let me. They said once you're in khaki, you'll never get out.

\*\*\*

I was assigned to the Twenty-second Regiment of the Sixth Marine Division at Guadalcanal. This was after the Guam campaign, long after the fight. I was with a rifle company. Our next campaign was Okinawa. We landed there on April Fool's Day, 1945. I carried a little portable typewriter and a carbine. We were told there

would be a tremendous number of casualties. There was nothing. The Japanese had gone into caves. I remember my first story of how we were greeted by the little Okinawan people.

Later on at Sugarloaf Hill a lot of people were slaughtered. I talked to the guys after an assault and they'd tell me about some kid who had been killed. These were the Joe Blow stories. That's what they were called. Marine private so-and-so, somewhere in the Pacific. You'd always said that, until the Washington office was allowed to say where. They were mostly the little human interest stories. They'd appear in hometown papers. A lot of people in my outfit were killed. And when I'd come back to the command post to type it out, the first sergeant would say, "Shit, you still alive?"

We were right outside the city of Naha. It was called the Chicago of Okinawa. When we finally took the island, a sort of city council was set up in Naha. Naturally, I compared it to the Chicago City Council. (Laughs.)

I was scared stiff very often. I remember being under attack and spending the night in a foxhole with a young lieutenant from Oklahoma City. The following night I was elsewhere, to follow up on a story. Otherwise I'd have been with him again. While I was away, he had his legs blown off. The assaults on Sugarloaf Hill were almost suicidal. I figured, what the hell, I ought to get a better view of what was going on. I went up there and was so intent on getting a story that I forgot to be afraid.

There was a sense of pride of having been in the Marine Corps, perhaps it was nuttiness. In a perverse, masochistic way, I even enjoyed boot camp. The one thing I carried away with me was the selflessness of some of these kids, with no great philosophical ideas about war or comradeship.

I've often wondered what would have happened to me if I'd never gone into the service. Would I have been a newspaper executive? (Laughs.) Had I not been in, had I not met some of these kids, I might have become a University of Chicago intellectual snob. It was not much different from the first newspaper jobs I had as a police reporter. You met a different class of people. But, I could have done without this experience. No matter how just a war it was, it was war. It never was a solution to anything. Fuck war.

**FRANK BROWN: *TRUMBULL PARK***

Frank Brown created a unique bridge between music and literature. Both a novelist and a jazz singer, he performed with the bold musical innovator Theolonius Monk and also wrote articles on jazz for *Downbeat* and *Ebony*. He was the first to read short stories rather than poetry to jazz accompaniment. His 1959 novel, *Trumbull Park*, based on an African American family moving into a Chicago Housing Authority project, was angry without being bitter. Following are excerpts from its final chapter:

And we moved on—the cops, the mob, and Harry and me.

Trumbull Park was in sight. Just a few more steps. If we could make it, we would have won. It was supposed to have been our first move. We were supposed to strike that first blow, draw the first gun, pull out the first knife. This wasn't in their plans. No fight. No first move. Just walking . . . walking. . . .

We got to an alley near the vacant lot right across the street from the project, and another mob crowded the streets in front of us, blocking the way between us and home. The cops slowed down, and as Harry

and I stepped into this alley:

"Look out!" one of the policemen screamed.

A wave of bricks flew at us from the vacant lot. Harry and I never stopped walking. We were too close to Trumbull Park to stop now. If the bricks killed us, then that would be the way it would be. But duck? Now? It was too late. There was no place to duck behind, no place to run to. No diesel, no mob, no bricks—nothing could stop us now! It seemed like it wasn't really me and Harry walking, but somebody else in a scene on a movie

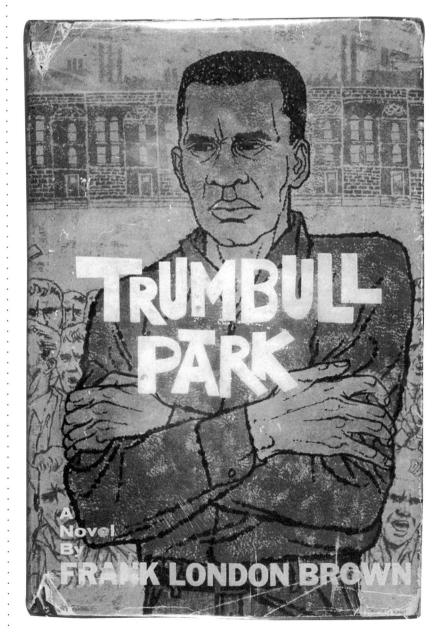

screen—somebody else who walked while we felt.

And even as I stared the faces down that would have liked to make us start the one little act that would have turned this mob on us and the policemen as well, I felt no hatred for them—nor pity. Just anger—the kind that one feels when you see somebody blocking the way between you and home. Anger—but no hate. These faces that moved by me and Harry were tired faces. Grime and filings from the steel mills lay on their faces like black veils—the old folks and young ones, screaming still. Once a rock hit me, and I almost fell it hurt so bad, but I didn't. I couldn't. Harry couldn't. To fall would have been to die; and we didn't want to die—we wanted to live. And we were going to, no matter what.

And we walked and walked and walked—walking through the great Trumbull Park, Buggy walking to Helen, Harry walking to his wife Margaret, walking to all of our friends there. Walking. Mobs screaming, throwing things, pushing us, pushing the policemen who had orders to take cover or else. Walking past 104th, past 105th, past the alley near 106th, almost there, almost home. Walking.

The Big Boys couldn't afford cold-blooded murder, and the Little Boys were afraid to commit cold-blooded murder—by themselves—and that's what it would have taken to stop us. That's what it would have taken to get Mona and Arthur Davis out before we came, and cold-blooded murder was what it would take to stop the others now—Kevin-Beverly, Terry Nadine, Carl-Ernestine, William-Christine, Norman-Armela—all of them. They'd walk now. I knew they would. So would the other "new guys" like Harry. So would guys not yet in Trumbull Park, and

their wives, and their children. They'd walk. They'd follow the path that Arthur and Mona and Harry and Helen and I had made—widen that path and wear it smooth. They'd let these people, the Big Boys and the Little Boys, let them know that death is not enough any more to keep Negroes from walking—and running and crawling and flying and singing and crying and even dying—for what we know is ours.

Oh, yes, the mob was still screaming; but now I heard singing Big Joe William wailing:

"Every day, every day . . . Well, it ain't nobody worried, and it ain't nobody cryin'!"

And we walked with our chests stuck out, and our heads way up in the air—just like that big, dark, blues-shouting stud.

And we took the long hip strides that Joe took as the women at the DeLisa screamed. There were women screaming at us— men too. So I started singing out loud, in the middle of cops, mobs, and everything else. Ol' Harry joined in, and I noticed a little water in his eyes. I felt a little choked up myself as we both sang loud and clear:

"Every day, every day . . . Well, it ain't nobody worried, and it ain't nobody cryin'!"

## THE LYRIC OPERA OF CHICAGO

Chicago's Lyric Opera is consistently able to stage world-class performances to full houses. The wonder is not what it will do next, but how it is that we can expect so much from such a still young company and how it achieved what it has. From 1947 to 1953, Chicago was without a resident opera company. "The city had all but gotten out of the opera habit," Ronald L. Davis wrote in his book *Opera in Chicago*.

Then came Carol Fox and Maria Callas. Fox, the daughter of a furniture manufacturer, had received voice training here and in Europe. Pulling together in the early 1950s a trio of cultural entrepreneurs that included herself, her former voice trainer and future conductor (Nicola Rescigno), and a real estate agent who loved opera (Lawrence Kelly), she set about incorporating the Lyric Opera.

One early performance by the Lyric that demonstrated what it aspired to and could attain was that of *Lucia di*

*Lammermoor* on November 15, 1954, with Maria Callas as Lucia. The young Callas had been lured to Chicago for a series of appearances by the committed and enthusiastic Fox. In his book, Davis describes the landmark performance:

The Callas zenith was not reached, however, until the final week, when she sang *Lucia di Lammermoor* and sang it as Chicago had never heard it before. She

**Maria Callas as Lucia**

*Chaos, Creativity, and Culture*

# 1940s

made Lucia a human being, not just a vehicle for coloratura display, as so many others had done. Her characterization was filled with heartrending poignancy, and her anguish in the scene with Enrico was a theatrical marvel. Vocally, she was exquisite, her first act "spun like warm silk, sometimes with an edge of steel."

"The most exciting soprano in the world," the *Chicago Daily News* wrote, "sang as she—or anybody else—may never have sung before and may never sing again." After the first division of the "Mad Scene," the house went into a prolonged ovation, while the singer, never stepping out of character, waited for the clapping and shouting to subside. It was a "Mad Scene" in which every phrase had dramatic and musical meaning. At its conclusion, "near pandemonium broke out," Claudia Cassidy wrote. "There was an avalanche of applause, a roar of cheers growing steadily hoarser, a standing ovation, and the aisles were full of men pushing as close to the stage as possible. I am sure they wished for bouquets to throw, and a carriage to pull in the streets. Myself, I wish they had both. For this creature called Callas is something special."

Carol Fox continued as general manager of the Lyric Opera of Chicago until 1981 when she was succeeded by Ardis Krainik, the third woman in Chicago to head the city's major opera company, with the first having been Mary Garden in the 1920s. Miss Krainik had served as a chorus member, a supporting singer, and in a variety of administrative positions before becoming general manager. She had been there from the beginning and initiated in 1990 its imaginative and successful decade-long program, "Toward the 20th Century." Before her death in

January 1997, she had also left behind a legacy that included a $100 million renovation and expansion of the Lyric Opera House. It was said that Miss Krainik "could charm a contribution to the Lyric out of the most stony-hearted Scrooge."

## CHESS RECORDS

The world first heard the electrified Chicago blues sound on the Chess Record Company label. The 1940s blues scene got its pop in 1945 on the day Muddy Waters switched to an electric guitar, one that could be heard over the noises of a bar. It was an instant hit. At this point, Leonard and Phil Chess, owners of the Macambo Lounge, started producing the city's blues sounds on the Aristocrat and Chess labels.

Unlike other musicians, given the opportunity, Muddy Waters did not feel a need to tour. He played the blues clubs in Chicago and recorded with the Chess brothers. Those they worked with were many, including Howlin' Wolf, Little Walter, and Buddy Guy. It was an electrified blues.

The sound, however, began to change to rhythm and blues in the 1950s as they recorded the very popular Bo Diddley and Chuck Berry. Although African American, Berry crashed into the white market by singing about such teenage themes as school, cars, and love. As Chess was popularizing it in the 1950s, the rhythm and blues sound was being transformed by others into yet another form of music—rock and roll.

In 1962, the record company hired a twenty-five-year-old arranger and composer from Detroit, Billy Davis. His efforts there had been instrumental in forming Motown Records. At Chess, he helped create a style unmistakably its own. It had the raw drive of Chicago blues and fervor of gospel. Its orchestration and arrangement were both powerful and sophisticated. Its performing stars included Etta James, the Radiants, the Dells, Billy Stewart, and Jackie Ross with "Selfish One."

*Chaos, Creativity, and Culture*

By the 1960s, once again the city was producing a unique sound—Chicago soul. Davis left Chess in 1968 and it never recaptured his creative direction. The company was purchased by the GRT Corporation in 1969 and moved to New York where it has recently reissued many of its early, now classic records.

## ALBERT HALPER

Someone once wrote of Albert Halper that his prose sounded as if it were written with the "L" rumbling past in the background. He was considered a 1930s proletarian novelist and a writer deeply affected by his Jewish roots. His novels, *The Chute, The Foundry, The Little People,* and *Sons of the Fathers* focus on the lives of lower-middle-class Chicagoans. His style became smoother in his later works, but that "L" rumble in his earlier ones, including *Union Square,* which was about New York, was pure Chicago.

As a writer whose dues had been collected many times over, Halper remained positive about his home base. He edited an anthology of local authors in 1952 titled *This Is Chicago.* The following is from his own contribution to the book, an essay on the subject of writing in Chicago:

Chicago has never been, nor tried to be, a city like New York, London, or Paris. It has always been, loudly and vociferously, itself. Though it strikes out at the one-day or one-hour visitor bluntly, like a huge fist, it possesses a subtle inner complexity that almost always escapes even the most discerning out-of-town eye.

Yet behind this strident horn-blowing often lurks a feeling of deep inadequacy, a sensitivity to fine things, an aching for the sun. This confused, collective yearning is about the best thing in Chicago, when you get to recognize it, to feel it.

Chicago is not only a city, it is a city of cities made up of great foreign blocs of population, impinging on one another. The Polish settlement here, next to Warsaw, is the largest Polish city in the world. There is also a sizeable German city, and a big Czech city, and an Italian town, and a Jewish city, and a Scandinavian borough that stretches for miles, and an Irish town. And out of this sprawling mass of neighborhoods has come a literature that does not have to play second fiddle to any body of literature in the land.

The "Chicago School" of writers has gripped the public mind since 1900, and some of its names are major ones—Dreiser, Sherwood Anderson, Sandburg, Masters,

ferber  algren  dillon  armstrong  condon
levin  wright  sandburg  farrell  zara
halper  masters  lewis  brooks  lardner
anderson  hecht  mc cormick  wendt  kieran
addams  darrow  kipling . . . and many others

## THIS IS CHICAGO
### AN ANTHOLOGY
Edited by *Albert Halper*

*Chaos, Creativity, and Culture*

Hecht, Richard Wright, Meyer Levin, James T. Farrell, Willard Motley, Algren—the list stretches on. And Ring Lardner, Hemingway, Willa Cather, Ferber, Frank Norris, and others, who sojourned here, did not escape the city's impact.

It's not a bad town for writers. It was never a bad town for writers. At this moment there must be a new young crop of them, totally unknown, writing painfully in family parlors and bedrooms on the North, South and West sides. It was always a good place for a writer to be born in, or to grow up in. And after a Chicago writer reaches adulthood it doesn't matter where he lives, in New York, Paris, or Rome. The silver cord is never cut, he never really gets away.

In offering this anthology to the public, the editor does not claim it to be a definitive one. No one can compile a definitive anthology on anything. But he does feel that the work of the authors gathered together between the covers of this volume—Chicagoans and non-Chicagoans alike—succeeds in painting an honest, sensitive, and extremely "viewable" portrait of a huge city that has always been exciting and newsworthy nationally and internationally.

In compiling this book, its editor came to feel, soon after he had begun to track down and sort out the pieces, that he was working with material that dealt not only with Chicago's past and present but also the past and present of the country as a whole. Chicago was indeed America only more so. To bolster this point of view, one had only to cast a cursory glance backward at the city's history. In its infancy, scholars tell us, Chicago was like most American frontier towns, only wilder, rawer. Its real estate booms were bigger, its collapses were greater; at times the values of its

business property bounded upward so startlingly as to make the eyes of out-of-town realtors pop. On the other hand, the debacle of the Insull Empire, together with its three hundred holding companies which controlled one per cent of the nation's wealth, was of such depth as to shake the financial foundations of public utility companies throughout North America.

People remember that when the depression existed in the thirties, this city was the most depressed city in the nation. Schoolteachers were not paid for years. Banks closed and stayed closed; primitive currency exchanges opened up to keep the financial gears grinding.

Yet when the upsurge came in 1940, Chicago became the boom-ingest town on earth, its factories working around the clock; the red fires from the South Side steel mills lighting up the sky.

When culture hit this town in the 1920s, it hit like a tornado; Mencken called Chicago the literary capital of the continent. And when a new kind of excitement was called for, scientists, squatting under the gridiron stands of Stagg Field on the South Side, touched off the world's first controlled atomic chain reaction and launched the age of atomic jitters.

The list could be extended. Yes, everything seems to be in sharper relief here, good things and bad. It's a town that never wears a mask; it lives forthrightly, take it or leave it. Even its political corruption, one of its aldermen recently bragged, is more honest than that of most cities.

This forthrightness, this inner honesty, seems to be the hallmark of its indigenous writers. These attributes do not make for fine stylistic cachets. A finely mannered Chicago writer is almost unthinkable. Yet the individual styles of the Chicago writers whose pieces are included in this volume are as carefully wrought, as evocative, as those of any group of American artists today.

## POLKA: A CHICAGO EXPORT

The polka was not born in Chicago, but like so many other forms of music, it got branded in the city, and "Chicago Style" polka, as a result, continues to be exported to the world, including Poland.

This enthusiastic form of music first swept the United States back in the 1840s, coming here from Bohemia and southern Poland. It was at that time a liberating dance, one with a unique incentive, for it allowed a Victorian Age man to put his hand and arm around a lady's waist. It became popular throughout the world in such places as England, Paris, North Africa, South America, and Mexico. The polka's popularity proved a fad, however, and soon passed. For the most part, the dance and the music that accompanied it lay dormant for a century, including Poland and Europe. Only in parts of the United States—in Eastern European enclaves, incredibly among certain Native American tribes, and in places in the Southwest—did it continue as an ethnic dance.

Then, following World War II, the polka found a robust new life, becoming a rallying dance and tradition that could be a lot of fun and that proved a symbolic bond between the American descendants of Eastern Europeans and their ancestral homelands, especially Poland.

The polka came to life in a big way in Pennsylvania but even more so in Chicago as such polka kings as "Li'l Wally" (Walter Jagiello) and Frankie Yankovic packed Southwest Side and Milwaukee Avenue polka halls, filled the radio waves, and cut records. The Chicago style, innovated to a large extent by Jagiello, relied on the old melodies more than did the Eastern or Pennsylvania style. It also had a different beat and was slower, making the Chicago polka an easier dance.

Li'l Wally cut his first two records using this style in 1946: "Our Break Up" and "Away From Chicago." He eventually cut seventeen gold and four platinum records in more than fifty years of recording.

The polka was originally a peasant dance, and many people in the United States and even in Poland still look down on it as lowbrow and long outdated. A lot of Chicagoans do not think so. They see the polka as much a genuine part of their cultural heritage as Chopin and Paderewski.

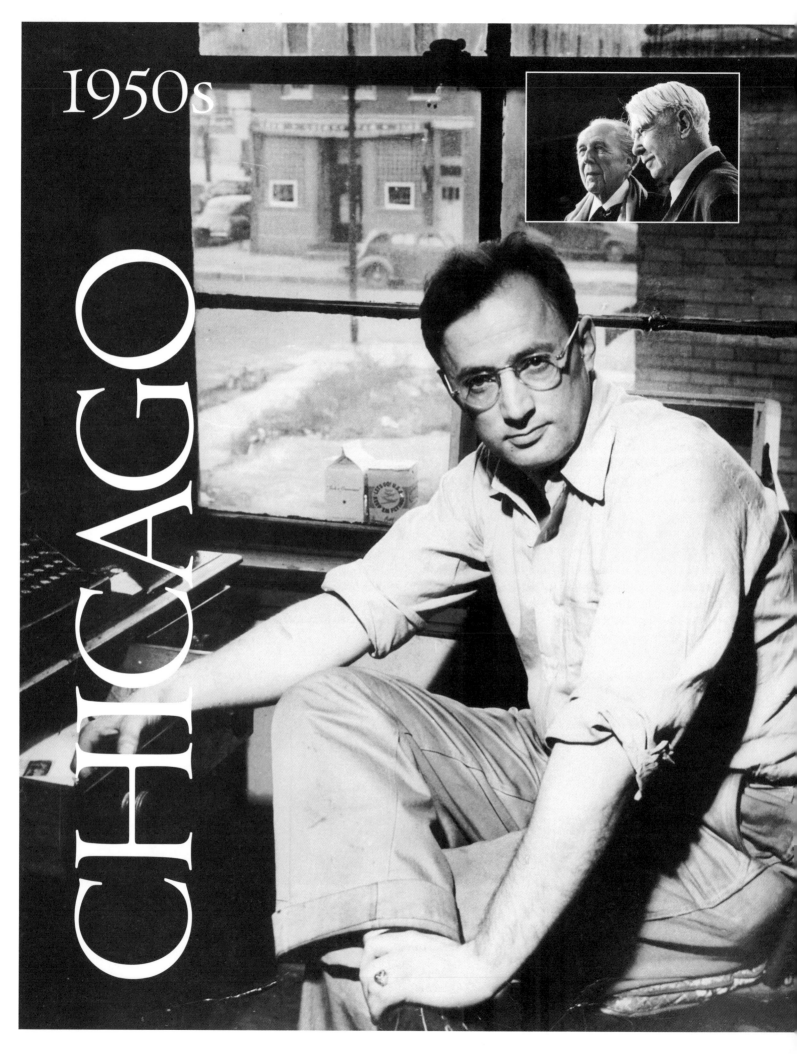

1950s

CHICAGO

# 1950s: Chicago: The Second City— the City on the Make

AJ. Liebling and some other visiting writers have labeled and libeled Chicago by saying it is rife with a sense of being inferior and has a "second city" complex. As with most patronizing statements, the words reflect more on the commentators than on the subject at hand.

Nelson Algren, in *Chicago: City on the Make,* was even harsher on the post–World War II Chicago in which he lived; but he had done his homework, woven his metaphors, and written with love of the city.

Chicago artists of the decade stood in a begrudgingly respected niche. Their efforts included the humanistic figure drawings of Leon Golub, the bronze and marble sculptures of Cosmo Campoli, the mirror and doll collages of George Cohen, and the surreal constructions of H. C. Westermann.

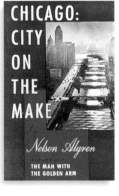

The Prudential Building, modeled more after the insurance firm's symbol of the Rock of Gibraltar rather than the traditions of the Chicago School of Architecture, nevertheless did inaugurate in 1955 almost two decades of commercial, high-rise building in and around the Loop. This has left a collection of buildings, paying homage to the great architectural traditions of the city.

At the same time, opera was rediscovering Chicago, improv theater was being born in the city, and Frank Lloyd Wright was trying to create a mile-high building.

On December 1, 1957, folksingers Win Stracke and Frank Hamilton founded the Old Town School of Folk Music, a bridge between the Carl Sandburg-trained Stracke in the 1930s and some of the most noted folksingers of the 1960s through the 1990s.

Chicago's writers—in addition to Saul Bellow, Gwendolyn Brooks, and

**Nelson Algren,
photograph by Art Shay**

# 1950s

Nelson Algren—included playwright Lorraine Hansberry as well as novelists Vera Caspary, W. R. Burnett, Max Sklovsky, Lillian Budd, Sam Ross, Frank Brown, Willard Motley, and Ira Morris, author of *Chicago Story*.

## THREE DIFFERING VIEWS OF CHICAGO IN THE EARLY 1950S

### Nelson Algren and *Chicago: City on the Make*

Gritty and, above all, lyrical, Nelson Algren's books stay in print, coming out in ever-new issues. His first editions of each are enthusiastically collected, and he is honored by an annual gathering of the faithful and a *Chicago Tribune*-sponsored short-story contest. Two of his works have been dramatized. His best-known novel, *The Man with the*

*Golden Arm,* won the National Book Award and became a film, starring Frank Sinatra. He speaks in a voice that is honest and authentic. The power of his words can be seen in the following passage from a chapter of his 1951 book, *Chicago: City on the Make:*

> love
> is
> for barflies

Before you earn the right to rap any sort of joint, you have to love it a little while. You have to belong to Chicago like a crosstown transfer out of the Armitage Avenue barns first; and you can't rap it then just because you've been crosstown.

Yet if you've tried New York for size and put in a stint in Paris, lived long enough in New Orleans to get the feel of the docks and belonged to old Marseilles awhile, if the streets of Naples have warmed you and those of London have chilled you, if you've seen the terrible green-gray African light moving low over the Sahara or even passed hurriedly through Cincinnati—then Chicago is your boy at last and you can say it and make it stick.

That it's a backstreet, backslum loudmouth whose challenges go ringing 'round the world like any green punk's around any neighborhood bar where mellower barflies make the allowances of older men: "The punk is just quackin' 'cause his knees is shakin' again."

"What's the percentage?" the punk demands like he really has a right to know. "Who's the fix on this corner?"

A town with many ways of fixing its corners as well as its boulevards, some secret and some wide open. A town of many angry sayings, some loud and some soft; some out of the corner of the mouth and some straight off the shoulder. . . .

### A. J. Liebling and *Chicago: The Second City*

Those on the East Coast—New Yorkers, mostly—have generally deemed Chicago a cultural wasteland. Few were as savage in their appraisal as was A. J. Liebling, who wrote a series of articles on the city for *The New Yorker*. The series was subsequently reprinted in a 1952 book entitled *Chicago: The Second City*. In contrast to Liebling's overreaching presentation of Chicago as a home for philistines, the book's illustrator, Steinberg, tweaked the city with good humor and interesting art on both the dust jacket and in its pages.

This excerpt is from Liebling's book:

There is an opinion, advanced by some men who worked in Chicago transiently during the twenties, as well as by many native Chicagoans, that the city did approximate the great, howling, hurrying, hog butchering, hog-mannered challenger for the empire of the world specified in the legend, but that at some time around 1930 it stopped as suddenly as a front-running horse at the head of the stretch with a poor man's last two dollars on its nose. What stopped it is a mystery, like what happened to Angkor Vat. There are only theories, most of them too materialistic to satisfy me, such as "Sam Insull took this town for all it had" and "The depression hit this town a wallop it never shook off."

Some skeptics have their own explanation of the disparity between the Chicago of the rhapsodists and the Chicago of today. It is that the rhapsodies were merely the result of mutual suggestion, like the St. Vitus's Dance epidemics of the Middle Ages. There may be some truth in that theory, too. "It was a wonderful place when I was a kid," a fellow who writes a column on foreign

affairs for a Chicago paper once told me. "Guys would be shot down every day on the busiest street corners."

A woman with a plaintive voice, calling me on the telephone after this appeared, dated Chicago's decline from the day Jane Addams boarded the Henry Ford peace ship in 1916. The intellectual life, as well as the social conscience of Chicago, centered on Jane Addams and Hull House before World War I, the woman said. Miss Addams's pacifism destroyed her prestige, consequently that of the whole group. Momentum carried some of the writers through the early twenties, and then they dispersed, having nothing to hold them together.

Liebling didn't bother to check this out. Jane Addams never boarded the peace ship and many believe the second part of his comment equally inaccurate.

### Alson J. Smith: Chicago—"Florence to New York's Rome"

In his *Chicago's Left Bank,* Alson J. Smith described the city in 1953 as "Florence to New York's Rome." A Connecticut Yankee, Smith had discovered Chicago in his student days during the early 1930s and was intrigued ever after by its "pork-and-poetry combination."

Here are some of his other observations about the city's culture:

The town is not provincial. It's friendly, and to those accustomed to cold-roast Boston, rigor mortis Philadelphia, phony Los Angeles, and go-to-hell New York, friendliness is a virtue so rare that it is likely to be confused with provincialism. And far from being a cultural Sahara, Chicago is actually the fertile seedbed for a good part of the native culture of the United States. What Boston and New England were to the country during

# 1950s

the first fifty years of the nineteenth century, Chicago and the Midwest have been during the first five decades of the twentieth.

Chicago is and can increasingly be the place of incubation, the seedbed, the creative center. It can be the locus of opportunity for the young, for those who wish to experiment, for the innovators. And of these there will always be some, like Nelson Algren and the Albright twins and Aaron Bohrod, who will clasp the city to their hearts and make it theirs, and who will never wish or need to go elsewhere.

For Chicago, in spite of the jungle competitiveness that so absorbs Algren, in spite of its open worship of the bastard-god Success, in spite of its monumental political corruption, in spite of its porcine, ubiquitous, and powerful hoodlums, is a tremendously alive and creative place; a place of dreary means, perhaps, but also of great and challenging extremes. So Carl Sandburg found it when he wrote, "Show me another city so glad to be alive," and so it is.

The measure of success the group will enjoy is problematical, since it has arrayed against it all the high brass of the big networks in both industries. But certainly it has gotten hold of an excellent name. Opportunity in Chicago for the young writer, artist, musician, architect, or actor is unlimited. Here, at a suitable distance from the commercial center of his craft, he is free to experiment and to develop in a way that is, if not impossible, at least difficult in New York or Hollywood. He does not have to fit any mold in Chicago, and he can draw for his inspiration on the electric vitality and the contagious brutality of the city.

For this is the most paradoxical city in the world, and in paradox there is the stuff of artistic creation in all fields of endeavor. How can a city be both brutal and friendly? Both radical and reactionary? Cultured and boorish? Corrupt and idealistic? Loved and hated?

It's true: Chicago is the most loved and most hated city in the United States and perhaps in the world. It is loved and hated by those who do not see the paradox; who see only the lovely or unlovely face of the city. And in Chicago these faces are not masked; they are there for everybody to see. When the artist does see the paradox, he is likely to want to stay and write about it as Algren does, or to paint it as Bohrod does. When he sees the paradox, sees both faces of the town, he is generally intrigued. He finds Chicago an exciting and emotionally rewarding place in which to live and work. If he doesn't see it, he will either uncritically love the place for its beauty and vitality or loathe it for its brutality and corruption. In either case he will not understand it.

## ADLAI STEVENSON

Political figures from Chicago and the Midwest, no less than its writers and artists, tend to use direct speech accompanied by an ability to explain their mission succinctly, to be with the people rather than attempt to be above them. This was true of Mayor Richard J. Daley and even the bombastic Big Bill Thompson as well as of the idealistic Illinois governor John Peter Altgeld, who sacrificed his political career to pardon men falsely convicted in the Haymarket Trial. It was especially obvious in the words of two national politicians who came from Illinois: Abraham Lincoln and Adlai Stevenson.

Lincoln was from Springfield; Stevenson, governor of Illinois from 1948 to 1952, was from a suburb north of Chicago, Libertyville. Abraham Lincoln helped focus the meaning of the Civil War in his Gettysburg Address

and the coming peace in his Second Inaugural Address. Stevenson, in his Speech of Acceptance in Chicago at the 1952 Democratic National Convention, successfully reached for the high notes of American politics and the presidency. The following excerpts are from the beginning and ending of that speech:

**Speech of Acceptance, Democratic National Convention, Chicago, Illinois, July 26, 1952**

I accept your nomination and your program.

I should have preferred to hear those words uttered by a stronger, a wiser, a better man than myself. But, after listening to the President's speech, I feel better about myself!

None of you, my friends, can wholly appreciate what is in my heart. I can only hope that you may understand my words. They will be few.

* * *

The ordeal of the twentieth century—the bloodiest, most turbulent era of the Christian age—is far from over. Sacrifice, patience, understanding and implacable purpose may be our lot for years to come. Let's face it. Let's talk sense to the American people. Let's tell

them the truth, that there are no gains without pains, that we are now on the eve of great decisions, not easy decisions, like resistance when you're attacked, but a long, patient, costly struggle which alone can assure triumph over the great enemies of man—war, poverty and tyranny—and the assaults upon human dignity which are the most grievous consequences of each.

Let's tell them that the victory to be won in the twentieth century, this portal to the Golden Age, mocks the pretensions of individual acumen and ingenuity. For it is a citadel guarded by thick walls of ignorance and of mistrust which do not fall before the trumpets' blast or the politicians' imprecations or even a general's baton. They are, my friends, walls that must be directly stormed by the hosts of courage, of morality and of vision, standing shoulder to shoulder, unafraid of ugly truth, contemptuous of lies, half truths, circuses and demagoguery.

The people are wise—wiser than the Republicans think. And the Democratic Party is the people's party, not the labor party, not the farmers' party, not the employers'

**Frank Lloyd Wright and Carl Sandburg, photograph by Archie Lieberman**

1950s

party—it is the party of no one because it is the party of everyone.

That I think, is our ancient mission. Where we have deserted it we have failed. With your help there will be no desertion now. Better we lose the election than mislead the people; and better we lose than misgovern the people. Help me to do the job in this autumn of conflict and of campaign; help me to do the job in these years of darkness, doubt and of crisis which stretch beyond the horizon of tonight's happy vision, and we will justify our glorious past and the loyalty of silent millions who look to us for compassion, for under-

standing and for honest purpose. Thus we will serve our great tradition greatly.

I ask of you all you have; I will give to you all I have, even as he who came here tonight and honored me, as he has honored you—the Democratic Party—by a lifetime of service and bravery that will find him an imperishable page in the history of the Republic and of the Democratic Party—President Harry S. Truman.

And finally, my friends, in the staggering task you have assigned me, I shall always try "to do justly and to love mercy and to walk humbly with my God."

## FRANK LLOYD WRIGHT AND CARL SANDBURG

Frank Lloyd Wright and Carl Sandburg followed parallel paths in becoming intimate voices of Chicago's soul. Wright said, "Every great architect is—necessarily—a great poet. He must be a great original interpreter of his time, his day, his age."

When they died (Wright in 1959 and Sandburg in 1967), each was acknowledged to have been a respected reminder of the youthful, rebellious Chicago—to represent its ability to create and to attract genius.

Wright, who started his architectural career in the offices of Louis Sullivan, carried Sullivan's "Form follows function" to brilliant and extraordinarily original conclusions in designing homes, hotels, commercial structures, museums, ornamentation, windows, and furniture. He established a school of architecture and assiduously pursued the development of its students. His ideas changed architecture throughout the world and brought creative patterns of the Midwest to places very reluctant to change, including Japan and Europe. His studio in Oak Park, his schools in Wisconsin and Arizona, and his works scattered throughout the world continue to carry his spirit and challenge those who encounter them.

Sandburg won a Pulitzer Prize for the *War Years* volumes of his biography of Abraham Lincoln and another for his *Collected Poems*. He also wrote fiction, autobiography, children's tales including *The Rootabaga Stories,* and other biographies including *Mary Lincoln.* Such poems as "Fog," "Chicago," "Grass," "Slabs of the Sunburnt West," "Cornhuskers," and "Halsted Street Streetcar" have long enthralled readers, but the greatest of all of his poetry was the 1936 book *The People, Yes* that reaffirmed his belief in America and in human beings. It followed his 1928 volume of poetry *Good Morning, America,* that seemed to lose it. As scholar, poet, and writer, Sandburg is enduring if one judges by the number of recent biographies and the almost twenty books of his that are still in print.

Both Wright and Sandburg rekindled their reputations in later life. Wright did it with his great Fallingwater house in the late 1930s, his Guggenheim Museum of Modern Art in New York, and his proposed mile-high building in Chicago. Sandburg renewed his credibility with his *War Years* in 1939, his *Remembrance Rock* and two autobiographical works, *Always the Young Stranger* and *Ever the Winds of Chance,* the latter being published after his death.

## BILL VEECK, DEMOCRACY IN SPORTS

Bill Veeck, born in suburban Hinsdale and later the principal owner of the Chicago White Sox, was unique in baseball and in his operating definition of popular sports culture. He believed both should be democratic. This philosophy differed widely from that of the wealthy playboys and corporate leaders who see a sports team as simply a money-making (or -losing) toy.

Prior to his two stints with the White Sox, Veeck had owned the St. Louis Browns and the Cleveland Indians. Several times over, he turned professional baseball upside down by bringing in fans by the millions and letting them be involved in the fun of it as he sat every day in the stands so they could argue his decisions with him.

Veeck held the reins of the White Sox from 1959 to 1961 and again from 1976 to 1980. When he purchased them, they were a team that had not won a pennant since the Black Sox scandal in 1919. Veeck found a way to fill seats, which helped reluctant owners see the national pastime as entertainment and not just a pedestaled opportunity for money and glory. He had no door on his office. He sat, during the games, in the bleachers.

The ensuing excerpt from his book, *Veeck as in Wreck,* shows the style of this Chicagoan, this man of the people:

# 1950s

Most of all, we showed the fans that we weren't just out for their money, that we cared about them and wanted them to have a good time. I can remember looking out the window after a game had been rained out and seeing a couple of hundred out-of-towners waiting disconsolately for their train at the Pennsylvania Railroad depot. [When he owned the Cleveland Indians,] I called down to the locker room and asked Boudreau and Feller to dash over and barber with them until the train came. Another time, about 700 school kids from Mahoning Valley were invited to a game as my guests. That game was rained out too, and I sent them all to a show so they wouldn't go home completely disappointed.

We didn't have to be geniuses in either Chicago or St. Louis to know that the people of the neighborhood weren't going to be overjoyed at having fireworks exploding all around them, night after night, so we held "Good Neighbor Night" and had them all to the game, on the theory that nobody is as upset when that noisy party in the apartment upstairs is being thrown by friends as he would be if the people upstairs were strangers. More than that—again—we were letting them know

we were well aware that we were imposing on their—we hoped—good nature.

We had special nights where 'A' students and their teachers were admitted free, because nobody else seemed to give them any recognition. We had special nights for bartenders and cabdrivers, always our prime sources of information. We had special days and nights for Boy Scouts and all youth groups. We had nights in which everybody who had worked for the Community Chest came as our guests, we had nights for the workers of Mayor's Youth Groups, we had nights for everybody who had contributed to the Combined Jewish Appeal. In many of these cases it wasn't the price of the ticket that was important, it was the knowledge that their work or their contributions were being recognized.

We wooed women shamelessly. We gave Cleveland women orchids and nylons at a time when orchids were still considered exotic and nylons were almost impossible to get. You can't get much more personal with women than that without meeting the family. Ten years later while I was stopping off at a Cleveland hotel overnight, my chambermaid came in with another chambermaid, pointed to me fondly and said, "That's the man. He gave me my first orchid."

The first thing we always have had to do in any park is to fix up the ladies' room. Baseball always seems to operate on the principle that women customers are just men customers in dresses. Ladies' rooms in most baseball parks are a shame and a disgrace. At Comiskey Park, the facilities were so bad that I forbade Mary Frances to use them until I was able to get them fixed up. By the time I was through, we had individual vanity tables and flattering fluorescent lighting. (I'd learned about that the hard way.) There were full-length mirrors so that the ladies could look themselves over and check the seams of their stockings before they went back out to face the world. Every now and then, we'd give out cosmetic kits as presents to everybody who entered. (I might as well say here that men's rooms are nothing to rave about in ball parks either. We've always had to make them fit for human beings too.)

## KATHERINE DUNHAM AND AFRICAN AMERICAN DANCE IN CHICAGO

Katherine Dunham, a dancer, choreographer and dance teacher originally from Joliet, went from a classroom at the University of Chicago in the early 1930s to the world stage and dramatically impacted the understanding and appreciation of African, African American, and Afro-Caribbean dance.

Dunham used her abilities as a dancer as well as the sociology she learned in her classes at University of Chicago and as a Rosenwald scholar to visit Africa, Brazil, and such Caribbean nations as Haiti, Martinique, and Trinidad to learn their dance traditions.

In the late 1930s and early 1940s, Dunham wrote about African-rooted dance in three books and put together groups that performed in the 1940s and 1950s throughout Europe, the United States, South America, Australia, New Zealand, and Japan.

Of Katherine Dunham and her group's performances at the Great Northern Theater in Chicago in October 1955, *Chicago American* dance critic Ann Barzel wrote:

Katherine Dunham started the vogue for "primitive" and West Indian dancing. She has been imitated extensively. Seeing the original makes one realize how pale and colorless the copies are. Miss Dunham's intellectual approach, her research in folk art have resulted in works that are more profoundly emotional than the superficial Calypso numbers that pop up on your TV screen and pep up too many night club floor shows.

**Katherine Dunham**

# 1950s

One of the attractions of the show is the variety it finds in Negro dance art. There are the Voodoo of Trinidad, the Samba of Brazil, the ritual of Africa, the shimmy, the Cakewalk and the Charleston of the North American Negro.

More than anything else, Dunham became a teacher. Through the Katherine Dunham School of Dance in post–World War II New York and later through her home and dance center in East St. Louis, Illinois, she continued to pass on dance that had come out of Africa, directing it to the soul of America.

In a November 13, 1946, *New York Times* article, John Martin called her school "a phenomenal institution" and wrote:

It has two, three, and five year courses leading to professional, teaching and research certificates; its faculty numbers thirty, its curriculum contains everything from dance notation through ballet, modern, and primitive techniques to psychology and philosophy, with acting, music, visual design, history and languages; its student body, unaffectedly interracial, numbers approximately 400, and its deficits are enormous.

In his book, *The Black Tradition in American Dance*, Richard A. Long adds an interesting footnote: "In addition to dancers, an array of other personalities passed through the classes of the Dunham School. These included Marlon Brando, James Dean, Jose Ferrer, Jennifer Jones, Butterfly McQueen, Shelly Winters and Doris Duke."

## THE SECOND CITY, IMPROV THEATER

Chicago makes a habit of surprising the world. Time and time again, it has created a stir. One of the most influential cultural shocks generated by Chicago took place in 1959. It happened with the founding of The Second City, an improvisational theater group, which altered the way America viewed comedy and spawned a stunning number of comedic artists, including Alan Arkin, Dan Aykroyd, John and Jim Belushi, John Candy, Severn Darden, Barbara Harris, Valerie Harper, Bill Murray, Gilda Radner, Joan Rivers, Paul Sand, Avery Schreiber, and George Wendt.

A great many of these actors, having graduated from The Second City, moved to New York, where they became regulars on the television show *Saturday Night Live,* and later changed addresses again to Hollywood, California. Other products, including David Mamet, went on to the established theater venues.

The Second City, on its part, was the product of The Compass Players, a group that originally came together on the campus of the University of Chicago. It had included David Shepherd, Paul Sills, Barbara Harris, Severn Dardin, Shelley Berman, Mike Nichols, and Elaine May.

The following is from *Something Wonderful Right Away,* by Jeffrey Sweet, a book of interviews with members of The Second City and The Compass Players:

The name they gave their enterprise was The Second City, a phrase adopted from a deprecating *New Yorker* magazine article about Chicago by journalist A. J. Liebling.

On December 6, 1959, The Second City opened its doors to a crowd too large for the barely completed 120 seat theater. First nighters were greeted by a lightning-paced program of scenes and songs that good naturedly skewered social and political concerns of the time. The most memorable sketch was "Businessman," from a scenario by Roger Bowen, depicting the thrilling adventures of a superhero who employed his superpowers to break strikes, construct tariff walls, and perform other deeds in the ser-

# 1950s

vice of the capitalist way of life. (His archenemy? Collective Man, of course!) In addition, Sills and company took on Eisenhower, grand opera, the medical profession and the cultural pretensions of FM radio ("broadcasting the best of everything worthwhile"). The troupe maintained its improvisational credentials by performing sketches based on suggestions from the audience after its set shows. The most promising of the improvs were then pulled into rehearsal, reworked, tested in the improv set again, pulled back into rehearsal for adjustments, and then included in The Second City show. (This method of developing new material is still in practice today.)

This was rich stuff for a city whose theatrical life till then had consisted largely of recycled Broadway and traditional stagings of museum pieces by the Goodman Theater.

## TWO PLAYS: TWO DIVERGENT VIEWS OF CHICAGO AND AMERICA IN THE 1950s

### Grease

*Grease,* a 1970 musical called a "sarcastic salute" to the 1950s, caught the country's imagination both as a Broadway play and in 1978 as a movie with John Travolta and Olivia Newton-John. Fictional Rydell High School (actually Taft High School) is the setting for the play, written by Chicagoans Jim Jacobs and Warren Casey and performed originally at the Kingston Mines Theater, a converted trolley barn on Lincoln Avenue. On opening night, the producers displayed real cool and theatrical savvy by having "greasers" in the audience and a real "Greased Lightnin'" jalopy as a prop. The play immortalized the Burger Palace Boys, the Pink Ladies, cigarette packs rolled up in sleeves, slicked-back hair, beehives, ducktails, and hubcap

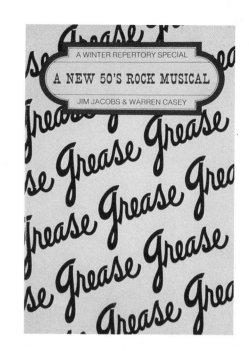

stealing. Nostalgic icons to most theatergoers in Chicago in the 1950s, these represented the arms of a rebellion to fight conformity rather than manifest it.

The following is a retrospective on *Grease* by Michael Feingold:

The greatest achievement of *Grease* (and the aspect which produces the loudest laughter in the packed house every night) is its perfect deadpan objectivity about everything in it: A d.a. haircut, a new guitar, a missed period, a falsetto backup group, a preposterously accurate handjive. It is a loving, funny, museum of where we were, perhaps even, when we scream and stomp our feet at it, a gentle attempt to exorcise the parts of ourselves we left back there, a tribute to the many small, stupid things that happened to us during "the decade when nothing happened."

### Lorraine Hansberry: *A Raisin in the Sun*

Lorraine Hansberry's *A Raisin in the Sun* opened on Broadway on March 11, 1959, as the civil rights movement of the 1960s was about to turn America

*Chaos, Creativity, and Culture*

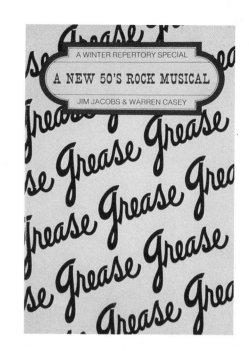

**106**

upside down. With a cast that included Sidney Poitier, Ruby Dee, and Louis Gossett, the play won the New York Drama Critics Circle Award. During a tryout a month earlier in Chicago, *Tribune* theater critic Claudia Cassidy had praised the play and cast and prophetically added, "More important to Chicago is that it has the fresh impact of something urgently on its way."

Hansberry, born on the city's South Side, graduated from Englewood High School. Her play, about the African American Younger family attempting to move into an all-white neighborhood, was partially autobiographical. The *Washington Post* called it, "One of a handful of great American plays—It belongs in the inner circle along with *Death of a Salesman, Long Day's Journey into Night* and *The Glass Menagerie.*"

Hansberry died of cancer at age thirty-four in 1965 but left behind this play, which helped open the doors for new racial attitudes by showing, as Ossie Davis said, "how much the Younger family was just like any other American family."

*A Raisin in the Sun:* Act III

WALTER: Don't cry, Mama. Under-stand. That white man is going to walk in that door able to write checks for more money than we ever had. It's important to him and I'm going to help him. . . . I'm going to put on the show, Mama.

MAMA: Son—I come from five generations of people who was slaves and sharecroppers but ain't nobody in my family never let nobody pay 'em no money that was a way of telling us we wasn't fit to walk the earth. We ain't never been that poor. (Raising her eyes and looking at him.) We ain't never been that dead inside.

BENEATHA: Well, we are dead now. All the talk about dreams and sunlight that goes on in this house. All dead.

WALTER: What's the matter with you all! I didn't make this world! It was give to me this way! Hell, yes, I want me some yachts someday! Yes, I want to hang some real pearls 'round my wife's neck. Ain't she supposed to wear no pearls? Somebody tell me—tell me, who decides which women is suppose to wear pearls in this world. I tell you I am a man—and I think my wife should wear some pearls in this world!

(This last line hangs a good while and WALTER begins to move about the room. The word "Man" has penetrated his consciousness; he mumbles it to himself repeatedly between strange agitated pauses as he moves about.)

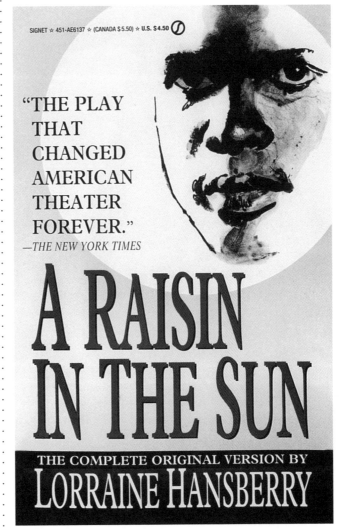

1960s

CHICAGO

# 1960s: Chicago Explodes

ayor Richard J. Daley was "Boss," "Da Mayor," and "The Man" in Chicago throughout the 1960s. The Black Panthers, the Democrats, the Yippees, Hippies, anti-Vietnam protesters, and members of the American Nazi party gathered in the city in an attempt to change the world. The events of the decade in Chicago, from demonstrations to riots to protests, were followed by accounts of each as first the newspapers, then television networks, magazines, and books tried to tell America what the Chicago happenings were all about.

Few such commentators have ever described the city as well as the people themselves did in *Division Street: America* (1967) by Studs Terkel, and those who were heard in his subsequent books.

—Harry Mark Petrakis, in *A Dream of Kings,* universalized the story of a Chicagoan who still kept one foot in his native Greece.

—Mike Royko, in 1963, began his nationally acclaimed column in the *Chicago Daily News,* also the home for syndicated columnist Sydney J. Harris.

—Emily Kimbrough, a former Marshall Field and Company employee and a prolific author of books of humor, who had attained a following with *Our*

*Hearts Were Young and Gay* in the early 1940s, continued to please a national audience.

—John R. Powers wrote about growing up Catholic in Chicago.

—Other Chicago novelists included Ronald L. Fair, S. W. Edwards, and Sam Siegel.

Chicago offered a unique group, or rather groups, of artists who went under the fanciful name, "The Hairy Who." Their works were often playfully

# 1960s

vulgar and had a direct impact on much of the art that two and three decades later has shown up in underground comics and newspapers. These artists included James Nutt, Karl Wirsum, and Gladys Nilsson.

The 1960s were the beginning of Sir Georg Solti's incredible era with the Chicago Symphony Orchestra and the end of the Mies van der Rohe age in urban architecture and the final days of Riverview Amusement Park.

Architecturally, Chicago was exploding with experimentation and designs often surprisingly socially conscious. South Commons, Prairie Shores, and Lake Meadows afforded integration and good apartments for renters with near-public-aid incomes to upper-middle-class ones. The late Bertrand Goldberg designed not only Marina City but also public housing, the Raymond Hilliard homes on the Near South Side.

## HARRY MARK PETRAKIS

Chicago has spawned, or at least had been home to, a long list of storytellers, including George Ade, L. Frank Baum, Edna Ferber, Ernest Hemingway,

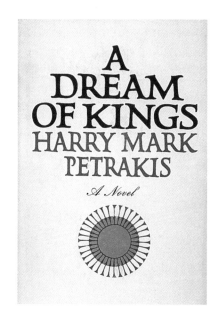

Richard Wright, Nelson Algren, Mike Royko, and Sara Paretsky. This list must include Harry Mark Petrakis. His collection of short stories, *Pericles on 31st Street,* was a finalist for the 1965 National Book Award, but his novel, *A Dream of Kings,* is recognized as Petrakis's finest effort. The rough-hewn main character, Leonidas Matsoukas, is a gambler, fighter, and operator of the Pindar Counseling Service—"Solutions provided for all problems of life and love." The much-flawed hero has the hubris to take on the gods themselves to rescue his son, who cannot speak and can barely move. In the following passage we meet the boy and read of his father's "dream":

Despite the distorted visage in the cracked glass, his head appeared hewn from some dark and basaltic rock, his craggy face a ravaged bas relief from a Greek column. His black hair, giving no hint of his forty-seven years, clustered thickly at his temples. His sharply peaked brows seemed reins haplessly seeking to restrain the wild, dark lunge of his eyes. His broad nose, broken and never properly mended after his match with Zahundos, exhaled into the forest of a roguish mustache that bristled about the ivory stockade of his strong white teeth. The only features that affronted his vanity were his long and unshapely ears, one a half-inch lower than the other, giving his head a lopsided appearance. In addition both ears had lobes so large they might have provided a pair of smaller ears for a conventional head.

He gathered his clothes and dressed in the damp and dingy kitchen. He slipped into the same shirt he had worn the day before, trying vainly to smooth the wrinkles, sniffing at the armpits, scowling at the frayed collar, feeling it an imposition to be reminded of his economic debilities so early in the day. He looped his tie into a wide knot and pulled it up to clasp his thick and muscle-corded throat.

Ready to leave, he walked quietly down the hall, holding his nose in bitter distaste as he passed his mother-in-law's lair, releasing it only when he came to the room in which his two small daughters slept. He pushed open the door gently and listened until he could hear the whispers of breath that rose from their beds.

He passed down the hall and entered the parlor. Within the bay formed by three high and narrow windows a single child's bed stood, a bed that resembled a cage because of the high bars and railings along the sides.

He stood beside the bed looking down at his sleeping son, Stavros, seeing the boy quiet for a beneficent interlude, undisturbed by the dreadful struggles that consumed him when awake. Yet even in sleep his flesh seemed an almost transparent shell spread tightly over the bone of his cheeks. His breath, coming in short spasms up the frail canal of his throat, fluttered a network of roots around his mouth, twisting his lips in sour little patterns. His whole body bore an affinity to shadow.

Matsoukas looked bitterly at the feeble sun barely visible in the sky. Everything was washed in a strange pallor, the window frame, the roofs of buildings, and the arabesque of the elevated tracks.

He began to speak to his son in a whisper so soft the words barely sounded beyond the edge of his lips.

"The sun has risen but you cannot see or feel it," he said. "It is pale and without strength and beneath it even the weeds wither

and die. But soon now, my beloved, we will leave this place of dark and rot, soon you will feel the sun of the old country, the sun of Hellas."

He closed his eyes and felt himself caught in a frenzy of recall.

"You have never seen a sun like that," he whispered. "It warms the flesh, toughens the heart, purifies the blood in its fire. It will make you well, will burn away your weakness with its flame, will heal you with its grace."

He fumbled in his pocket and brought out a small cube of sugar. He peeled off the paper and slipped the cube under the boy's pillow. He kissed the tips of his fingers and placed them softly against his son's moist cheek.

He left the flat, drawing the door closed quietly behind him.

## POETRY, A CHICAGO TRADITION

The first page of a 1966 anthology, *Port Chicago Poets,* recalls the following comment about Chicago and poetry by a visitor to the city ninety-nine years before in 1867:

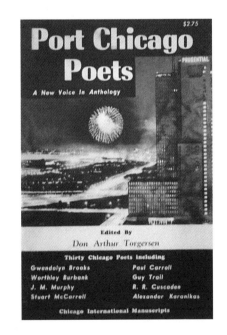

# 1960s

In good time, the western bottom lands will spontaneously grow poets. The American mind will be brought to maturity along the chain of Great Lakes, the banks of the Mississippi, the Missouri and their tributaries in the far Northwest. There, on the rolling plains, will be formed a republic of letters, which, not governed like that on our seaboard by the great literary powers of Europe, shall be free indeed. . . . The winds sweep unhindered from the Lakes to the Gulf and from the Alleghenies to the Rocky Mountains; and so do the thoughts of the Lord of the prairie. . . . Some day he will make his own books as well as his own laws. . . . He will remain on his prairie and all the arts of the world will come and make obeisance to him like the sheaves in his fields. He will be the American man and beside him there will be none else.

The city had indeed "grown" poets. *Port Chicago Poets* contains the works of thirty of them, including Gwendolyn Brooks, Paul Carroll, Stuart McCarrell, Edith Meinecke, Don Torgersen, and Ralph Hayashida, to name a few.

The 1996 winner of the Pulitzer Prize for poetry, Lisel Mueller, who won it for her volume, *Alive Together,* was a former book reviewer for the *Chicago Daily News* and a founder of the Chicago Poetry Center.

Also in 1996 contemporary Chicago poet Sterling Plumpp published the noteworthy *Ballad of Harriet Tubman.*

In addition, a long list of editors of *Poetry* magazine have been notable poets themselves. These have included Harriet Monroe, George Dillon, Henry Rago, John Nims, Karl Shapiro, and Daryl Hine.

Other lists of the city's poets could include not only this handful of accepted writers but also literally thousands who receive no such formal recognition. These Chicagoans are filling the poetry magazines of the country with their contributions, publishing books of their poems, and enlivening the city with powerful and sometimes rousing poetry slams, holding quieter but no less enthusiastic readings such as those sponsored by the Poetry Club of Chicago.

Chicago, for more than twenty-five years, has seen a flourishing poetry, man-woman-or-youth-in-the-street movement among the city's Hispanics inaugurated by among others the enthusiastic, driven David Hernandez, who published his first volume of poetry, *Despertando or Waking Up in 1971.*

The city's many colleges and universities all continue to contribute individuals to the list of Chicago poets. These have included Michael Anania at the University of Illinois/Chicago, Reginald Gibbons at Northwestern, Paul Carroll from the University of Chicago, Martha Vertreace at Kennedy-King College, Paul Hoover at Columbia College, and R. Craig Sautter at De Paul University.

The poetry of Chicagoans has consistently born the stamp of the city's culture and especially its writers. It has been vigorous not only in its style but also in its message. The outcasts of the city's past, its strong ideas, and its poets in Bughouse Square are a metaphor in the closing lines from Sautter's book, *Expresslanes Through the Inevitable City:*

Bughouse the forgotten dowry of 19th-century-outcast immigrant intellectuals whose battles for free speech became our initiation into unrestricted expeditions of infidel incantations . . .

Bughouse birth of our anti-materialistic aspirations and altruistic idealizations, of our still thriving thankfulness . . .

Bughouse now at the fringe of myth and legend, never lamenting its redeemable revelations totally irreconcilable with subrealities of TV politics or advertising addictions . . .

Bughouse so far away now in the all-too-confident commercial colossus, surrounded by high-rise gentrification, still whispering to me of its historical hopes and proclamations of enlightenment and emancipation for a waiting humanity. . . .

To understand there is such a thing as Chicago poetry and not just poetry by Chicagoans, one needs to follow the lines of original thought and authentic style of the city's poets in early issues of *Poetry;* the works of Carl Sandburg, Nicholas Vachel Lindsay, Edgar Lee Masters, and Harriet Monroe; the poems of Gwendolyn Brooks and Li-Young Lee; the city's ethnic poets; its academic ones; its slammers and rappers; current poets such as Eloise Fink, Luis Rodriguez, John Dickson, Hy Hirshfield, Gertrude Rubin, and thousands more whose poems have helped enliven anthologies, poetry slams, readings, and magazines such as *Poetry, Chicago Review,* and *TriQuarterly.*

"I write poetry too," is a catchphrase in all parts of this city and metropolitan area.

## CREATIVITY AND THE CHICAGO SCHOOL OF ADVERTISING

Chicago's unique style and its creativity have been part not only of the city's architecture, writing, and other artistic efforts but also of its language and even business. One could find this imprint at the turn of the century in the Sears, Roebuck & Company and Montgomery Ward & Company catalogs. These books talked directly to the people and demonstrated trust with an approach of giving refunds based on the customer's word that he or she was not satisfied.

Again, this closeness to the American people, mixed with imagination and inventiveness, was Chicago's as it pioneered radio soap operas and live television.

In the following excerpts from an August 30, 1965, article in the *Chicago Tribune,* the late advertising executive

## A CHICAGO AD: "WHERE'S THE BEEF?"

"Nine-tenths of the commercials you watch are like wallpaper—you don't even see them," observed Chicago ad film producer Joe Sedelmaier. Not so his contributions to the ad world; they are noticed. An example of his work was his 1985 "Where's the beef?" commercial belted out by octogenarian Clara Peller against Wendy's competitors. It was a TV spot viewers didn't tire of and the phrase became part of the presidential campaign and the American language. For the fast-food chain, it helped bring double-digit growth that year. Sedelmaier's humor, imagination, and good read on his audience and product earned him recognition as one of the most creative ad people in the country.

# 1960s

Robert R. Burton pointed to the strength and the uniqueness of the Chicago School of Advertising:

Perhaps at the heart of our sometime feelings of doubt and insecurity—client and agency alike—is that we look only at billing comparisons. It is true that "the East" outbills the Midwest about 3 to 1. But I can remember when it was 10 to 1.

And what has that to do with the absolute quality of the thinking or the freshness of the creativity? The East also "outbills" the Midwest in banking—textiles, cybernetics, shipbuilding, and government contracts. But dollar-volume is only one of many possible comparative measurements. We in the agency business may have been guilty of making it the only one. Largely because digits are easier to quote and agree on than depth of thinking.

Chicago retains many top accounts. It certainly isn't charity or chauvinism that keeps the nation's No. 1 cereal, No. 1 TV brand, No. 1 greeting card, No. 1 domestic airline, No. 1 food association, No. 1 wax, No. 1 auto insurer tied to Chicago agencies.

Dominant domestic and international brands using Chicago agencies year after year are to be found in every consumer category: beer, candy, detergents, meats, sporting goods, shoes, salt, movie cameras, hair-care, food-retailing, personal-finance, steelmaking, and others.

Someone, somewhere in Chicago must be doing the thinking that is helping these firms grow, lead, and dominate all comers—with or without eastern agency relationships.

When one carefully compares the essential contributions with the long term trend of our business—as I have done from the vantage point of a New York office—it must be agreed that more basic pattern-cutting has been accomplished in Chicago than New York. At least in the last 20 years.

Breakthrough ideas in photography, typography, TV animation, media, merchandising, and ad design have occurred. There is a refreshing air of practicality in the Chicago school of advertising. An insistence on testing of ideas and alternatives—whereas New York shops more often rely on instinct and outworn esthetic judgment. A long-term brand-share trend can mercifully fog out their bigger mistakes.

It's pretty hard to duck out here on the prairie!

## THE PICASSO

The *Picasso*, a statue created by the Spanish sculptor Pablo Picasso, was erected in the Civic Center Plaza in 1967 and many—if not most—Chicagoans seemed confused about what it represented. To some, it looked like a bird; to others, a woman's face; and, to a few, the profile of then Mayor Richard J. Daley. This did not mean the residents of the city do not like it, just that they don't always know what to make of it. With the following verse recited at the dedication, Gwendolyn Brooks helped the city reflect on its new symbol with her poem from *Blacks,* published by Third World Press in 1991:

Chicago/Kezys

64 Photographs of Chicago
By Algimantas Kezys

# The Chicago Picasso
*August 15, 1967*

"Mayor Daley tugged a white ribbon, loosing the blue
percale wrap. A hearty cheer went up as the covering
slipped off the big steel sculpture that looks at once
like a bird and a woman."
—*Chicago Sun-Times*

(Seiji Ozawa leads the Symphony. The Mayor smiles.
And 50,000 See.)

Does man love Art? Man visits Art, but squirms.
Art hurts. Art urges voyages—
and it is easier to stay at home,
the nice beer ready.
    In common rooms
we belch, or sniff, or scratch.
Are raw.

But we must cook ourselves and style ourselves for Art,
    who
is a requiring courtesan.
We squirm.
We do not hug the *Mona Lisa*.
We
may touch or tolerate
an astounding fountain, or a horse-and-rider.
At most, another Lion.

Observe the tall cold of a Flower
which is as innocent and as guilty,
as meaningful and as meaningless as any
other flower in the western field.

**Below is a list of some artists with
public sculptures in the Loop area and
the buildings or streets they are near:**

**Henri Azaz**
*Hands of Peace*—Clark and Madison
**Henry Bertoia**
*Offering to the Wind*—Amoco Plaza
**Joseph A. Burlini**
*Circus City*—Amoco Plaza
*Reflections*—Amoco Plaza
**Alexander Calder**
*Flamingo*—Dirksen Federal Building
*Flying Dragon*—The Chicago
Art Institute
*Universe*—Sears Tower
**Marc Chagall**
*The Four Seasons*—First Chicago
Bank Plaza
**Jean Dubuffet**
*Monument a la Bete Debout*—State
of Illinois Building
**Ruth Duckworth**
*Clouds Over Lake Michigan*—Sherman
and Van Buren
**Richard Hunt**
*Winged Form*—Amoco Plaza
**John Kearney**
*Two Deer* and *The Fawn*—Amoco Plaza
**Joan Miro**
*Miro's Chicago*—south of Daley Plaza
**Henry Moore**
*Large Internal Form*—The Chicago
Art Institute
*Large Upright Internal/External Form*—
north of First Chicago Bank Building
**Louise Nevelson**
*Dawn Shadows*—Madison and Wells
**Claes Oldenburg**
*Batcolumn*—Jackson and Madison

**GWENDOLYN BROOKS**

Gwendolyn Brooks is a cultural and poetry maven. She is also an exciting and fine poet in touch with the city's heart. Ms. Brooks continues to find imaginative ways to awaken a liking and a love for poetry in even the youngest of school children and to help struggling poets find the rung right above them. She won the Pulitzer Prize for *Annie Allen,* but her most esteemed book was *A Street in Bronzeville.* Chicagoans know her through her kindness, her poetry readings, and her very popular book *Selected Poems.*

The following poem is from *Blacks,* published by Third World Press in 1991:

# of De Witt Williams on his way to Lincoln Cemetery

He was born in Alabama.
He was bred in Illinois.
He was nothing but a
Plain black boy.

Swing low swing low sweet sweet chariot.
Nothing but a plain black boy.

Drive him past the Pool Hall.
Drive him past the Show.
Blind within his casket,
But maybe he will know.

Down through Forty-seventh Street
Underneath the L,
And—Northwest Corner, Prairie,
That he loved so well.

Don't forget the Dance Halls—
Warwick and Savoy,
Where he picked his women, where
He drank his liquid joy.

Born in Alabama.
Bred in Illinois.
He was nothing but a
Plain black boy.

Swing low swing low sweet sweet chariot.
Nothing but a plain black boy.

Gwendolyn Brooks

# 1960s

**RICHARD J. DALEY**

Richard J. Daley was mayor from 1955 until his death in 1976. "Chicago," the pundits said, "was Daley's city." In the 1970 book, *Daley of Chicago,* Bill Gleason, a sportswriter and a Chicago original himself, gave us this description of the man who was mayor:

When he arrives at a funeral home, he whirls through the entrance door, members of the retinue taking large steps to keep pace, and if it is not a Catholic wake and no kneeler upon which a man can say a prayer beside the casket, he looks to be in motion even when he is talking earnestly and comfortingly to the widow. He moves, moves, moves, making things happen.

His carriage and his posture carefully cultivated are magnificent. Chins in, abdomen tucked up. Because he looks so much like the politicians of the editorial page cartoons, he does everything possible to avoid the stereotype. He is not a tall man. He is not a slim man. But he walks tall and slim. This is a trick he learned well from others. He has disciplined his body, but his face got away from him. Its a good face, but instead of having been stretched it was folded and piled. Just as he has an extra chin, he has a profusion of jowls. There are within the jowls great dimples and small crevasses. At times students of his face see Mr. Pickwick there; at other times they see Santa Claus; and at still other times the character portrayed so often by Sidney Greenstreet, the late movie villain. In 1955 critics made fun of the clothes worn by Daley. Now he makes "best-dressed man" lists, an accomplishment that amuses him.

His malapropisms, tautologies and syntactical errors are collectors items. But he is not the "dese, dem and dose" mispronouncer that some among the literati have made him out to be. His basic speech impediment is one shared by most Irish-Americans, even to the third and fourth generation. There is something in Gaelic language that makes the sounding of "th" all but impossible. For Richard J. Daley and millions like him, thanks becomes "tanks" and think becomes "tink." Even *the* is difficult—it usually emerges sounding like thu—and these, them and those are more so.

**THE CHICAGO CONSPIRACY SEVEN**

The 1969 trial of radicals involved in demonstrations during the Democratic National Convention in Chicago a year earlier attracted international attention. The number was reduced from eight to seven when United States District Judge Julius Hoffman separated out black activist Bobby Seale. It then became the Chicago Seven Conspiracy Trial.

The following from *The Great Conspiracy Trial,* by Jason Epstein, explores the inner workings of the famous show trial:

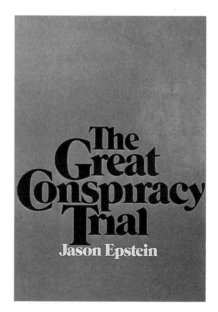

The judge sat impassively throughout this outburst. When William Kunstler had returned to his chair and the marshals had restored order, he began to read the sentences for each of (David) Dellinger's contempts. For reading the names of the dead on moratorium day, he sentenced him to five months. Altogether he sentenced Dellinger to twenty-nine months and thirteen days.

He then proceeded to deal with (Rennie) Davis, whom he sentenced to twenty-five months and fourteen days on twenty-three counts of contempt.

***

The judge next sentenced (Tom) Hayden to fourteen months and fourteen days for eleven separate contempts. For rising to object that Bobby Seale "should not be put in a position of slavery" he was sentenced to three months. He was sentenced to four months for saying in the presence of the jury that the marshals were beating Seale. He was sentenced to six months for saying loudly enough for the jury to hear him that Ramsey Clark had not been allowed to testify. When Hayden rose to speak, he told the judge that American youth had turned its back on the system represented by the Court.

"Before your eyes," he said, "you see the most vital element of your system collapsing."

### NELSON ALGREN ON *PLAYBOY* MAGAZINE

Hugh Hefner, a cartoonist in Chicago for *Esquire* magazine, started *Playboy* in 1957, which was to prove one of the most successful magazines in history. The image of this new "girlie" publication was that it represented a broad-ranged American rebellion against the restrictive moral code of the past. And secondly—a somewhat distant second—was that it was making a contribution to

**Hugh Hefner**

this nation's culture. Stories and articles appeared in *Playboy* that were written by many of the nation's top writers. Their names seemed to indicate their solid support for this male fantasy of what a sexual revolution could be. Nelson Algren, who was foursquare in favor of both sex and revolution, was not above writing for *Dude* and other equally less ambitious publications but chose not to march in *Playboy*'s parade, criticizing it in his book, *Who Lost an American?*

The following is an excerpt from Algren's book chapter:

*Playboy* speaks to those who wish desperately to know what it means to be male. It speaks to the reader whose masculinity depends upon

## 1960s

# 1960s

his choice of deodorant or cigar, one who can maintain respect for a woman only as long as she abides by a tacit assurance not to arouse him sexually. It does not sell sex. It sells a way out of sex.

Sex that—in Karl Barth's meaning when he names the basic relationship of man's life Mitmensch—co-humanity—is out of bounds to the *Playboy* believer. For him sex can be indulged in only as a recreation—"virtue in those areas where virtue is important." Virtue, like an assertive weskit, may be put on for an evening or for the fall season, but is not something to which one is to commit oneself.

Because one is not to commit oneself at any time, any where: not to a weskit, not to another human being nor to an issue alive in the world.

"We hold that man is free," Simone de Beauvoir writes, "but his freedom is real and concrete only to the degree that it is committed to something, only if it pursues some end and strives to effect some change in the world. Man is free only if he sets himself concrete ends and strives to realize these: but an end can be called such only if it is chosen freely. The cult of money, which one encounters here, does not spring from avarice or meanness: it expresses the fact that the individual is unable to commit his freedom in any concrete realm; making money is the only aim one can set oneself in a world in which all aims have been reduced to this common denominator."

To seek to be free by avoiding involvement with the world, which is the commodity *Playboy* pitches, cannot be achieved. There never was a world—or a woman—who could be turned on and off like a faucet. The woman may run hot and she may run cold, but in all Man's time she has never been turned off.

The man who constitutes the backbone of *Playboy* readership by buying the magazine from a news-stand for sixty cents is a man under thirty. After thirty readership drops off abruptly: something happens to most of its readers between twenty-eight and thirty-one. You know what I think? I think he finds out you can't turn her off.

The reassurance that *Playboy* thinking offers the young American is that, by going into a blind retreat upon himself, arranging his own room comfortably and adopting those attitudes prescribed by the world of advertising, he has jus-tified his existence; simply by protecting himself from disap-pointment, risked by falling in love with either the world or a woman, he has fulfilled himself.

"The reality of a man is not hidden in the mists of his own fancy," Mme. de Beauvoir wrote before these mists began to rise, "but lies beyond him, in the world, and can only be disclosed there . . . it is in economic success that the American finds a way of affirming his personal independence remains wholly abstract, for it does not know on what to bestow itself."

Male failure is always attribut-able, with Montherlant, to mother, sister, or wife.

"The only place on his body where Achilles was vulnerable," he writes, "was where his mother had held him."

## SIR GEORG SOLTI AND THE CHICAGO SYMPHONY ORCHESTRA

A Chicago newspaper photographer who over many years had covered the Chicago Symphony Orchestra was speaking of its phenomenal rise to greatness: "We just got lucky. The orchestra has a lot of fine musicians who work very hard at it. And then, then there was Solti . . ."

Maestro Solti (1912–1997) became

*Chaos, Creativity, and Culture*

**120**

the principal conductor of the CSO in 1969. Born in Budapest, he had previously conducted in Bavaria, Frankfurt, and London, where he was knighted by Queen Elizabeth II. Arriving in Chicago with a vitality and a commanding presence, he tamed and mellowed the orchestra, which had been known as "the world's loudest," and reaped praise in Chicago, on the East Coast, and in Europe.

*Chicago Tribune* music critic John von Rhein, in Solti's obituary September 6, 1997, commented: "All his life, Solti seemed driven by a single desire: to make an indelible, unmistakable impact upon the symphonic and operatic music of our time. He succeeded perhaps better than the far-from-modest maestro ever would have imagined."

His first performance as maestro of the orchestra is described in the following excerpt from William Barry Furlong's 1974 book, *Season with Solti:*

Then came Solti—bald, intense, filled with a machismo that only Wagner could understand. He mellowed the orchestra's hard-diamond glints, shaped and honed its sonorous rumble, and built on it a logical edifice of telling detailed and perfect dramatic emphasis that could leave even the most indifferent of audiences spellbound. Thus, in one long gush, like a city that survived a siege, the Chicago Symphony came to greatness on a world scale.

What happens in the season is a reflection—and a continuation—of that greatness. It was not, in candor, built alone on a cascade of flashing arpeggios or the darkling glances of a single conductor. Rather, it was built on a cascade of flashing arpeggios or the darkling glances of a single conductor. It was built on a million tiny details, the minutiae of men and music, that affect and color every minute and hour every day and week of their lives, on stage

Just before he stepped down as maestro in 1991, Solti talked with *Tribune* music critic John von Rhein and repeated comments he had made to the members of the Chicago Symphony Orchestra during their last practice. The following quote is from that interview:

Yesterday in rehearsal I said to my orchestra, "The good thing about you and me is that we take every concert and every rehearsal seriously." We are not doing a job we are doing a love affair. We seriously understand each other. When I finish my official tenure, we will have produced about 1,000 concerts and roughly 100 recordings, plus many tours and TV appearances.

I am enormously proud of that achievement.

As I have said many times, I don't value how long I have served, but how well. I wanted the quality of the orchestra to be recognized worldwide. I think I have accomplished this. There is no doubt in my mind that it is the No. 1 orchestra in the world.

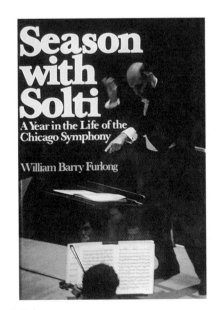

1960s

# 1960s

It is the subject that counts. I'm interested in revealing the subject in a new way to intensify it. A photo is able to capture a moment that people can't always see. Wanting to see more makes you grow as a person and growing makes you want to see more of life around you. In each exploration or concern for the subject, I continue in the area for a great length of time.

**—Harry Callahan**

and off. "Behind every musician," wrote Deems Taylor, "lurks a man who is fully as interesting as the art he pursues."

There are some qualities that all great orchestras have in common: they can, for example, save a charlatan and make him seem like a Toscanini on the podium. There are some qualities that they do not have in common: the Cleveland Orchestra, under George Szell, was a great ensemble made up of generally anonymous men who overcame their anonymity by playing with unparalleled unity. The Chicago Symphony, by way of contrast, is a virtuoso orchestra—it is made up of many stars in the musical world; it was harder for them—given the primal instinct of the musician—to sublimate their skills within the orchestra, but the manner and style with which they've done it have produced not only an incredibly unified sound but a personality of heightened exaltation.

## CHICAGO PHOTOGRAPHERS

Because of special needs and unusual opportunities, Chicago has produced an ever-renewing list of extraordinary photographers, ones capable of producing at a level that clearly delineates their work as art.

Beginning in the early twentieth century with the visits of documentary photographer Lewis Hine, the city showed a deep interest in realism as well as talent in photography. Hine, closely identified with haunting portraits of children at work, was inspired by what he found at Jane Addams's Hull House, and returned there time and again to photograph its activities and people.

By the 1920s, the city's press corps photographers were replacing the artwork that had long decorated Chicago's Sunday newspapers with exciting, breathtaking photos. At the same time, the city's unique architecture was being captured by the photographers of the Chicago Architectural Photographing Company as well as the partnership of Kaufmann-Fabry. These two firms attained an international reputation from the excellence of their work, especially in capturing the structures of the 1933–1934 world's fairs.

The late 1930s saw the beginning of one of this country's unique ventures into artistic photography: the New Bauhaus and its successor, the Institute of Design. Beginning with Moholy-Nagy's foundation course there, elaborated upon in his book *Vision in Motion,* the school housed such photographic innovator instructors as Harry Callahan, Nathan Lerner, Arthur Siegel, and Aaron Siskind.

"In the 1950s and early 1960s," according to Gail Buckland, "the Institute of Design was virtually the only institution in the United States where photography was taught as an art." Her comment appeared in a foreword to a 1978 Museum of Contemporary Art exhibit, *The City and the Photographer,* which gave recognition to "the response of the photographic artist to Chicago. Many of the modern masters of the art," she added, "have their origins here and have worked or continue to work in the city."

From the 1940s through the 1970s, Chicago-based magazines, including *Ebony, Coronet, Chicago,* and *Playboy,* helped put to work a band of competitive and highly qualified photographers. These were joined by ones employed by the advertising industry and national publications such as *Time, Life,* and *Look.* To stay employed, they had to be good, imaginative, fresh, and at the cutting edge of their profession.

A list of the names of some of those photographers who made their mark in Chicago would include Harold Allen, Harry Callahan, Barbara Crane, Stephen Deutch, Yasuhiro Ishimoto, Kenneth Josephson, Algimantas Kezys, Archie Lieberman, Ray Metzker, Mickey Pallas, Art Shay, Arthur Siegel, Victor Skrebneski, and Ruth Thorne-Thomsen.

# 1960s

**Photograph of Mickey Pallas**

*Above:* **Photograph by Art Shay**
*Left:* **Photograph by Ovie Carter**

# 1960s

The names must also include newspaper street shooters, among them Ovie Carter from the *Chicago Tribune* and John White from the *Chicago Sun Times*, each of whom has won a Pulitzer Prize.

Two of the nation's top advertising photographers during recent years were studio partners Jim Brady and Eddie Van Baerle. The former was known for his Marlborough Man shoots and the latter especially for his work with food products for Kraft and Pillsbury, among others. Their processing lab was unquestionably the best dye-transfer lab in the country for catching precise and true color.

David R. Phillips, considered a photographer's photographer, is noted for picture shoots both in Chicago and around the world. He is respected also as a genius on all aspects of repairing and using sophisticated and complex equipment, and often has been consulted by the very top photographers across the country.

The late Mickey Pallas earned a similar recognition for starting and operating Gamma Photo Labs, Incoporated, which provided the best in processing for professionals and aspiring amateurs. He later opened the Center for Photographic Arts to give recognition to others in his profession.

Several photographers have earned popular acclaim along with their very highly respected professional recognition as the result of books with which they have been associated. One is Archie Lieberman, whose powerful photograph of Frank Lloyd Wright and Carl Sandburg appears elsewhere in this book. He joined with one of the best writers in the city, Bob Cromie, to create the finely written and illustrated book *Chicago*. His photographs have been intense and in the Chicago tradition of social realism. They included such diverse subjects as men on death row, farmlife, inner-city vice scenes, drug addicts, and Israelites.

Art Shay's dramatic photographs also portray multiple slices of Chicago, including the world of Nelson Algren in the 1940s, 1950s, and 1960s. Some of these, along with his reminiscences, gave us an extraordinary book, *Nelson Algren's Chicago*. Shay, according to his count, has produced the covers for 1,004 magazines, books, and annual reports. He has won twenty art director awards and, in 1959, took *Life* magazine's "picture of the year."

The tradition of exceptional photography is still alive at a shooting level on the streets with the men and women who work for the town's newspapers or in its studios. Chicago's ability to create artist photographers continues on at the Institute of Design and now in such schools as that of the Art Institute of Chicago and Columbia College.

**Photograph by Art Shay**

1970s

CHICAGO

Ana Castillo

My Father Was a Toltec and selected poems

CHICAGO SOUL

ROBERT PRUTER

# 1970s: Chicago Has Something to Say

For a seventy-year period, Ruth Page was a great gift to the Chicago dance scene as, first, a ballerina, then a director and choreographer. In 1970, she established the Ruth Page Foundation and School of Dance, continuing to stress and create American themes for dance.

Another Chicago legend, Richard Nickel, considered one of the great architectural photographers on the American scene, died in 1972 while photographically recording the tearing down of Adler and Sullivan's Stock Exchange Building.

In 1972, Mike Royko won a Pulitzer Prize, one of the many honors accorded his daily column, then appearing in the *Chicago Daily News.*

Chicago suddenly had numerous small but wonderful and well-attended legitimate theaters. The Steppenwolf Theater Company, one of the best of these, was to produce some of the nation's most respected actors, including Gary Sinese, John Malkovich, and others.

In 1974, Saul Bellow was awarded the Pulitzer Prize for his novel *Humboldt's Gift* and, for the body of his writings, the 1976 Nobel Prize for Literature.

The city's authors included Stuart Dybek, who incorporated the vitality of the city in his short stories; two other novelists, Cyrus Colter and Leon Forrest, each of whom produced memorable works; novelist and *TriQuarterly* magazine editor Laurence Gonzales; Bill Brashler, who authored *City Dogs* and *The Bingo Long Traveling All-Stars and Motor Kings.* Father Andrew Greeley, who had by the late 1970s already produced almost one hundred books on a wide variety of religious and ethnic subjects, broke into the popular fiction field and became a best-seller. Last but not least, the *Chicago Tribune's* Paul Gapp garnered a Pulitzer Prize in 1979 for his architectural criticism.

Also during the seventies, the one hundred ten-story Sears Tower was constructed, utilizing a very efficient "bundled tubular" method of construction that has best been compared in physical appearance to the tubes of a pipe organ.

On an artistic note, with the addition of sculptures by Marc Chagall, Alexander Calder, Chicagoan John Henry, and Claes Oldenburg, the Loop and downtown area of Chicago continued to be transformed into what Franz Schulze has called "a veritable public museum of modern art on a gargantuan outdoor urban scale."

Finally, in other areas, the University of Chicago continued to add to its extraordinary list of creative scholars who have won the Nobel Prize in areas such as medicine, science, and economics.

## CHICAGO BALLET AND RUTH PAGE (1899–1991)

Ruth Page—for more than seventy years the heart of ballet in Chicago—was respected nationally as one of the most eminent pioneers of the dance as an American art form. She shared, according to ballet historian George Amberg, that distinction with William Christensen in San Francisco and Catherine Littlefield in Philadelphia. Of the three, he found her "the most progressive and intellectually and artistically curious."

June Sawyers wrote of Page in *Chicago Portraits:*

Ruth Page was a pioneer of American Dance, and for more than seven decades she was a formidable presence on the Chicago dance scene. At a time when the best dance was almost exclusively identified with foreign countries, Page departed from tradition and dared to choreograph ballets with peculiarly American themes. She worked with virtually every Chicago opera company at one time or another. Further, she is credited with creating a new art form, opera into ballet, a repertoire that included *La Traviata, Carmen* and *The Barber of Seville.*

As a teenager in the era before World War I, she had toured internationally with Anna Pavlova's company. Over subsequent decades, she excelled time and time again in the city as a ballerina, a director, a choreographer, and a founder of several ballet companies.

At age seventy-one, she started the Ruth Page Foundation and School of Dance on Chicago's Near North Side. And, from the ages of sixty-three to ninety-two, Ruth Page directed and choreographed the annual Airie Crown Theatre rendition of the *Nutcracker.*

The following assessment of her is from the 1949 book *Ballet in America: The Emergence of an American Art,* by George Amberg:

In the twenties the Chicago Allied Arts had an importance similar to that of the Ballet Society today and her connection with this vital little organization offered an aesthetic education such as few young artists in the American ballet got. During this time, Miss Page became thoroughly acquainted with the theatrical work and ideas of the Russian painter Nicolas Remisoff who later collaborated on most of her ballets. However, in her creative work, both as a concert dancer and as a choreographer, Miss Page was stimulated, rather than dominated, by these influences and she developed very definitely in her own way. Compositions such as "Frankie and Johnny" or "Hear ye! Hear ye!" are of an uncompromising, dramatic directness without precedent or parallel on the ballet stage.

Every one of her creations has drama, whether it be a solo dance or a duet or a group composition, whether it be conceived in abstract nonrepresentational, symbolic, terms, like Ravel's *Bolero,* which he called *Iberian Monotone* and *The Bells,* or presented as straight drama, like *Guns and Castanets,* which is actually the *Carmen* story. The basic structure of her work is determined by her acute sense of the theater and of the need for dramatic accentuation. In her own words, she tends "to emphasize the drama or dramatic purpose of the movement" and she does not hesitate to employ expressional or "modern" movement, if she feels that "the work will be more effective dramatically." For the same reason, she has experimented with the use of speech in connection with the dance. She argues that "In our western civilization the theater arts have been so separated that a few spoken words in a ballet seem to be quite revolutionary."

## TWO WOMEN ON THE AISLE
### Claudia Cassidy

From the early 1940s through the 1970s, those who dared perform publicly in Chicago's theater, dance, or music worlds had to contend with a *Chicago Tribune* critic often called "that witch" or "that witch in Chicago." She was Claudia Cassidy, author of a column called "On the Aisle." Whether based locally or on tour, individuals, troupes, or ensembles had to face the gauntlet of her words.

She detested mediocrity and did not much like people trying to make money from it. The writers, performers, and promoters whom she castigated rarely realized she was usually right and always honest. In a day when the ink of a pen or that of a typewriter ribbon was the blood of journalism, her enemies—and they were many—believed

**Claudia Cassidy**

she had substituted acid when writing her reviews.

An honest culture such as Chicago's tends to spawn critics with integrity and its review readers are apt to prefer their criticism blunt and direct. Ms. Cassidy, who died in 1996, worked until she was almost ninety. She once wrote: "Sometimes the shows that shoot at the moon and fail are more interesting than those that aim at mediocrity and score a bull's eye."

*1970s*

*Chaos, Creativity, and Culture*

**Ann Barzel and
Ruth Page**

**Ann Barzel**

Dance critic Ann Barzel will be remembered in Chicago for assembling and donating her 80,000-item collection on dance in the city and the Midwest to the Newberry Library. It is a researcher's treasure trove covering 150 years of performances that includes the souvenirs of a young Isadora Duncan who performed in a cabaret at State and Washington Streets, Anna Pavlova who resided here during World War I, and, among others, the city's own Ruth Page and Maria Tallchief.

In the 1960s and early 1970s, Ms. Barzel served as dance critic for two newspapers—*Chicago's American* and *Chicago Today*. She also wrote for major dance publications across the country. Her words were like her personality—spirited, committed, and passionate about the dance and about life.

The depth of her character and commitment is shown in a comment she once made. It was the early 1960s, before the Civil Rights Movement had become a reality, when she personally boycotted a major Chicago-area cultural institution because it gave out free passes that did not include the young people who lived south of Madison Street, which meant most of the city's

African American children. For her, dance and the arts were for everybody.

## ALLIGATOR RECORDS THE BLUES

Alligator Records, with its slogan, "Genuine Houserockin' Music," has accomplished since the early 1970s what Chess Records did in the 1940s and 1950s. It has gotten the "Chicago sound" out to the world. Alligator was started in spring 1971 to record the single "Hound Dog Taylor and the HouseRockers." The blues man and his band played in an obscure club in the heart of the city's South Side. Bruce Iglauer, the recording company's founder, operated it for the next four years from his apartment in Uptown. In a promotion booklet on the twentieth anniversary of Alligator, he wrote:

The corner of 54th Place and Shields Avenue on the South Side of Chicago is a weed-filled vacant lot now. It's impossible to see the outlines of the foundation of the building that used to stand there. But for dozens of neighborhood fans, this corner is fondly remembered as the site of Florence's Lounge, one of Chicago's friendliest and loosest blues clubs. Unlike the more famous Windy City blues joints—Theresa's, Pepper's, Silvio's, Walton's Corner, The Blue Flame, and a dozen more—Florence's didn't have a band every night. Six days a week, Florence's was just another anonymous tavern in the heart of the city's black community. But every Sunday afternoon, beginning in the early 1960s and continuing for a decade, Florence's rocked to the music of Hound Dog Taylor and the HouseRockers. Blues musicians from all over the city and all over the world dropped by to jam and party with some of Chicago's staunchest (and hardest-drinking) blues fans. Just to get into Florence's, you had to circle around the pig ear sandwich truck parked in front, pass the sidewalk dice game, and slip through the clump of men outside the door drinking from brown paper bags. Once you got in, it was hard to see the band over the crowd. Florence's wasn't even big enough to have a bandstand. They just moved a few tables from the back of the club, the band rolled in their amps, the folks danced in the narrow aisle between the bar and the rickety booths.

In addition to Hound Dog Taylor, blues performers that Alligator recorded

during the 1970s included Big Walter Horton ("Trouble In Mind," 1972); the "Queen of the Blues," Koko Taylor ("I Got What It Takes," 1975); Son Seals ("Going Back Home," 1976); Jimmy Johnson ("Serves Me Right to Suffer," 1978) and Pinetop Perkins ("Blues After Hours," 1978).

## MARY HERRICK ON THE CHICAGO PUBLIC SCHOOLS

Over the years, several themes have worked their way through in the efforts of those fighting on behalf of Chicago public education. The basic one, which goes back to the common school movement in the 1840s, is the belief that public education itself can work. The second, expressed in the approach of Francis Parker, John Dewey, and superintendents William Harvey Wells and Ella Flag Young, is that the goal of education is not to make students more successful members of the workforce, but rather to assist each in developing his or her full human potential. Education, in other words, should not be seen as one thing for the children of the wealthy and upper classes but something else for those of other people. No one has expressed this combination of optimism and democracy better than Mary Herrick in her 1971 book, *The Chicago Public Schools: A Social and Political History.* The following is from the final pages of that book. The chapter is entitled, "It Can Be Done":

A few people through the years who insisted that the purpose of public education was to give every child the opportunity, full and equal for all, to develop his abilities and his special talents, whatever they might be, in order to become, to the extent these allowed, a self directed, creative human being, able not only to make a constructive contribution to society, but also to live his own life with satisfaction. This last goal has been frequently mentioned in respectful oratory on formal occasions, but it has never been seriously considered as a basis for the operation of a school system by any considerable number of legislators, mayors, city councilmen, or Board of Education members. Parents may say they want such a goal for their own children, but too few have been concerned with what happens to other people's children. Those among the teaching staffs who have sought to make the schools a path to such a goal have found little support in the past from those in power.

It is this confused conflict of narrow, limited purpose which has precipitated the Chicago Public Schools into successive financial crises. There never has been any sustained, conscious effort to find the funds to finance any one of the conflicting goals, except, perhaps, just to maintain the existence of a school. Other major enterprises in the city—and the nation—have not been forced to drift so helplessly.

When it was decided to turn the Chicago River backward in order to stop typhoid fever, engineers estimated the cost, and the money was found. When the cost was more than the original estimate, for whatever reasons, more money was found. When wars have been declared, or fought without a declaration, there has seemed to be no limit to the billions paid for them out of current taxation and debts passed on to future generations. When Congress determined that it was in the national interest to send men to the moon, billions were spent on experiments to find the most effective way to achieve this scientific feat, and more billions to carry out the operation. This huge expense was justified as advancing mankind's basic knowledge of the origin of earth and moon and the physical make-up of the universe and before the Russians did it.

No responsible agency has ever taken careful thought as to how present knowledge of the physical and social sciences could be employed to help children develop bodies, minds, and personal and social values with which to continue the search for truth for themselves and for the shrunken world of which our nation is a decreasingly important part. Nor has any estimate ever been set on how much such exploration might cost, to say nothing of estimates of putting such findings into effect. Is money spent for such ends, or the use of human knowledge for such purposes, of any less value to the human race than finding out the exact content of the moon's dust or strengthening one theory or another of how our lifeless globe came to be, eons ago—or beating the Russians in a game? The affluent United States could feed its hungry, educate its children well and send a man to Mars

if its people wanted these things; it is the only nation in the troubled history of the world which could. The affluent state of Illinois, third among the fifty in its personal wealth per capita, most certainly could contribute as large a share of that wealth to its schools as Mississippi and Arkansas contribute to theirs, from their lesser resources. The city of Chicago could at least provide a seat for every child in its public schools—never done since the first school opened—and could give all its children a real opportunity to learn at least the basic tool subjects of learning, which it has never given all of them and it is not giving all of them today.

## SAUL BELLOW

A one-man Chicago literary phenomenon, Saul Bellow has won three National Book Awards, the 1974 Pulitzer Prize, and, in 1976, the Nobel

Prize for literature. The way to deal with Chicago, he once said, is "to accept it for what it is." Many of his novels and short stories are set in this city and do exactly that. Bellow's understanding of the ever-changing city is demonstrated in this excerpt from his book *It All Adds Up:*

Chicago builds itself up, knocks itself down again, scrapes away the rubble, and starts over. European cities destroyed in the war were painstakingly restored. Chicago does not restore; it makes something wildly different. To count on stability here is madness. A Parisian can always see the Paris that was, as it has been for centuries. A Venetian, as long as Venice is not swallowed up in mud, has before him the things his ancestors saw. But a Chicagoan as he wanders about the city feels like a man who has lost many teeth. His tongue explores the gaps— let's see now: Here the 55th Streetcar turned into Harper Avenue at the end of the trolley line; then the conductor hurried through the car, reversing the cane seats. Then he reset the trolley on the power line. On this corner stood Kootich Castle, a bohemian rooming house and hangout for graduate students, photographers, would-be painters, philosophical radicals, and lab technicians (one young woman keeps white mice as pets.) Harper Avenue wasn't exactly the banks of the Seine; none of the buildings resembled Sainte-Chapelle. They were downright ugly, but they were familiar, they were ours, and the survival of what is ours gives life its continuity. It is not our destiny here to get comfort from old familiar places. We can't, we Chicagoans, settle back sentimentally among our souvenirs.

## THREE CHICAGO HISPANIC VOICES
### Ana Castillo

Ana Castillo climbed the mountain, the one that establishes a person as a writer. For her, it was far steeper than for most. While she was growing up in Chicago in the 1950s and 1960s, her father was a member of the Toltec street gang. She pushed herself into getting an education so she could escape having to work in a factory. As she did, she found herself in the ferment of the 1970s Latino Movement in the Midwest and its drive toward recognition and dignity. It was not, however, about women. In a 1994 introduction to her book *My Father Was a Toltec,* she wrote: "Addressing such issues, especially those related to sexuality, was seen as the territory of privileged white women and even interpreted as a betrayal by many Latino activists, both men and women."

But Castillo found her path and followed it. Since then she has written several novels, including *The Mixquiahuala Letters, Sapogonia,* and the well-received *So Far From God.* She has received an American Book Award, a Carl Sandburg Award, and a Mountains and Plains Booksellers Award for her fiction, along with a 1990 National Endowment for the Arts grant for her poetry.

The two following poems are from *My Father Was a Toltec and Selected Poems:*

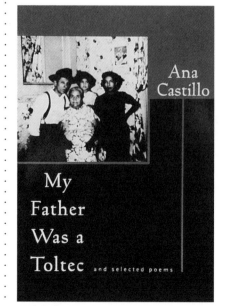

# The Toltec

c. 1955

My father was a Toltec.
Everyone knows he was bad.
Kicked the Irish-boys-from-Bridgeport's ass.
Once went down to South Chicago
to stick someone
got chased to the hood
running through the gangway
swish of blade in his back
the emblemed jacket split in half.

Next morning, Mami threw
it away.

# Women Are Not Roses

Women have no
beginning
only continual
flows.

Though rivers flow
women are not
rivers.

Women are not
roses
they are not oceans
or stars.

i would like to tell
her this but
i think she
already knows.

# 1970s

**David Hernandez**

David Hernandez is as different from any other performer at a poetry reading as an electric guitar is from an acoustic one. The energy he exudes is more than an increase in volume and intensity. Connected to a strong sincerity, his exuberance directs the rhythm, the flow, and even the message of his work. It seems to say, "I, my background, my experience, my outlook are worth your hearing about. So stay awake, pay attention, listen up, here I come at you."

Then, it is over. There is quiet. And upon reflection, listeners realize Hernandez has given them, as he was reciting, something to feel and to think about.

In *Street Sounds,* published in Chicago in 1972, Hernandez combined poetry with folk, jazz, and Latin musical elements. He was commissioned in 1987 to write a poem commemorating the city's 150th anniversary.

The following is from his 1991 book of poetry, *Rooftop Piper:*

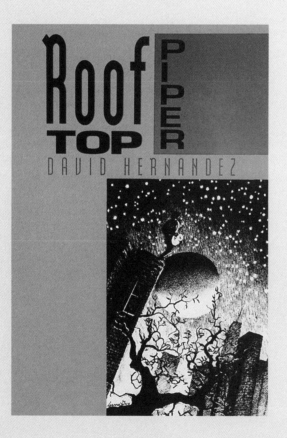

## the big picture

comes in a blade
of green with
the moon above
and the sun below
somewhere in China.

If I dig fast enough
right through the heart
of the earth, I can have
morning tea in Tibet
and return on time to watch the last lap
of the lake when night
fully blossoms silhouettes
and city dreams.

## the old women eating

Times like today
the only voice
she hears
     comes with
    the mashed potatoes
  and coffee
    at the restaurant.
75 winters already.

COYOTE SUN

CARLOS CUMPIÁN

## Carlos Cumpián

Carlos Cumpián, a Latino poet, writes his verses using the metaphors of the streets of Chicago, the city in which he lives, and the images of San Antonio and the Southwest where he was born and grew up. His poems have been published in two volumes, *Coyote Sun* and *Armadillo Charm,* as well as in a children's book, *Latino Rainbow.* His fervor and intensity are not limited to his words, but extend to the zeal with which he attempts to reach out and touch people through his poetry. His subjects are offbeat: Bophal, a bus ride in Chicago, El Cinco de Mayo, his landlord, and an armadillo.

His freshness comes in lines such as:

Smart armadillos amble jobless,
   happy not to work in a zoo,
they stroll
   plush river grass and smooth
red pebble paths,
   far from fast two-legged foreigners.

## MIKE ROYKO

Mike Royko, the late syndicated columnist for the *Chicago Sun-Times* and then the *Chicago Tribune,* started his column with the *Chicago Daily News* in 1963 and quickly became the city's main political and cultural curmudgeon, establishing an extraordinary record that ended at his death, April 29, 1997. His acerbic humor and often antiestablishment approach were not a mask, but rather the clothes worn by this extraordinary storyteller. To some, a few of his opinions in later years seemed outdated, but his talents were not diminished a bit. One of his major assets was that he was never afraid to offend. Royko's Chicago was the one newspaper readers around the country had available for more than three decades because his column was syndicated in papers around the country. He created an everyman character, Slats Grobnik, much longer on common sense than on education. A Slats column that appeared in the *Chicago Daily News* on May 8, 1972, follows:

### How Slats Lost His Marbles

Since the warm weather arrived, I haven't seen one kid playing marbles. It looks like the game is dead.

**Mike Royko painting by Arlene Marks**

But what killed it? The sociologists haven't explained so we can only guess.

Maybe it's because today's youths are so rich. They have seized the nation's economy and can buy what they want. A bag of marbles isn't an impressive possession. The only people poor enough to appreciate a bag of marbles are the parents, but they are too busy working for their children to have time for marbles.

Maybe it is because nobody plays marbles on TV. Most of the games youngsters play have been popularized on TV. Golf, bowling, and sex, for example.

Frankly, I don't feel any sense of loss at the decline of marbles. I played it a lot, but I wasn't very good. But, then, nobody in the neighborhood was in the same league as Slats Grobnik.

Many great athletes are born with special physical gifts that make them "naturals."

Wilt Chamberlain, with his height, was a born basketball player, and Teddy Williams, with his remarkable eyesight was a natural hitter.

With Slats, it was his thumb.

He was blessed with an extraordinarily long, double-jointed thumb. Nobody had a thumb as long as Slats'. Nobody had fingers as long as Slats' thumb.

And it was powerful. He was constantly exercising it, sitting for hours every night and just flicking it. His thumb muscle got bigger than his biceps. The girls at the North Avenue Beach laughed at his strange physique, but he didn't care. He'd pick up a rock and flick it out past the breakwaters.

When he'd kneel, dig his knuckles in the dirt, and unleash his shot, his thumb made a wooshing sound like that of a golf swing.

Then Slats also had the confidence of a natural athlete. When he heard the story of David and Goliath, Slats shrugged and said: I could of done the same thing with a marble.

He became so well known that his alderman heard about him and got excited. There used to be a big-city marble championship and the alderman figured that if someone from his ward won, he'd get his picture in the paper for something besides a malfeasance indictment.

The alderman went to Slats' house and promised his parents that if Slats won he would have a city job some day. Slats cried hysterically until his mother explained that he wouldn't really have to work.

After that Slats did nothing but practice and polish his supershooter.

He thought his shooter had mysterious powers of its own, because it had been given to him by his late Aunt Wanda, who was well known for her spiritual consultations and fortunes. Slats even called the shooter Aunt Wanda and believed he could not lose with it, or win without it.

On the morning of the tournament, Slats was calm. He ate a hearty breakfast of Twinkies and Pepsi.

Then it happened.

The shooter rolled off the kitchen table and fell to the floor, where his baby brother, Fats Grobnik, was crawling. Fats popped it into his mouth and swallowed it. He swallowed everything, which is why he is called Fats.

Slats was pale when he came out and announced:

Fats swallowed Aunt Wanda. I ain't playing.

The alderman showed up with a quart of mineral oil, but Mrs. Grobink wouldn't let him in her house.

After that, Slats never again

played marbles. And it was a long time before he lost his bitterness and stopped dropping shoehorns and roller skate keys near his brother.

## RICHARD NICKEL, PHOTOGRAPHER OF A CITY LOST TO THE WRECKING BALL

Richard Nickel, an architectural photographer, lies buried in Graceland Cemetery, not far from the graves of Chicago architects John Wellborn Root, Daniel Burnham, and Louis Sullivan. His tragic death bore the aura of martyrdom. He loved their buildings and fought with great urgency to save them from the wrecking ball that swung indiscriminately in Chicago in the 1960s and 1970s. As Louis Sullivan's Stock Exchange Building—one of the great urban structures of all time in Chicago—was being torn down, Nickel lost his life; the building collapsed on him as he photographed the process.

Many of his pictures have achieved the immortality the buildings themselves couldn't. One of these perhaps better than any other captured the drama of architecture. The photo, taken of the Stock Exchange facade, became

*Chaos, Creativity, and Culture*

familiar to the city as the cover of David's Lowe's excellent book, *Lost Chicago*. It came to be accepted as a memorial to Nickel himself and to all the buildings that the city had lost.

In the book *They All Fall Down: Richard Nickel's Struggle to Save America's Architecture*, Richard Cahan used the following words to sum up the man whose photographs are helping to preserve the dignity and memory of many of the great buildings Chicago has lost:

To Nickel, buildings were like people. Beautiful when young, they acquired character as they grew older. He could feel buildings. Each had a soul.

To him, genius had rubbed off onto the mortar, and stone, and steel of structures built by the lions of architecture. The destruction of their buildings was no less shocking than the ravaging of a museum masterpiece by a madman. It had to be stopped.

Chicago in the impatient 1950s and 1960s would not be concerned with coddling the past. This sturdy city with its eye on tomorrow was in the firm grip of Mayor Richard J. Daley, a Sphinx-faced, malapropism-popping political boss determined to live forever through great public works projects. Daley wanted to clear the terrain for Chicago as neatly as had the Great Chicago Fire in 1871. He wanted to rebuild. Miles of homes, thousands of buildings, even entire neighborhoods were cleared in the name of growth and increased tax dollars.

Nowhere was the city's rebuilding more apparent than downtown, in and around Chicago's 35-square-block Loop. Completion of the 41-story Prudential Building in 1955 marked the start of a downtown building boom, and with it came a wave of destruction unprecedented since the fire. The

buildings that were razed—the Pullman Building, Reaper Block, Columbus Memorial, Venetian, Austin, Hartford, and dozens more—had names and personalities. They were demolished without any protest to make way for corporate addresses and parking lots.

Nickel was one of the first to stand up against the demolition of skyscrapers. In the words of *Kansas City Star* architecture critic Donald Hoffmann, Nickel hit the barricades before anybody knew there was a war. Nickel hoisted the first picket sign in front of the Garrick Theater Building in 1960, prompting attorneys for the theater to drive their limousines up to the building and ask Nickel what the hell he was doing.

All I could say, Nickel later told a reporter, was that I didn't want the building wrecked. His feelings went deeper. His unsuccessful year-long fight to save Garrick gained national attention. Even Daley was forced to take notice. As scaffolding laced the Garrick Theater, marking its execution, a passerby with no architectural background walked up to the grimy structure and sighed: I don't want to see these old buildings torn down.

It was part of Nickel's quarrel with his time that he could not stop the destruction of fine architecture. He grew to learn that picketing and emotional pleas had little effect. "The forces are so great that there is really almost nothing you can do," he wrote. Economics, the bottom line, demand the death of these buildings when they stopped bringing a profit.

Sparked by a college assignment during the early 1950s, Nickel embarked on a lifelong search to find and document the work of

Louis Sullivan, the fountainhead of modern architecture.

"His passion about building impressed me at first," Nickel recounted years later. "He showed this total devotion to building. Then there were his ideas about functionalism and his devotion to nature, things that I had an affinity toward myself. Now, I wasn't very well read at that point, but I never had encountered a personality like that, one that was so involved with life."

Nickel hunted down dozens of little-known Sullivan buildings and drawings. As his search continued, Nickel went on a rescue mission.

At first he saved what he found on film, taking intense, quiet, resolute photographs. He was a super "crisp documentarian," using the proper lens and the proper camera to show structures just as he saw them. His work, never well known outside Chicago, was described by photographer Aaron Siskind as "simple and correct and quite beautiful." The photographs became landmarks themselves.

Nickel spoke of himself as "just a photographer who happens to take pictures of buildings." By trade, he was an architectural photographer, but he was no more limited by his subject than Edgar Degas had been bound by ballerinas. Nickel's original purpose was to create a comprehensive photographic record of Sullivan's work. He eventually found that he could use his camera to express himself and confront his audience. Depressed about the imperiled masterpieces he found in his rangefinder, Nickel took photos as a last resort against what he was witnessing.

By returning to wrecking sites, Nickel made a statement that went beyond his effort to document what Sullivan had created. Nickel insisted on being a witness, a recorder of vanishing beauty. More than anything, he wanted to portray death—death before its time.

## DAVID MAMET

In a 1982 *Chicago Tribune* article on the emerging playwright David Mamet, Richard Christiansen wrote:

[Mamet's] *American Buffalo* . . . opened in October 1975, and if you're looking for significant dates in the history of Chicago—

# 1970s

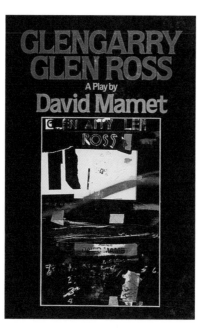

slangy *Stories of the Streets and Town,* Ring Lardner in his baseball classics, Gwendolyn Brooks in her poetry, and Studs Terkel in his many books of interviews.

Mamet's theatrical career began as a teenager doing backstage chores and a little acting at the Jane Addams Theater in Chicago's Lake View neighborhood. He spent his college summers working as a busboy at Second City and stopping every once and awhile to take notes. After having encountered mixed reviews for his first two plays, *Duck Variations* and *Sexual Perversity in Chicago,* the playwright—still in his early twenties—established his own theater group, calling it the St. Nicholas Company.

It was part of a wonderful era for the stage in Chicago. Small theaters including the Organic, North Light, Victory Gardens, Wisdom Bridge, and the extraordinary Steppenwolf along with dozens of overnight efforts throughout Chicago's suburbs gave the city yet another cultural garland to wear on its brow. They offered variety—the good try and the surprising success, the profound insight and the bizarre one, experimentation, stellar and amateurish acting, and above all—excitement.

Mamet, who made use of the creative impulses he felt in the city of his birth, quickly became recognized as the "young lion of Chicago theater." *American Buffalo* won the New York Drama Critics Circle Award for the best new play of the year. This award was followed by the Pulitzer Prize for his play *Glengarry Glen Ross.*

Films were next for Mamet as he became both a Hollywood writer and director. His first work was a remake of *The Postman Always Rings Twice,* followed by the mystery trial story *The Verdict* and his recreation of 1930s Chicago gangsterdom *The Untouchables.* Other efforts demonstrated his humor and his fascination with con artists as in *The House of Cards.*

and American—theater, there's one to remember.

What Mamet first described to Mosher as "a play with three characters set in a junk shop" became a work rich in echoes and resonance. Its brilliant, poetic use of brutal street language captured the futility and desperation of the lives it examined.

Continuing his commentary, Christiansen added that the play's theme was neither the three's bungling attempt at a get-rich scheme nor the European interpretation of the play as an attack on the capitalist system. Rather, according to Christiansen, the ultimate point: ". . . As Mamet was to make clear in all of his plays, was the failure to connect with and care for other human beings."

Mamet epitomizes Chicago's literary/theatrical tradition not only in dealing with such a theme, but also in being one of the writers who very carefully listens to how people say things as well as to what they are saying.

It was this good ear that informed Finley Peter Dunne in his Irish brogue tales of Mr. Dooley, George Ade in his

In addition to his film work, he continued to write books for both children and adults. In a book of his essays *Writing in Restaurants*, Mamet described his hometown, Chicago:

**"Windville"**

In our beloved Windville we curse the cold and revel in being the most senseless spot in North America to spend the winter in. But the air feels new, and all things still seem possible, as they did to Willa Cather and Sherwood Anderson and Willard Motley and Hemingway and Frank Norris and Saul Bellow and all the Chicago writers who—when speaking of home—finally write the same story. It was and is a story of possibility, because the idea in the air is that the West is beginning, and that life is capable of being both understood and enjoyed.

Those writers exhorted us, as did their philosophical confrere Alderman Hinky Dink Kenna—Bathhouse John's partner in crime:

"Whatever the endeavor, make of it a lollapalooza."

**"Wall of Respect," photographed by Robert Sengstacke**

## STREET MURALS: CHICAGO'S "WALLS WITH TONGUES"

A 1978 guide to Chicago murals, published by the Chicago Council on Fine Arts, located 226 of them. The guide referred to these pieces of public art as "wall flowers" and, even more appropriately, as "walls with tongues."

Its list included:

■ the pioneering "Wall of Respect" and short-lived "Wall of Truth" at 43rd Street and Langley Avenue, both initiated by African American artist William Walker;

■ the Hispanic "Wall of Brotherhood" by Mario Castillo at 18th and Halsted Streets;

■ "Good-bye Gallery" at 600 West Hubbard Street, commemorating endangered species;

■ the revolutionary ones inside and outside Casa Aztlan, 1831 South Racine Avenue;

■ "The Four Seasons," done with glass-and-stone fragment by Marc Chagall in the First National Bank Plaza in the Loop;

■ "La Crucifixion De Don Pedro Albizu Campos," painted by the Puerto Rican Art Association at Artesian and North Avenues;

■ a wide variety of other murals with such titles as "The Wall of Love," "Wall of Black Saints," "History of the Packinghouse Workers," "Black Women Emerging," "History of the American Red Cross," "The Wall of Games," and "Break the Grip of the Absentee Landlord."

The guide quotes a 1974 appraisal of such art in Chicago:

Among the waste lots and semi-demolished buildings of Boston and South Side Chicago, I came across a new kind of art. These . . . districts, where derelict car bodies rust quietly on the pavements and the roads are bumpy and unmade, have given birth to an original school of mural painting. . . . The subject matter of the paintings is rooted in urban ghetto life—drugs, aggression and segregation are the dominant themes. Many of the artists are unknown and some of the murals are collective works created by entire communities.

The murals I saw were ephemeral. When I returned a few weeks later to take a second look, many of them had disappeared, along with the walls on which they were painted. They had appeared mysteriously, like a flower on a bomb site. A particular combination of circumstances had produced them, and new circumstances wiped them away. They are part of the hectic American cycle of destruction and reconstruction. In Europe we are used to thinking of art as permanent, and to seeing it cloistered in art galleries and museums. Here among the rubble and the rust, it springs to life like a one-day lilly.

—Helene de Nicolay
"Wall Flowers" (*Realites,* No. 279; February 1974)

## THE CHICAGO IMAGISTS: THREE VIEWS

During the 1960s, 1970s, and early 1980s, a school of Chicago artists saw itself dramatically swept to international acclaim through reviews, galleries, showings, and public exhibitions. Their movement, recognized as radical and revolutionary in the world of art, was given the name "Chicago Imagism" by art critic Franz Schulze.

A major exhibit of Chicago Imagists found itself in the British Isles in 1980 and 1981, playing to the art critics of London, Tyne and Wear, Glasgow, Edinburgh, and Belfast. Represented in the showing that tarried in each city for up to two months were the works of fourteen of Chicago's artists.

The following comments about the Imagists and their movement are those of three art critics: Victor Musgrave, Russell Bowman, and Franz Schulze.

In introductory comments for a

1980 book, *Who Chicago?*, published to accompany the British exhibit, British critic and gallery director Victor Musgrave wrote:

Chicago, a tough, iconoclastic city on the edge of the Great Lakes, with a killing climate, has for long been gestating what amounts to an all-out assault on prevailing cultural norms. With New York and West Coast establishments setting their faces grimly against the strident interlopers, Europe was hardly likely to become aware of them, although certain European-style artists from Chicago, being "safe," have succeeded in getting some attention from critics in London. For a long time it was as if the Imagists did not exist for anyone outside their native city. It was an invisibility that applied to the British art institutions when they looked westward while galleries like the Tate succumbed—belatedly, as is their wont—to the powerful commercial exploitation behind such artists as Warhol, Lichtenstein and Stella.

In the same book, Russell Bowman, a noted writer on Chicago artists, contributed an essay on "Chicago Imagism: The Movement and the Style." The following is an excerpt from it:

During the last fifteen years a unique art has developed in Chicago. It is the product of a group of artists working in association with each other and sharing certain assumptions about the

**147**

# 1970s

making of art: it is a movement. This group of artists, despite varying individual modes, produces work with a certain common formal and expressive characteristic: it is a style. While this style—now largely called Chicago Imagism—undoubtedly belongs to certain tradition and owes something to artistic attitudes prevalent among earlier Chicago artists, it does not resemble anything that came before it, not in Chicago, not elsewhere. The interest of this art lies not only in the extraordinary vitality, originality and import of the works themselves, but also in the degree to which aspects of this style have gained currency as art moves into the 80s.

Franz Schulze, one of the most articulate and incisive cultural critics in the city's history, has made unique contributions with his books and articles both on architecture and art. The following is from his long-out-of-print and much-treasured *Fantastic Images: Chicago Art Since 1945*:

In the worlds of studios, galleries, and museums, contemporary Chicago art conjures an image every bit as distinctive as Chicago architecture, but one almost diametrically opposite in character and expressive motive. "Chicago-type" art is not only not rational, it is anti rational to the point of perversity. It does not at all cherish logic, or clarity, or the open, declamatory mode of artistic statement that characterizes Chicago building—or, for that matter, most post–World War II American painting. It tends rather toward highly personal, introverted and obsessive styles, and those who create it are usually more doggedly infatuated with symbol, image, dream and pungent anecdote than they are concerned

with the need to give these elements articulate form.

Not surprisingly, then, art in Chicago has become known, especially during the past decade, as predominantly surrealist. Here fantasy married funk, it is said, and produced a progeny of young painters and sculptors who like to show their work corporately, under group names and exhibition titles that recall rock combos and suggest a compulsion toward word play: The Hairy Who, The Non-Plussed Some, The Sunken City Rises, Marriage Chicago Style, Chicago Antigua. It is also understood that Chicago's collectors adore them, that the whole city's art world is fixated on a surrealist point.

Some of this is true, some of it partly true, some of it simply overstated. The sensibility common to Chicago-type art is surely broader than a craving for surrealism, and its origins can be traced back to well before the late 1960s, when the groups just mentioned came to light. Indeed the first generation to give clear evidence that some shared attitude was forming in Chicago was already working seriously in the late 1940s, and its bias was, if anything, expressionistic. The term Monster Roster, coined in the late 1950s to describe some of the members of that generation, distinctly implied a bold, heavy-handed expressionism. It is reasonable to say that permutations of expressionism and surrealism compose the manners of the several dozen artists who have given Chicago art an identity over the past twenty-five years, but even then considerable qualification is called for. For one thing, the two modes are seldom employed here without conscious reference or close resemblance to European or even American prototypes. Chicago surrealism does not emulate that of Paris or New York, and Chicago expressionism has little kinship with, say, German models. Moreover, among Chicago artists themselves there is a wide latitude of styles. Leon Golub's expressionism is somber and portentous most of the time, and there is nothing surreal about it. Yet on occasion, and without any relaxation of gravity, it will take on a serene, almost classical air. Cosmo Campoli is probably also an expressionist—or if he is not, then he is surely nothing else—but the consistent lyricism of his inventions is so much his own that it is impossible to hang any standard label on it. Some other Chicagoans Seymour Rosofsky and June Leaf come to mind—but each of them mixes that vehemence with his own degree of surrealist hysteria. George Cohen, Theodore Halkin, Evelyn Statsinger, Irving Petlin, Robert Barnes, Don Baum, Ellen Lanyon and H. C. Westermann are fantasts of very broad range; what unites them is the intensity and privacy of their feelings rather than the stylistic gesture of their work. The rattling, discursive narratives and cheerful vulgar mood of the later artists— Gladys Nilsson, James Nutt, Karl Wirsum, Ed Paschke—add diversity to the picture. And Steven Urry, another of the later group, doesn't work with readily recognizable images at all.

This very variety would seem to substantiate the contention of some observers, more vocal within Chicago than without, that there really is no such thing as "Chicago-type" art. Nothing, they say, has appeared in Chicago art in the last couple of decades which has not surfaced in one form or another in American art as a whole. Furthermore, a notable number of good artists identified with Chicago (such as Richard Hunt, Roland Ginzel and Harry Bouras) cannot be considered expressionist or surrealist except by stretching the term out of shape.

Yet these claims of no unity overcomplicate what the prevailing view of "Surrealist Chicago" oversimplifies. Chicago has long been a wholesale supplier of talent to New York City—and a rather richly productive one at that. It has almost, although never quite, become accustomed to watching its most gifted artists depart as soon as they are ready to "make it" on the more competitive and more lucrative Manhattan scene. (Of the artists so far named, all of whom matured in Chicago and did some of their best work here, eight—Barnes, Golub, Leaf, Nilsson, Nutt, Petlin, Westermann and Wirsum—now live elsewhere.) Younger artists who might have grown powerful enough to launch a clear-cut Chicago-related school or movement have never stayed here long enough, or in sufficient numbers, or with adequate promotional machinery, to do so. It is all the more remarkable, then, in a situation where continuity is constantly interrupted, that there has been so persistent a strain of image conscious art, heavily loaded with symbolic and associational overtones. The strain vanishes, reappears and alters its coloration over the decades, so that by 1970 Gladys Nilsson is painting pictures that are much more cooly tongue-in-cheek, fey and fastidious, than the shaggy, dead-serious icons which Cohen and Golub did about 1950, or the delicately hushed hallucinations of Barnes and Petlin in 1960.

But all five painters—and too many of their Chicago colleagues to ignore—enunciate a private,

# 1970s

TOTEMS
WITHOUT
TABOOS
THE EXQUISITE CORPSE
LIVES!

A Surrealist Group Exhibition
October 22 / November 23
HEARTLAND GALLERY
7000 North Glenwood, Chicago

idiosyncratic message. The bond, then, is more an attitude than a style, but it is recognizable over the years, and it does seem to follow from the artist's inverted experience of Chicago as surely as the Chicago architect's frank rationalism is the vitality he has as an artist cannot help but to admire, and even love; this, despite the fact that the vitality has little to do with his concerns, since it is composed more of commercial and physical than of cultural energies. In New York and Paris the artist is accepted as a professional member of the community. Paris has wrapped him in a mystique of his own, while in New York—albeit he is still subject to a lingering American suspicion of the fine arts—he is nevertheless an instrument by which the character of Manhattan Island is measured. On the other hand, one is ordinarily inclined to size up or get the feel of Chicago some other way: by looking at its politicians or its businessmen, its journalists, its novelists or its social critics, but surely not by studying its painters and sculptors.

Nevertheless, the city is big enough, technologically sophisticated enough, bumptious and unruly enough, to have produced a steady stream of lively, inquisitive, original, hungry and—particularly—tough minds. This together with its midwestern fastness, has produced in Chicago a vigorous and unique American urban personality and a hardy, ingrown art that has much of an "in-spite-of" quality about it. Thus the artist in Chicago works largely to remind or persuade himself that, after all, art is possible here, in fact to affirm that he as an artist, and above all as a person, is real. He is likely to care less—perhaps even to rationalize a distaste—for the

niceties of line, color and form or esthetic theory, because of these luxuries, and Chicago is no place to acquire them or talk about them. But he can explore his own dreams, fits, visions, and obsessions, because they are the only and the most important subjects available to him.

Chicago art is not native, but it is fiercely, resolutely hermetic, as so many visitors from New York and Europe have noticed so many times, and it interests itself only a little in concepts like the historic mainstream, or in the condition and locus of the garde, be it avant- or arriere-. But just as some biological species have evolved in geographical isolation and hostile climates, the art of the Chicago Imagists has grown since World War II into a body of work which has its own sense, and its own dimension, within the broader American whole.

There is a disagreement between Bowman and Schulze over the date the Chicago school began. The latter gave the date of 1945 and included many Chicago artists that Bowman would rather see as precursors to the Chicago Imagist movement.

## THE SURREALIST GROUP OF CHICAGO

Surrealists, with their strong penchant for freedom of expression and focus on content rather than the rules, tend to find Chicago a stimulating, supportive environment. One of the Loop's most prominent pieces of public sculpture, "Miro's Chicago," was created by surrealist Joan Miro. The Art Institute of Chicago, its other museums and many of its galleries have long found space for Max Ernst, Salvador Dali, Rene Magritte, as well as lesser-known surrealists.

Chicago has an even more intimate bond with surrealism, however, one underlined in 1976 with the World Surrealist Exhibition in the city. At it, 600 works by 150 surrealist artists from thirty-one countries were shown.

The program for the exhibition stated:

> We must emphasize that nothing has been further from our intention than the mere act of hanging new works on old walls, to provide some ridiculous "esthetic" diversion. The very character of an "exhibition" has always been and remains suspect in our eyes, carrying with it limitations and risks. Rejecting in advance any and all opportunist distractions of an "exhibitionist" tendency, the World Surrealist Exhibition is designed as an act of war against all forces of miserabilism.

The Surrealist Group of Chicago was instrumental to a large extent in revitalizing the surrealist art and literary movement that had flourished strongly in Europe between World War I and World War II. It played a key role in pulling together the exhibition. Formed in the 1960s, its members were referred to at the time as "the left wing of the Beat Generation."

Two of them, Franklin and Penelope Rosemont, became full-fledged members of the surrealist movement in Paris in 1965 at the invitation of Andre Breton, who introduced them into that group's activities for several months. Franklin has written poetry and treatises on surrealism, and Penelope has been an innovative artist and poet working in "landscapades, alchemograms and prehensilouhettes [sic]."

In early 1998, the Chicago Surrealist Group published through Black Swan Press a volume entitled *The Forecast Is Hot.* In typical surrealist fashion, it explains existentially what it is, adding to the title that it is a "compilation of leaflets, diatribes, celebrations, tracts, exhortations, denunciations, clarifications, announcements, prefaces, polemics," and others.

Contributions by other group members have included, according to Mark Rosenzweig writing in the Fall 1993 issue of *Progressive Librarian,* a reinterpretation of the blues by Paul Garon, Joseph Jablonski's exploration of millennial and utopian currents, Philip Lamantia's critique of the so-called "New American Poetics" and Nancy Joyce Peters's discussions of "Women and Surrealism."

The same publication gives a two hundred-item bibliography of the Chicago-based Black Swan Press and the Surrealist Group of Chicago.

*Chaos, Creativity, and Culture*

1980s

CHICAGO

CONTEMPORARY AMERICAN FICTION

He was a ghost of a man, haunted by the ghosts of Vietnam.

WINNER OF THE NATIONAL BOOK AWARD

PACO'S STORY

THIS IS STRONG, HEART-WRENCHING STUFF BY ONE OF AMERICA'S MOST IMPORTANT LIVING AUTHORS.
ROBERT MASON, AUTHOR OF CHICKENHAWK

LARRY HEINEMANN

HAIR TRIGGER 14
A STORY WORKSHOP ANTHOLOGY
Columbia College Chicago

FIRST PLACE

# 1980s: Experiences for a Nation

**B**y the early 1980s, the Near North Side alone had expanded to include sixty art galleries as the city's interest in art, especially contemporary, American, and Native American, exploded.

The most exciting example of the very vibrant Chicago theater scene was David Mamet. In 1984, he won both the Pulitzer Prize and New York Drama Critics Circle Award for his *Glengarry Glen Ross*. He was soon using his talents writing scripts for movies as well as directing them.

The poetic scene, supported and encouraged by the city's poetic maven, Gwendolyn Brooks, grew to encompass readings, slams, books, contests, and even a phone number that allowed callers to hear the works of local poets. In addition to *Poetry* magazine, the Chicago area was publishing more than a dozen other magazines that accepted poetry. These included *Aim Magazine, Alternative Fiction and Poetry, Poetry East, Night Roses, Rambunctious Press,* and *TriQuarterly*.

In 1985, Columbia College's undergraduate literary magazine, *Hair Trigger,* was awarded the first-place prize in the United States for the second time, and in 1988 a Columbia graduate, Larry Heinemann, won the National Book Award for *Paco's Story*.

Northwestern University's *TriQuarterly* magazine published a special 1984 issue on Chicago featuring such nationally read Chicago writers as Richard Stern, Norbert Blei, Leon Forrest, Angela Jackson, David Hernandez, Paul Carroll, John Dickinson, Tony Ardizzone, James McManus, Dave Etter, Maxine Chernoff, Cyrus Colter, Stuart Dybek, Harry Mark Petrakis, Larry Heinemann, and Gwendolyn Brooks.

Other excellent writers of the decade included Jack Fuller, author of *Convergence*

**Harold Washington**

## 1980s

### HAROLD WASHINGTON

Harold Washington was Chicago's first black mayor. Elected in 1983, he immediately started delivering services and bringing outside resources to neighborhoods long abandoned by past administrations. With that, the healing had begun. In a 1987 speech on the 150th anniversary of the incorporation of the city of Chicago, he articulated his vision and dreams for the city.

The following is an excerpt from that speech:

Across the country and around the world, we've made it clear: there's a new Spirit of Chicago, building on the old. Chicago is not simply the City that Works. The word is out—Chicago Works Together.

We fought for this economic and social and spiritual renewal at a critical time, and we won that struggle just in time because Chicago in 1987, like every other major American municipality, is facing unprecedented challenges to its survival as a world city.

Everywhere we look across our land, we see the American city in peril—endangered by economic challenge from abroad, threatened by a failure of the will from within.

\*\*\*

Now, more than ever, Chicago is challenged to take the lead. Just as we are finally able to leave local petty political bickering behind us, the new Spirit of Chicago is aroused to greater trials, perhaps the most important challenges our generation will face.

\*\*\*

Now, once again, our way of life is in trouble—and it is in our cities where we know that firsthand. America is bleeding, in our streets and alleys, in our stairwells and in the corridors of our schools.

and *Mass*; Edith Freund, whose *Chicago Girls* contained the spirit of the city in the 1890s; Joseph Epstein, essayist and editor of *The American Scholar*; Bob Greene, syndicated columnist and author of a whole shelf full of books; Bill Granger, one of the top spy story writers in the country; and June Brindel, who was writing novels about ancient Crete.

On the music scene, the Chicago Symphony Orchestra under Sir Georg Solti was proclaimed by many critics to be the best orchestra in the world. Under the maestro, it had eleven invigorating international tours and won an even greater number of Grammy Awards.

*Chaos, Creativity, and Culture*

America's cities are on the critical list, and we must not be timid or halfway in our response.

We have found that we must act to save ourselves, not just in Chicago, but all across that entire commonwealth of cities that has created an urban America.

We have mobilized, through the United States Conference of Mayors, the League of Cities, and other coalitions, to take care of our people. We have acted urgently, because the need is great.

Today, almost one-fourth of our children are living in poverty, two-fifths of Hispanic children, over one half of black children, little ones younger than seven years old, wake up each morning suffering the physical abuse of hunger. These are the highest rates we've ever seen, ever in the history of this country. Their hunger is unacceptable.

Nationally, one-fourth of our graduating classes are not graduating, an incurable waste for our society. In Chicago, almost half of our boys and girls never finish school, a tragic human loss for them and their families, and an economic injury for our city and our nation. That dropout rate is unacceptable.

Mothers and babies, children and youth, the elderly, all those whose shelter depends on federal assistance, are threatened by the prospect that they may join the ranks of the homeless, as 70,000 units of public housing are abandoned each year; it is reported that 900,000 federally subsidized but privately owned apartments could vanish in the next decade. That destruction of our homes is unacceptable.

The economic inequality worsens: while the overall poverty rate in America is at 11 percent, it is 32 percent for blacks, and 25 percent for Hispanic people. The inequality, that "We the people" versus "They the people," is unacceptable.

We do not accept the abandonment of the people of America's cities. We will not allow our citizens to be written off as bad debts.

## THREE CHICAGO WOMEN WRITERS
### Bette Howland

Race is a recurring theme in the literature of Chicago. The great writers don't give us answers, but rather help in thinking about it, in broadening our experience of this extraordinary enigma of our time and place.

In the following passage from her 1978 novel *Blue in Chicago*, Bette Howland uses her first-person character to talk about the impact of Richard Wright's *Native Son* on a woman heading north through the predominantly African American South Side of the city. She is on her way to the Loop from the University of Chicago enclave and neighborhood, Hyde Park:

I glanced up the aisle. The thing I'd forgotten is how the bus kept turning. Up Fifty-first Street to Drexel; down Drexel to Forty-seventh; up Forty-seventh to Martin Luther King Drive; down King to Forty-third—every few blocks it nosed onward, plunging deeper and deeper into the black ghetto. The coins clicked and rolled in the fare box.

The South Side has always been Chicago's black belt; these slums were here years before I was born. But in the past when I used to travel back and forth this way almost every day, I never noticed if I was white and all the other passengers were black. Blacks had not yet pressed the issue. And it must be said right off that the fact that I didn't notice, that it didn't matter to me, did not improve the situation in any way.

I remember becoming fully aware of this discrepancy reading *Native Son*, when the rich girl and her

Communist boyfriend think that their liberal sentiments will make up to Bigger for everything. The trouble is that these one-to-one solutions—I love you, you love me; you shoot me, I shoot you—are no good. Just no use. Still, this ignorance or innocence or whatever you want to call it was long gone—and I would have given a great deal to have it back again. Today I was very much aware of the color of everyone else's skin, and I was sure that everyone on the bus was just as much aware of mine.

This was manifestly not so. No one was paying attention to me, any more than I was paying attention to the pages of the book lying open on my lap. As a matter of fact, almost everyone else seemed to be reading—the news sheets crackling, the murder black in the headlines.

The bus was getting crowded; passengers swayed in the aisle and grabbed for the strap hangers. A girl was groping her way, arm over arm, along the rails, an unlighted cigarette in her fingers. Hot pants, vinyl stretch boots, turban. Her face flat expressionless, artificially pale—an Oriental effect. She leaned her shaved eyebrows over my seat.

"Gotta match?"

I gave her matches.

This has got to stop. I've got to stop reacting to people according to color. This is what has been happening to me; happening to everyone I know. White and Black. Race is a prominent fact of life in Chicago, a partitioned city, walled and wired. You can't help reacting in this way. Try it. Try it walking down the street some night. It's a reflex. Everyone is becoming conditioned. And for some reason I realized this all of a sudden listening to the news this morning, realized that I've been allowing myself

to become conditioned—letting this fear, this racism, run away with me. I'm not sure why a murder in the streets—even around the corner—should have had such a bracing effect. But you've got to come up for air sometime; maybe that's why I got on the bus today. I used to know these things.

### Maxine Chernoff

Maxine Chernoff has admitted what few writers ever acknowledge: that they need a place, a familiar one, in a special way. They need it to write about. In a panel discussion reprinted for the special Spring/Summer 1984 "Chicago" issue of *TriQuarterly,* she commented: "I think that there is a wealth of material for me that was sitting here for some thirty years, that I didn't really pay much attention to because I was interested in pretending I wasn't from anywhere."

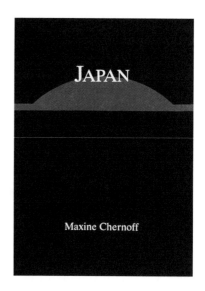

The following is a letter that is part of Maxine Chernoff's short story "Bop," reprinted in the same issue of *TriQuarterly.* Its narrator is an immigrant (here, three years) from Russia:

Dear Readers of Chicago:

It strikes me as new American that much is made of largeness in your country. Examine if you please Mount Rushmore. Here are the great stone faces of the profound leaders of men. But here is a man also. He is cleaning the stone faces. Up the nostril of Abraham Lincoln, freer of slaves, the cleaner of limbs, as a fly, without notice. Or, let us say, a family on vacation takes his photo. There is the great stone Lincoln. There is the tiny man with huge brush for nostril cleaning. Thus is humor because the size of man is made small by large design of beauty.

In America I hear many jokes. Some are about women whose husbands cannot meet their desires, which are too large. In others, several members of Polish nation are trying to accomplish small goal, the removing of a lightbulb. Their effort is too large for smallness of task.

On a certain Sunday I was driving with American acquaintance down the Madison Street. My American said, "You'll never believe what we waste our money on here," and it is true that in Soviet Union largeness is always minor premise of grandeur. There are large monuments to workers, huge squares to fill with people cheering for politics, heads of Lenin the size of cathedrals and many women with large breasts, who are called stately by the Russian men. Now on American Sunday I look to right and there stands a huge bat of metal. It stands, perhaps fifty feet tall like apartment building. I say to my friend, "The baseball is grand American entertainment. The baseball is your Lenin."

"No," says American friend. "The bat is a joke about wasting money. It has nothing to do with baseball."

The bat is then humorous. I believe words of my friend who is businessman. In poor or undemoc-ratic countries there is no humorous public art. History is the only public art. The huge stone pyramids are not meant as joke. In America the bat of abundance is cynic's joke. Same cynic points at huge genitals of corpse. He makes public monument to frozen bat. The lover of art points to the living genitals or makes the beautiful statue like Michelangelo's *David.*

As the huge Gulliver was tied down by the little citizens for possible harm done, so the public shows the disdain for size, even with its power. Thus is opposite, humor from largeness. The bully is, yes, strong, but he is also a fool. He is laborer digging in dirt. His brain is mushroom producing no truths. Largeness is victory and also defeat. To largeness we prostrate ourselves and then up our sleeves die laughing.

Thank you,
Oleg Lum

### Sara Paretsky

Sara Paretsky arrived in Chicago in the 1960s as a Vista volunteer, part of a Great Society-inspired program to make a contribution to the city. She worked in a neighborhood on the Southwest Side. Eventually, she found

another niche: writing mystery novels around the fictional character V. I. Warshawski, a name that sounds more like an auto parts dealer in the city than the ace woman detective she is.

The following is from *Burn Marks,* one of the author's many best-selling books:

The kinds of places Elena could afford didn't seem to advertise in the papers. The only residential hotels listed in the classifieds were in Lincoln Park and started at a hundred a week. Elena had paid seventy-five a month for her little room at the Indiana Arms.

I spent four hours futilely pounding the pavements. I combed the Near South Side, covering Cermak Road between Indiana and Halsted. A century ago it housed the Fields, the Sears, and the Armours. When they moved to the North Shore the area collapsed rapidly. Today it consists of vacant lots, auto dealers, public housing, and the occasional SRO. A few years ago someone decided to restore a blockful of the original mansions. They stand like a macabre ghost town, empty opulent shells in the midst of the decay that permeates the neighborhood.

The stilts of the Dan Ryan L running overhead made me feel tiny and useless as I went door to door, asking drunk or indifferent supers about a room for my aunt. I vaguely remembered reading about all the SROs that came down when Presidential Towers went up, but somehow the impact this had on the street hadn't hit me before. There just wasn't housing available for people with Elena's limited means. The hotels I did find were all full—and victims of last night's fire, savvier than me, had been there at dawn renting the few rooms available. I realized that

the fourth time a blowsy manager said, "Sorry, if you'd gotten here first thing this morning when we had something . . . "

At three I called off the search. Panicked at the prospect of housing Elena for some indefinite future, I drove into my Loop office to call my uncle Peter. It was a decision I could make only while panicked.

Peter was the first member of my family to make something substantial of his life. Maybe the only member besides my cousin Boom-Boom. Nine years younger than Elena, Peter had gone to work in the stockyards when he returned from Korea. He quickly realized that the people getting rich weren't the Poles hitting cows over the head with hammers. Scraping together a few bucks from friends and relations, he started his own sausage manufacturing firm. The rest was the classic story of the American dream.

He followed the yards to Kansas City when they moved there in the early seventies. Now he lived in a huge house in the tony Mission Hills district, sent his wife to Paris to buy her spring clothes, shipped my cousin off to expensive private schools and summer camps, and drove late model Nissans. Only in America. Peter also distanced himself as much as possible from the low-budget end of the family.

My office in the Pulteney Building was definitely down market. Most of the Loop expansion in recent years has been to the west. The Pulteney is at the southeast fringe where peep shows and pawn shops push the rents down. The Wabash L rattles the fourth floor windows, disturbing the pigeons and dirt that normally roost there. My furnishings are spartan gleanings from police auctions and resale shops. I used to hang an engraved sketch of the Uffizi over the filing cabinet, but last year I decided its intricate black detail looked too drab with the olive furniture. In its place I'd put up some splashy posters of paintings by Nell Blain and Georgia O'Keeffe. They gave the room a little color, but no one would mistake it for the hub of an international business.

Peter had been there once, when he brought his three children to Chicago for a tour several years ago. I had watched him swell visibly as he calculated the gap between our net present values.

## THREE EXTRAORDINARY NATURE WRITERS

### Allan W. Eckert

Allan W. Eckert, one of the most highly acclaimed nature writers in American history, scripted for fifteen years the very successful television series *Wild Kingdom*. Among his nature books have been the *Great Auk, The*

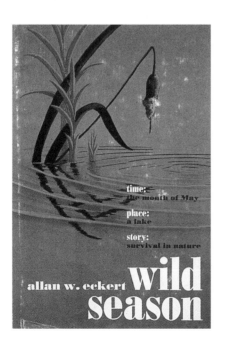

*Owls of North America,* and *The Silent Sky.* Other works that have helped him win seven Pulitzer Prize nominations have focused on the years in the Midwest when the Indians and pioneers competed for the land. After living for some years in the Chicago area, he moved to the Everglades and then to Ohio, but Eckert, a native of Chicago, is a writer whose works make the city proud.

The following excerpt is from a fine volume of his writing, *Wild Season.* It is about wildlife in a glacial lake on the border of Wisconsin and Illinois. The prologue tells of the factors that formed the lake:

Prologue

Newly wakened from its eons-long slumber, the glacier had become a hungry monster ponderously grinding its way across a defenseless land. Its frosted teeth sank deeply into the earth in a hundred, a thousand, a hundred thousand individual bites. Its appetite was immense and in its gullet the ingested forests and fields, hills and dunes were masticated by great ground granite boulders.

One day this irresistible mass of ice would come to be known as the Labradorean Sheet, but for now it was merely a great glacier which gnawed its way southward out of its bleak northern lair, eating the land and drinking rivers of the land, and its appetite was immense.

But even such an appetite as this had its limitations and when—in the area that would eventually come to be known as Wisconsin and Illinois—the glacier overestimated its own capacity, it ground to a halt, seemed to ponder its limitation for an era, as it perspired mightily under a warming sun, and then retreated toward the far north to resume hibernation.

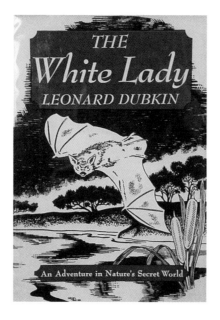

THE
*White Lady*
LEONARD DUBKIN

An Adventure in Nature's Secret World

### Leonard Dubkin

Leonard Dubkin, a Chicago journalist, found the mysteries of nature more interesting to cover than murder, mayhem, or the latest political press conference. He quit reporting and wrote with grace, originality, and gentle humor about the animals with whom he shared space in the city. His nature columns about such prosaic city inhabitants as pigeons, bats, starlings, grackles, squirrels, and robins touched something special in the heart of readers. His books included the award-winning *The White Lady* about a bat, *Murmur of Wings,* and *My Secret Places: One Man's Love Affair with Nature in the City.*

The following excerpt is from *The White Lady:*

Did it count for nothing that for a whole summer I had lived with a thing of beauty; did not that have some bearing on the summation I was making? I had watched the white lady being born, I had seen her grow and develop, observed her first flight, and even had a small part in the molding of her character, in the formation of some of her habits. It was as though I had spent the summer observing the production of a

work of art, as though I alone of all the people on the earth had watched it grow from an insignificant beginning to an object of loveliness. So even if I had learned no new facts about bats, nor evolved any theories concerning them, my intimacy with the white lady had more than justified the time I had spent in the grotto.

### Scott Holingue

In his 1994 book *Tales from an Urban Wilderness,* artist and nature sensitive Scott Holingue presented stories of his almost fifty years of involvement with wildlife in Lincoln Park on Chicago's lakefront. There, he has searched and continues to search for ailing, mistreated, or wounded animals, intervening on their behalf. Retired newspaper reporter Bob Cromie has said of Holingue's book: "The result is a fascinating below-the-surface look at another world, one whose suffering and problems, tragedy and humor, usually are unseen by the thoughtless or uncaring."

Following is an excerpt from Holingue's book:

Incredible though it might be, I have witnessed every kind of pet from a guinea pig to an alligator being dumped in Lincoln Park. The list is long and it includes

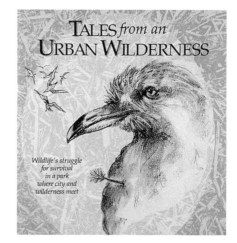

TALES *from an*
URBAN WILDERNESS

Wildlife's struggle
for survival
in a park
where city and
wilderness meet

ferrets, ducks, rabbits, ring-neck doves, and turtles as well as innumerable dogs and cats. Actually "pet" is the wrong word. It is a misnomer. There is no such thing as a wild creature that is or can be made into a household animal or vice versa.

## CARLOS A. CORTEZ

Mexico had its Diego Rivera, and Chicago has Carlos Cortez—painter, poet, and propagandist. Cortez's life has been that of the son of a father who was a Mexican-Indian (and a member of the Industrial Workers of the World) and a mother who was German-American and a socialist.

"My parents," he likes to say, "did not go to the same radical church."

Somehow, their son, through his art, expresses both of their heritages and their commitments to American radicalism. He has spent his life doing construction work and preaching ideas about labor being more important than capital, and workers more significant than bosses. Holding to his own radical ideas about the struggle of workers for justice, he spent World War II in jail for refusing to sign up for the draft.

In the 1950s, he was illustrating stories for the *Industrial Worker,* but making electro-engraved plates grew too expensive and he started using linoleum to do it. Linocuts brought out the best in him: his focus on the hard life of ordinary people, his penchant for propaganda, his almost primitive art style, and, above all, his passionate soul.

Both his subject matter and style called for him to produce posters, and he did. To them, he added soul-baring slogans such as one for a nursing woman that says, "Soy creadora, no soy creada." or "I am a creator, not a servant." Another one he did for a woman from Guatemala, whose husband had "disappeared." He depicted the military taking her husband from their home and titled the work, "Before the Disappearance."

He also created posters of such radical stalwarts as IWW martyr Joe Hill, Haymarket widow Lucy Parsons, and Mother Jones, turn-of-the-century organizer of mine workers. His style is uniquely his own, but shows clearly his Chicano heritage.

He refuses to number copies of prints or make limited editions of them. He has left instructions so that after his death the price will not go up because they have become scarce and working people would not be able to buy them.

One critic has commented that Cortez's "eccentrically patterned shadows suggest an obscure point of contact to the Chicago Imagists." One can find many different ingredients in his works. The works of few painters could ever better be described with the metaphor of a fine, rich, and very hearty stew than those of Carlos Cortez.

Created from a piece of floor tile, Cortez's linoblock *Field Workers* portrays *campesinos,* or farm workers, toiling among the endless rows of vegetables. It was originally an illustration for the

**Larry Heinemann**

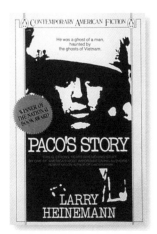

## PACO'S STORY, BY LARRY HEINEMANN

*Paco's Story,* by lifelong Chicagoan Larry Heinemann, is a dramatic and relevant tale about Vietnam, but it is more than that, just as Remarque's *All Quiet on the Western Front* was more than just a relevant tale of World War I. It presents us with Paco Sullivan, returning from the brutality of Vietnam with metal in his smashed legs and antidepressants and painkillers in his blood. The story is told by the ghosts of his Alpha Company in language that is jarring, somewhere between prose and poetry. The experiences related are powerful, violent, and full of emotion. This is not a book for everyone, but the reasons it was chosen for the National Book Award are easily found in its pages as it breaks the boundaries that confine most other novels.

The following excerpt is from chapter five of *Paco's Story:*

And Paco finishes up the last of the deep baking pans—tomorrow's special will be turkey loaf with stewed tomatoes—remembering how Gallagher had short thick arms and how the red-and-black tattoo of that dragon twisted and twined up and down his forearm; how when Gallagher showed it he always made a big fist and would roll his wrist. Later that night, when Paco leans back into his pillows, luxuriating in the stupefying doses of Librium and Valium, he recalls the fascination all of us had with Gallagher's red-and-black, blue-and-green tattoo.

It may come as some surprise, James, but Paco for all his trouble, has never asked, Why me?—the dumbest, dipstick question only the most ignorant fucking new guy would even bother to ask.

Why you? Don't you know? It's your turn, Jack!

Not in all the hours that he lay terrifically wounded—the rest of us gone, Paco as good as left for dead—did he ask. Not on that

publication the *Industrial Worker,* the mouthpiece of the Industrial Workers of the World. Because the small radical newspaper could not afford to have illustrations photo-engraved, they were for many years printed on a flatbed press for which Cortez made linoblocks.

The linoblock *Chicago Sings* was commissioned by one of Cortez's friends who was contemplating making a record label. Using the theme "Chicago Sings in Many Voices," Cortez placed in the center Big Red, the reggae singer, surrounded by diverse faces of people of Asian, Indian, and other descents. He also included his self-portrait as well as the face of his friend's wife on the left.

dust-off chopper with the medics delicately and expertly plucking debris from his wounds, Paco bursting with gratitude, whimpering and shivering from the cold. And not on any of these nights lately, after work, when Paco would sit up in bed, sore and exhausted, gazing down at himself—bitterly confronted with the mosaic of scars—waiting for his nightly doses of Librium and Valium to overwhelm him (like a showering torrent of sparks, some nights, or an avalanche of fluffy, suffocating feathers).

No, James, Paco has never asked, why me? It is we—the ghosts, the dead—who ask, Why him?

So Paco is made to dream and remember, and we make it happen in this way, particularly on those nights when his work—washing the last of the dishes, cleaning up and stowing down after closing—goes particularly well with no one to pester him, and he settles into a work rhythm, a trance almost ("I wash and God dries," he'll tell you, James). Even the burgeoning pain in his legs and back—that permanent aggravating condition of his life—blossoms and swells, warming him like a good steady fire of bottom coals. It is at those moments that he is least wary, most receptive and dreamy. So we bestir and descend. We hover around him like an aura, and declare (some of the townsmen have bragged and sworn they have seen us). Paco would finish his work virtually in the dark; Ernest, the boss, long gone to deposit the day's receipts; Paco turning around in his astonished pleasure at discovering the work so agreeable—entranced by the surprising ease of it—reaching around, dipping his hand into the last of the greasy bus pans for the next thing to soak and scrub and rinse clean. But everything is done, and dry; and his work is ended.

The following is part of a *Chicago Tribune Sunday Magazine* article on Heinemann by Jeff Lyon:

Larry Heinemann came home from Vietnam with a story to tell, and it earned him a National Book Award.

Then came the Big-Bang, the moment last fall when Chicago writer Larry Heinemann was reborn as a fiery celestial object in the literary firmament. In one awesome instant Heinemann, former Army reconnaissance sergeant, Convenient Food Mart counterman, bus driver, cabbie, and creative writing instructor who two years ago threw job and security out the window to devote himself full time to the onanism of novel-writing, came from left field to win what is arguably the most coveted American prize, the National Book Award.

It was on a Monday night in early November that Heinemann left the pack of struggling no-names behind. The bramins of the New York publishing world had gathered expectantly in the gold-leaf splendor of the grand ballroom of Manhattan's Pierre Hotel. Sipped champagne and showered admiring glances on the odds-on favorite to win the award, Toni Morrison, author of the highly acclaimed novel, *Beloved.* Morrison, with several best-selling books to her credit, including the much honored *Song of Solomon,* is black, popular and very commercial, the right political ingredients in the industry's eyes for anointment as the country's top writer of fiction. But if Morrison was to be denied, then almost certainly the prize would have gone to Philip Roth, the celebrated author of *The Counterlife,* who, having won a long ago (1960) National Book Award for his first significant work, *Goodbye, Columbus,* was something of a sentimental favorite. The black-tie crowd had to make do, however, with Roth's aura that evening, rather than his presence, for he was in Poland to attend a theatrical event of no little irony in that country of ancient anti-Semitism and modern Communist squeamishness: a stage adaptation of *Portnoy's Complaint.*

Lost in the chic literary parlando swirling about him was Heinemann, author of the 1986 portrait of a hollowed-out Vietnam veteran, *Paco's Story,* for which he had been nominated, and the 1976 Vietnam war novel *Close Quarters.* Paco's Story had received critical plaudits, to be sure—*Los Angeles Times* critic Richard Eder called it "deeply original and affecting" but it was hardly on the tip of everybody's tongue. Truly, the *New York Times Book Review* hadn't even bothered to review the novel until the day before the awards ceremony—though it had been published 11 months before. Seated next to his wife, Edie, Heinemann rustled loosely in his rented tuxedo—"For a person in my financial circumstances, it was a very odd way to blow $55," he says, "but I figure it's one night of my life, let's make it memorable."

# 1980s

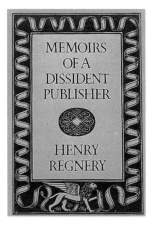

He would slip off his apron, soaking wet and sour with sweat, and hang it on a nail, straighten his T-shirt, take up his black hickory cane, and take that droning, warm feeling for the work out the back door and across the street to the Geronimo Hotel, up to his dingy little room overlooking the brick railroad alley at the back of Earl and Myrna's Bar downstairs.

## CHICAGO BOOK PUBLISHERS

Chicago book publishers, despite operating in a field increasingly dominated by major firms located on the East Coast, have nevertheless made some distinct contributions to the American literary scene.

In the late 1890s and early 1900s, Stone and Kimball and the successor publishing firm of H. S. Stone and Company issued 309 titles including first editions of works by George Bernard Shaw and Robert Louis Stevenson as well as a plethora of Midwestern authors. Among the latter were George Ade, Hamlin Garland, George Barr McCutcheon, and temporary and tempestuous Chicagoan, Mary MacLane. The book designs and covers included the work of artists such as Aubrey Beardsley, art and book design that is still collected 100 years later.

Chicago publisher George M. Hill at the same time issued the extraordinary book *The Wonderful Wizard of Oz.* Two junior partners in the firm Frank Reilly and Charles Britton took a special interest in the project and became friends of Baum. They retained enough of his high standards in publishing subsequent Oz books to market them successfully to the children of this country.

In the 1920s, Chicago publisher Pascal Covici, before moving to New York, left a heritage of having published books by local writers, including Ben Hecht, Maxwell Bodenheim, and Vincent Starrett.

The city has been enriched by many small, artistic publishers. The results have ranged from the books published by artist Ralph Fletcher Seymour and such well-known private ones as the Blue Sky and Black Cat presses to the current, larger, highly respected Academy Chicago and the special niche Evanston Publishing.

The long list of solid Chicago publishers has included the turn-of-the-century McClurg as well as the current *Tribune*-owned Contemporary Books, Bonus Books, Chicago Review Press, and December Press.

The city has university presses that include Illinois, Loyola, Northwestern, and Chicago. The last is the largest university press in the United States and even published the best-selling novel *A River Runs Through It,* by Norman Maclean. Loyola publishes books dealing with Chicago using the Wild Onion imprint.

Third World Press was founded in the city in 1967 by Haki Madhubuti with a few dollars, plenty of hope, and a clear vision. Its publications have ranged from the writings of Gwendolyn Brooks to those of the legal scholar Derrick Bell. Chicago's other minority presses include Abrazo Press and other newly developing publishers of Hispanic writers in the city.

The oldest and one of the most distinct of Chicago publishers is the Charles H. Kerr Company, a socialist publishing house that has been around the longest in the United States. In 1986, on its 100th anniversary, Crain's *Chicago Business* profiled it, saying: "A few people at Kerr do a lot of very hard, very fine work, which meets a real need for radical, socialist and labor history."

December Press, which was founded at the University of Iowa as a literary underground publisher, has been operating in Chicago since the mid 1950s, and published a magazine and short books of fiction by emerging writers from Raymond Carver to Norbert Blei.

Few, if any, publishers have contributed more to Chicago writing and

*Chaos, Creativity, and Culture*

literature than the late Henry Regnery. Known across the country and around the world for publishing philosophically conservative books by William Buckley Jr., Russell Kirk, Arthur Nock, Henry Chamberlin, and Wyndham Lewis, Regnery also issued dozens of Chicago manuscripts that had little or nothing to do with his conservative outlook. He published books on and by Blacks in the 1950s when others wouldn't. Regnery was the publisher of Mike Royko's and Bob Greene's first books as well as several titles on the city's writers, one on sports, another about gangsters, and a quiet one by Leonard Dubkin about nature in Chicago.

Regnery, a man with politically set views, could also be open-minded. One aspect seemed to be his yin and the other his yang. Part of the reason must be attributed to his love of Chicago. In his own book *Creative Chicago,* he wrote some of the most complimentary words ever penned about the city:

It is characteristic of Chicago that during World War II when the Japanese interred on the West Coast were released, Chicago was one of the few cities willing to accept them, to its great advantage it turned out, since they quickly became productive and useful members of the city. New York and Philadelphia would have none of them. Tolerance, of course, can degenerate into indifference, but Chicago's quality of acceptance of others is one of its better attributes.

## CHICAGO'S LITERARY FUTURE AND COLUMBIA COLLEGE'S *HAIR TRIGGER*

Chicago could not have a more vibrant sign of continued literary energy than *Hair Trigger,* an undergraduate literary magazine published by the students of Columbia College, a fast-growing off-Loop college, that has an open enrollment, attracting its students, for the most part, from the working-class neighborhoods of Chicago and its suburbs.

In 1985, as it had done in 1979, *Hair Trigger* won first prize for undergraduate literary magazines from the coordinating Council of Literary Magazines. *The Harvard Advocate* and *The Amherst Review* placed second and third.

In 1993, *Hair Trigger* received the Gold Crown award from the Columbia University Scholastic Press Association, again competing against the top schools in the country. In 1995, it won the association's Silver Crown award. It has also stacked up innumerable honors for individual stories and essays.

The judges have commented: "Big, energetic, original throughout . . . ," "The writing is thoughtful, realistic, sensual, exciting . . ." and "Each story is fresh, evolving with its own energy, its own design. There is no reliance on formulae or quick tricks."

The school's Fiction Writing Department uses the Story Workshop Method developed thirty years ago by its retired head, John Schultz. Among its graduates is National Book Award winner Larry Heinemann. Through other graduates, the department has spawned four independent, nationally recognized and distributed literary magazines: *Private Arts, Hyphen, Emergence,* and *Sport Literate.*

*Chaos, Creativity, and Culture*

1990s

CHICAGO

# 1990s: A Passion for the Future

By the early 1990s, a new imaginative and expanded architecture enhanced Chicago's skyline in scattered sites throughout Chicago and its suburbs. This transformation marked the city, especially North Michigan Avenue, the Loop, and the areas immediately surrounding it. In a unique 1993 book, *AIA Guide to Chicago,* the city's architectural structures were cataloged and critiqued, not by professional architects but by a caring group of amateurs.

The summertime Chicago Blues Festival in Grant Park started attracting upwards of 500,000 people, while street blues continued to be played on street corners everyday and in empty Maxwell Street lots on Sunday mornings. The *Original Chicago Blues Annual* listed almost 150 spots throughout the city where blues music could be enjoyed regularly.

At the 1995 Modern Language Association convention in Chicago, Columbia College professor Fred Gardaphè created a major stir with a talk on the "new Chicago literature." He might have held up a copy of *Chicago Works: A Collection of Chicago Authors' Best Stories.* It and two sequel collections again remind the public of the wide variety of writers working in Chicago. Its cover listed twenty-one established local authors. The list ranged from the venerable Harry Mark Petrakis, Cyrus Colter, poet Michael Anania, and *TriQuarterly* editor Reginald Gibbons to the less well-known Eugene Wildman and Marsha Froelke Coburn, along with top writers such as Charles Dickinson, Richard Stern, and Larry Heinemann. Other authors of the decade included novelist Richard Martins, Grace Arons, Sara Paretsky, and Tony Ardizzone.

Also in the 1990s, the city lost some of its finest actors, artists, photographers, and creative personalities to

AIDS. Among them was Jim Nash, a force as a publisher and retailer of industrial-rock records.

Lee Godie, a homeless woman who had sold her paintings on the steps of the Art Institute of Chicago for many years was given a well-deserved, twenty-year, retrospective of her work at the Cultural Center. Other homeless individuals earned recognition for their poetry when it appeared in a newspaper, *StreetWise Chicago,* that they themselves sold on the streets of the city.

The 1990s art scene in Chicago, fueled by its deep sources of the creative spirit, continued to produce innovative artists such as the justice-demanding Pearl Hirshfield and the Chicago "dottist" Arlene Marks.

## CHICAGO ARCHITECTURE: A DEMOCRATIC AND COMPREHENSIVE CRITIQUE

Chicago has not only extraordinary architecture but also a populace that has long been unusually involved with the structures that make up and represent the city.

In his 1893 book, *Outré Mer,* a visitor to the city, M. Paul Bourget, wrote about a basic force loose in Chicago:

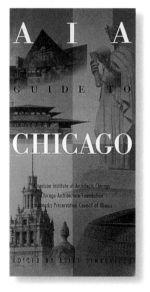

At one moment you have around you only "buildings." They scale the sky with their eighteen, with their twenty stories. The architect who has built, or rather who has plotted them, has renounced colonnades, moldings, classical embellishments. He has frankly accepted the condition imposed by the speculator; multiplying as many times as possible the value of the bit of ground at the base in multiplying the supposed offices. It is a problem capable of interesting only an engineer, one would suppose. Nothing of the kind. The simple force of need is such a principle of beauty and these buildings so conspicuously manifest that need that in contemplating them

you experience a singular emotion. The sketch appears here of a new kind of art, an art of democracy, made by the crowd, an art of science in which the certainty of natural laws gives to audacity's in appearance the most unbridled tranquility of geometrical figures.

Chicago's great architect Louis Sullivan, who wrote a book in 1908 titled *Democracy: A Man-Search,* repeatedly came back to it as his central theme. "Form follows function," he told us, casting out what he called "feudal thinking" and replacing it with the people-centered culture.

Following in this deep-rooted tradition, the Chicago Chapter of the American Institute of Architects issued a book in 1993 entitled *AIA Guide to Chicago.* Edited by Alice Sinkevitch, this modest 541-page guidebook has a brilliant democratic attitude toward Chicago's architecture.

For once those evaluating the city's buildings were not professionals or critics, but "the people" or "the crowd," as Bourget called them. They were the volunteer docents at the Chicago Architectural Foundation, interested amateurs whose most apt qualifications were their love of the city and willingness to be critical.

When this book makes reference in the title to Chicago, it refers to the whole city—the neighborhoods as well as the Loop, the Back of the Yards area as much as Michigan Avenue and the suburbs. As a result, the jewel of downtown architecture is presented in the diadem of the whole metropolitan area.

The following is from the preface written for the book by John F. Hartrey Jr.:

This guide should clarify our vision of Chicago. For the past two years Alice Sinkevitch has sent into our neighborhoods a dedicated troop of scouts who have trained themselves to see the city with open minds and keen eyes. There were a few practicing architects among them, but the majority were amateurs in the most loving sense of the word. Many are docents for the Chicago Architectural Foundation and have had a critical part in creating a political and educational environment in which preservation is possible. Others are dedicated preservationists who have worked within the city government and cultural institutions.

Their greatest accomplishment, however, was not only to have cataloged the city's famous buildings but also to have captured the rich diversity of the built environment. There is a gritty integrity to Chicago's neighborhoods. Their buildings remind us that, until quite recently, architecture was a craft handed down through the generations. Our city was built by people who could not legally be called architects today. This book amply demonstrates that the loss of this craft tradition has not improved the quality of our lives.

This guide is a monument to the breadth of our scouts' interests and to the clarity of their observations. It will help us to see Chicago as a whole and to recognize in it a much richer architectural culture than many of us might have expected.

## PEARL HIRSHFIELD: ARTIST-ACTIVIST

Chicago has long claimed a special position in helping to expand the role of the artist. The challenge to do so is inherent in such battle cries as the "Form follows function" of Louis Sullivan, the "Less is more" of Mies van der Rohe, the "Constructionism is the socialism of wisdom" of Laszlo Moholy-Nagy, the political activism of Richard Wright, and the radical posters of Carlos Cortez.

The 1968 Democratic National Convention was arguably Chicago's most political moment in the twentieth century as the city became a magnet for the radicals of the country and then housed the federal courtroom that passed judgment on their behavior. This trial, in turn, attracted many of the nation's top artists, a number of whom felt that art must interact with the issues of the world as well as the roller coaster of life.

Thirteen such artists—including Claes Oldenberg, Nancy Spero, Leon Golub, and Alexander Calder—contributed original art to create a limited edition portfolio, *Conspiracy: The Artist As Witness.* It was then published, with the proceeds going to help defray the legal expenses of the defendants in the "Conspiracy 7" trial.

The conceiver and organizer of this project was a suburban Evanston woman, Pearl Hirshfield, who is involved personally and through her art in local and global issues. Her installations are intended to bring the viewer inside to experience it. Her various works include the use of light, shadow, reflection, water in motion, and audio text or sound.

One of her installations, *Shadows of Auschwitz,* is a fence-like suggestion of a cattle car, enclosed in a narrow dark space. Revolving searchlight tattoo numbers of concentration camp inmates, collected through personal contact around the world, are written on mirrors on the back of the "fence." A person walking through can see his or her own image covered with tattoos. The work is part of a traveling exhibit and is scheduled to be seen in museums throughout the country.

*Nuclear War Games Plans,* a series of five small works that suggest games of chance, was exhibited in Hiroshima, Japan, by invitation only during that city's 100th anniversary in 1989.

Another installation is a hanging painting-collage with a working replica of an electroshock box and an audio text by an expert on torture. The shock box

**Gene Siskel and
Roger Ebert**

## 1990s

was one of several devices once used by Chicago's white police on African American prisoners to gain confessions. Attention by Amnesty International, a lawsuit, and exhibits of her work all helped move Chicago to fire the police commander of the district involved.

## CHICAGO CRITICS

Chicago has provided an ample number of Pulitzer Prize winners in criticism and commentary since these categories were begun in 1970. The city's critics have tended to be more direct, less pretentious since the days

*Chaos, Creativity, and Culture*

of columnist (and poet) Eugene Field, who was quick to remind those Chicagoans who wanted to put on airs that their city was noted for its stockyards.

In recent years, its winners of the Pulitzer in criticism or commentary have included Mike Royko, then columnist of the *Chicago Daily News;* Ronald Powers, television critic of the *Chicago Sun-Times;* Roger Ebert, movie critic of the *Sun-Times;* the late Paul Gapp, architectural critic of the *Chicago Tribune;* and Clarence Page, columnist of the *Tribune.*

You can add to these such Chicago editorial cartoonists as John T. McCutcheon, Vaughn Shoemaker (twice), Jacob Burck, Bill Mauldin, John Fischetti, Richard Locher, and Jeff MacNelly.

Unquestionably, the best-known Chicago critics are Gene Siskel and Roger Ebert, who critique movies for the *Chicago Tribune* and *Chicago Sun-Times* respectively and who host a top-rated syndicated television show. These two newspapermen have elevated their work to that form of human endeavor that *Webster's Third International Dictionary* describes in defining art as "the conscious use of skill, taste and creative imagination in the practical definition or production of beauty." Their reviews are appreciated because they can understand and enjoy the beauty in moviemaking or be incensed at the lack of it.

Chicago critics in publications such as the *Reader, New City,* the *Windy City Times,* and many local as well as suburban newspapers share the touch of their more-famous colleagues in the *Tribune* and the *Chicago Sun-Times.*

The following excerpt is a pithy example of Chicago criticism. It is from a 1996 review of the movie *Bottle Rocket* by the *Tribune* movie critic, Michael Wilmington: "Watching *Bottle Rocket* doesn't just make you laugh. It makes you smile between the laughs, think beneath the smiles."

## SOME RECENT CHICAGO WRITERS: A ONCE-OVER

**Carol Anshaw:** A literary critic, Anshaw received the National Book Critics Award in 1990 for excellence in reviewing. She also won the Carl Sandburg Award for her novel, *Aquamarine.* Her voice in it has been called "strong"—her theme, "original."

**Jean Auel:** Born and raised in Chicago, Jean Auel attended Jones Commercial High School. After her marriage, Auel moved to Oregon where she received an MBA from the University of Portland. Her innovative and best-selling *The Earth's Children Series* about Ayla, a Cro-Magnon girl adopted by Neanderthals, started in 1980 with *The Clan of the Cave Bear,* followed by *The Valley of the Horses, The Mammoth Hunters,* and *The Plains Passage.*

**Norbert Blei:** Even though Blei eventually moved to Door County, Wisconsin, much of his award-winning writing has been 100-percent authentic Chicago. He grew up in Cicero and knows the Chicago area's ethnicity and style intimately. His short stories, *The Ghost of Sandburg Phizzog,* was a 1987 Pushcart Selection. *Chi Town* is wonderfully biographical. His *Neighborhood* was called by the *New York Times* "a refreshing alternative to much of the autobiographical fiction written today."

**William Brashler:** When reading Brashler's 1976 novel, *City Dogs,* the reader feels like he or she is sampling a stew of such Chicago writers as Lardner,

*Chaos, Creativity, and Culture*

# 1990s

Algren, Petrakis, and Paretsky, with a dash of Mamet. Here's a sample: "So this crowd, with two wagons, three squads, unmarked dicks' cars—and Harry knew them all—double-parked like flies, and the neighborhood hangers-on, some leaning from second- and third-story windows throwing french fries on the cops, drew Harry like the scent of reduced-price port." Brashler is in the mode but not imitative. His first novel, *The Bingo Long Traveling All Stars and Motor Kings* about the African American baseball leagues, had earned him the sobriquet "gifted" and was made into an outstanding movie. His titles include a series of Duffy House baseball mysteries under the pen name Crabbe Evers.

**Philip Caputo:** Caputo's *A Rumor of War,* published in 1977, has been praised as "one of a handful of classic nonfiction accounts of the Vietnam War." John Gregory Dunne wrote in the *Los Angeles Times* of it, "Heartbreaking, terrifying and enraging, it belongs to the literature of men at arms." He has since written novels that have included *Indian Country, Del Corso's Gallery, Horn of Africa,* and *Equation for Evil* as well as his autobiographical *Means of Escape.* As a *Chicago Tribune* reporter in the 1970s, he shared in a Pulitzer Prize for investigative reporting. He also won the Overseas Press Club's George Polk Citation for his work as a foreign correspondent. The *New Yorker* called Caputo, "an extremely good writer."

**Sandra Cisneros:** This promising young writer has moved to San Antonio, but Cisneros is a graduate of Loyola University and has won hard-earned recognition for her works. Notable among them is a book of poems, *Loose Women,* published in 1994 by Knopf. A book that helped her gain recognition and respect was her *House on Mango Street.*

**Cyrus Colter:** Colter, a lawyer who served as a member of the Illinois Commerce Commission, found another life and respect as an award-winning fiction writer. A collection of his stories, *The Beach Umbrella,* won the 1970 Iowa School of Letters for Short Fiction Award. James Hurt, in his *Writing Illinois,* commented that "the characters in *The Beach Umbrella* are as intertwined with the city they live in as the characters in *The Dubliners* are." *The River of Eros,* Colter's first novel, was reviewed in the *Chicago Tribune* as not being "the South Side we are accustomed to reading about, with its gang warfare and street violence. Colter takes us deeper into the ghetto than that."

**Mary Francis Shura Craig:** An extraordinarily prolific writer, Mary Craig also wrote under the names "M. S. Craig" and "Mary Shura." She authored 250 short stories and sixty-nine novels that included ones in the mystery, children's, and historical genres. Her many awards included the Carl Sandburg Literary Arts Award for Children's Literature. She also was the president of the Chicago Chapter of the Mystery Writers of America and gave writing workshops across the country. She died tragically in a home fire January 12, 1991.

**Barbara D'Amato:** Although D'Amato won both the Agatha and Anthony awards for true crime books, she became perhaps even better known for her mystery novels. They feature detective Cat Marsala, and the titles include *Hard Case, Hard Women, Hard Luck, Hard Tack, Hardball,* and *Hard Christmas.* She served several times as president of the Midwest Chapter of the Mystery Writers of America.

**Charles Dickinson:** An editor and writer for the *Chicago Tribune* and before that of the *Chicago Sun-Times,* Dickinson has earned a reputation as compelling novelist with a list of titles that included *Waltz in the Marathon, Crows,* and *The Widow's Adventures.* His novel *Rumor Has It* follows a long tradition of Chicago newspaper writers using their work experiences as the background for fiction.

**Stuart Dybek:** Through his *Childhood and Other Neighborhoods* and *The Coast of Chicago,* Dybek has proven himself one of the city's best-ever storytellers.

James Hurt wrote, "The larger theme that runs through Dybek's stories is the nature of culture." Norbert Blei has said of him: "Dybek is not just good, he's damn good. If you like Algren, Motley, Wright, Farrell, Dreiser, Anderson, Bellow, Petrakis, Brashler's *City Dogs*, the neighborhood columns of Mike Royko, the spirit of Studs Terkel's Chicago voices, then you'll like Dybek. His stories are of that tradition. I'll throw in Sandburg too. I'm talking neighborhood here (Chicago's unique sense of it), and every writer from these parts who comes out alive, eyes wide open, blood gurgling, has a piece of it, a separate vision that marks his words no matter what."

**Joseph Epstein:** Longtime editor of the *Phi Beta Kappa* magazine, *The American Scholar*, Epstein has also taught writing and literature at Northwestern University. As an author, he has fine-tuned the essay as has no other Chicago-area literary commentator since Floyd Dell. His laid-back, thought-provoking pieces have appeared in his magazine and have been published in book form. His short stories, which have been carried in *Commentary* and other magazines, were collected in the 1991 volume *The Golden Boys.*

**Leon Forrest:** Forrest, who was a Northwestern University professor and chairman of African American studies there, got launched as a novelist in the 1970s. A reviewer in *The Atlantic* said his writing style "demonstrates superbly the literary possibilities of the blues idiom." His titles included *There Is a Tree More Ancient Than Eden* and *The Bloodworth Orphans*, followed by his 1983 novel *Two Wings to Veil My Face.* In 1992, he created probably the city's all-time epic (1,200 pages), *Divine Days.* Another Chicago Press, a small publisher, issued it, but a fire at the publisher's then destroyed most of the expensive, limited copies of the novel. Other calamities ensued, including a *New York Times* reviewer dying before completing his write-up. Although the gods seemed to be snarling at *Divine Days,* it is a true celebration of the feel and texture of the much-maligned South Side and ultimately of Chicago. Fortunately, a new edition was published in hardcover and paperback by Norton. Commenting about the favorable reception it has since received, Forrest said, "Nobody seems to notice the length." He died November 6, 1997, of cancer.

**Edith Freund:** Freund was a good book waiting to happen. An excellent magazine writer and journalist, she was asked to research the history of a wealthy and long-prominent family in Chicago. When they backed out, she recycled her material in 1985 into *Chicago Girls,* an excellent novel set in Chicago's 1890s. She has also written *Hazzard & Truelove,* a novel published in 1992 in England.

**Hoyt Fuller:** Fuller's poetry and his 1975 novel, *A Plundered World,* along with his essays, *Introduction Toward a Black Aesthetic,* left road signs for other writers when he died in 1981. They are still being read. Robert L. Harris wrote of him: "He was a consummate Black man with a profound sense of his people's past, a fervent attachment to Africa, a tireless devotion to the Black aesthetic and unflappable dedication to the integrity of his people and their culture."

**Jack Fuller:** On his way to becoming president of the *Chicago Tribune,* Fuller graduated from Northwestern University and Yale Law School, served as correspondent for the *Stars and Stripes* in Vietnam, and worked his way up as a reporter, foreign correspondent, and editor of the *Tribune.* In 1989, he was awarded the Pulitzer Prize for his work as the paper's chief editorial writer. While doing all this, he was also producing novels. These included *Convergence* (winner of the 1983 Cliff Dwellers Award from the Friends of Literature) and *Mass, Fragments,* and *Our Fathers' Shadows.*

**Laurence Gonzales:** A former coeditor of Northwestern University's

# 1990s

*TriQuarterly,* poet, musician, and award-winning journalist, Gonzales has written a number of novels that include *Jambeaux* (which has been compared to Kerouac), *The Last Deal,* and *El Vago.* Much of the power of his writings comes from his refusal to be in the rut of what's expected of a writer.

**Bill Granger:** Granger, from the 1970s through the 1990s, has proved one of Chicago's most respected writers. Using his experiences as a police reporter, he wrote his first novel, *Public Murders.* It won the Edgar Award from the Mystery Writers of America. He followed it with three more novels, *Priestly Murders, Newspaper Murders,* and *The El Murders.* He also wrote eleven *November Man* international spy novels as well as three others, *Time for Frankie Coolin, Queen's Crossing,* and *Sweeps.* Like Algren and Bellow, he has acquainted himself with the city's history and its past writers and has used flavorings from them in almost everything he concocts.

**Andrew Greeley:** If Greeley— Catholic priest, University of Chicago sociologist, and popular genre novelist—is not the most prolific writer Chicago has produced, it is difficult to find anyone who's outdone him. In the early 1980s, he acknowledged that up until that time he had produced more than one hundred books. He has probably more than doubled it since. These include religious and sociological books as well as many, very many, novels. His characters most often are upper-middle-class Catholics or ones fallen away from Catholicism and now confronting the world, the church, various forms of affluence, and sex. While his books do not tend to wind up in the literature per se sections of bookstores, they do often belong in the category of escape literature with a message.

**Bob Greene:** *Chicago Tribune* syndicated columnist Greene is a conundrum that many cannot figure out. His column appears in more than 200 newspapers and he is both loved and criticized for the persistence he often displays in

it. Tom Wolfe said of him, "Bob Greene is a virtuoso of the things that bring journalism alive: literary talent, hard reporting, a taste for mixing it up haunch-to-paunch, shank-to-flank, and elbow-to-rib with people of all sorts." His books, written fast but often well, have been about rock bands, presidential campaigns, Michael Jordan, his small child, and reminiscences of his high school days. His fiction has included *Bagtime,* which was made into a play, and *All Summer Long.*

**Hugh Holton:** Other prominent police and detective writers, including Robin Moore (*The French Connection*) and Sara Paretsky, have favorable things to say about Holton's novels *Presumed Dead* and *Windy City.* He has been a Chicago policeman for more than twenty-five years and writes a column, *Cop's Corner,* for *Mystery Scene* magazine.

**Harry Homewood:** A submariner during World War II, Homewood has used his experiences to create three fine novels, *Final Harbor, Silent Sea,* and *Torpedo.* He was the former chief editorial writer for the *Chicago Sun-Times.*

**Paul Hoover:** In his *Saigon, Illinois,* Paul Hoover joined fellow Chicago authors Phil Caputo, Jack Fuller, and Larry Heinemann in writing memoirs or memorable novels about Vietnam and/or its impact on the Midwest. The protagonist of the novel is doing body counts and alternative service at Cook County Hospital instead of in Vietnam. Hoover's characters and writing share an anarchistic style that has long offered itself as part of the Chicago tradition and heritage.

**Eugene Izzi:** A reviewer in *Chicago Magazine* called lifelong Chicago-area resident Izzi "the new master artist of crime fiction." Helping him earn such praise is a long list of Chicago-based crime novels that several observers have said have gotten better as the list grew longer. It has included *Bad Guys, The Eighth Victim, King of the Hustlers, The Take,* and *Tribal Secrets.* Izzi took his own life in an enigmatic, bizarre episode that reflected his fiction more than anything else.

**Angela Jackson:** A powerful poet, Jackson has received over the last three decades a string of honors that recognize her work. Her volumes of poetry have included *Voodoo/Love Magic, The Greenville Club, Solo in the Boxcar, Third Floor E,* and *The Man with the White Liver.* She was anthologized in *15 Chicago Poets.* Among her dramas are *Witness: A Voice Anthology, Comfort Stew,* and *Shango Diaspora, Dark Legs and Silk Kisses.*

**Stuart Kaminsky:** It doesn't hurt for a successful writer to have an area of specialty. With Kaminsky, a professor at Northwestern and the author of several books on the movies, it was an expertise in films. He used it to create the settings for his Toby Peters mysteries. They avail themselves of settings that have included the sets for *The Wizard of Oz* and *The Maltese Falcon* as well as the life of moviemaker Howard Hughes. Another featured Fred Astaire, Rita Hayworth, and Betty Grable. He also has been an author in the Inspector Rostnikov mystery series that included the acclaimed *Man Who Walked Like A Bear* and the 1988 Edgar-winning *Cold Red Sunrise.*

**Eugene Kennedy:** As have James Farrell, Father Greeley, and many a Chicago politician, Kennedy represents a bridge across the expanse between religious and secular culture in a city where the divisions are, to many, not neighborhoods, but rather parishes. Kennedy, a longtime professor of psychology at Loyola University, is a former Catholic priest. Like Greeley, he has produced a fairly long list of religious and sociological books as well as novels. While Greeley tends more to critique the church and its politics, Kennedy can more often be found looking into the city and its political life.

**Haki Madhubuti:** A multitalented author and poet, Madhubuti has been the publisher of Third World Press books since 1967 and a professor of English at Chicago State University.

His work has appeared in many anthologies and more than a dozen books.

**Grace Marks:** Grace Marks has written a delightful novel about Chicago, *The Dream Seekers,* set at the time of the World's Columbian Exposition of 1893.

**Richard Martins:** A critic and book reviewer with many bylined articles in the *Chicago Tribune,* he wrote two novels. The first, *The Cinch,* is about a man caught in the middle of an FBI plot to bankrupt the kingpins of illegal gambling in Chicago. The second was a well-received Middle Eastern spy novel, *The Sandman.*

**James McManus:** Like many other writers in this listing, McManus showed how one can have talents in a variety of areas. Having served as a teacher at the School of the Art Institute of Chicago, he also has written the book of prose poems *Antonio Salazar Is Dead* and the collection of short stories *Curtains.* His novels include *Chin Music, Out of the Blue,* and *Ghost Waves.*

**Judith Michael:** Using their first names together as a pen name, this Chicago couple—Judith Barnard and Michael Fain—have created a writing team and a list of very readable, best-selling novels that have included their first, *Deceptions,* followed by many more, such as *Possession, Inheritance, A Tangled Web, Sleeping Beauty, A Pot of Gold,* and *Acts of Love.*

**Morris Philipson:** A researcher, publisher, and author, Philipson served as director of the University of Chicago Press. He has written several scholarly books as well as novels. His novels, full of witty and scintillating dialogue, have been highly praised as exposes in such areas as the life of the affluent and the counterfeiting of art. Among these works are *Secret Understandings, The Wallpaper Fox, A Man in Charge,* and *Somebody Else's Life.*

**Michael Raleigh:** Raleigh's Chicago-based mystery novels feature Paul

Whelan. These have included *The Maxwell Street Blues, A Body in Belmont Harbor, Death in Uptown,* and *Killer on Argyle Street.* Just reading the titles gives readers a lesson in Chicago geography.

**Sam Ross:** The author of more than a dozen novels, Ross proved through works such as *Windy City* that he understood not only the mystique of the city, but also about growing up in it and what it can do to you. Other of his books are *The Sidewalks Are Free* and *He Ran All the Way,* which was made into a film starring John Garfield.

**Richard Stern:** One of the city's most respected authors, Richard Stern is recognized as a writers' writer who followed in a tradition that has included many excellent fiction writers who also taught at the University of Chicago. These have included Robert Herrick, James Weber Linn, and Saul Bellow. Among Stern's novels are *Golk, Stitch, In Any Case,* and *Other Men's Daughters.*

**Chuck Stone:** Stone had served as editor of the Black newspapers in New York, Washington, D. C., and Chicago. Holder of a master's degree in sociology from the University of Chicago, he wrote two books on Black power as well as the acclaimed 1970 novel about Chicago politics *King Strut.*

**Susan Sussman:** Sussman is an Evanston author with a talent for food writing. She parlayed it into a 1989 "delicious" novel, *The Dieter,* that piled up sales and won her critical acclaim. She followed it up with the 1991 *Time Off for Good Behavior* and has written a number of children's books.

**Scott Turow:** A vision not inconsistent with the facts one might have of Turow is that of a lawyer riding the Chicago & Northwestern Railroad to his law office and at the same time busily scribbling the words of yet another mystery thriller involving the law. His earlier book, *One L,* about his first year in law school, was compared in a *New York Times* review to "the most absorbing of thrillers." His 1987 novel, *Presumed Innocent,* quickly became a best-

seller and was made into a first-rate movie starring Harrison Ford.

**Judith Wax:** A wonderful humorist and storyteller, Wax wrote *Starting in the Middle,* which was wise, witty, and promising. Sadly, she lost her life in the crash of Flight 191 at O'Hare Field in 1979.

**Richard Whittingham:** A sportswriter and native Chicagoan, Whittingham has written books about the Bears and one about being a Chicago street cop. His novels include *State Street, Their Kind of Town,* and his 1997 *Martial Justice.*

## OUTSIDERS
### Lee Godie

From the late 1960s to the 1990s, Lee Godie attempted to sell her paintings for $5 or $10 apiece on the steps of the Art Institute of Chicago. To many, she was a street person, someone to ignore or to offer a handout. Few saw her as the kind and quality of painter whose works might hang in their homes, in galleries, or on the walls of the Art Institute itself. She resented being viewed as a charity case and would cause a ruckus if someone offered her a dollar or some coins. She saw herself as an Impressionist living in Paris between the wars. When she died March 2, 1994, she had become appreciated as the city's most famous "outsider" artist. At a Cultural Center twenty-year retrospective, it was reported that her

paintings were being resold in galleries for thousands of dollars. Critic David Syrek stated, "Lee's paintings have an intensity not found in a great deal of outsider art. I think they will stand the test of time." In the brochure for her retrospective, critic Gregory C. Knight wrote: "We can speculate that Godie is by now included in more collections in this metropolitan area than any other artist."

## Jim Nash

Technically, Jim Nash was not an outsider, but somehow he also profoundly was one. He was the cofounder in Chicago of the Wax Trax record label and coproprietor of a store with the same name in the 2400 block of Lincoln Avenue. In a 1995 eulogy to him, *Tribune* rock critic Greg Kot wrote, "In 1978, Chicago's music scene became hip again," attributing the change to the arrival that year of Nash and his partner, Dannie Flesher. The pair opened their record emporium on Lincoln Avenue and started a recording company that eventually put out more than 200 labels of early industrial-rock music.

"Jim Nash leaves his mark on Chicago," by Greg Kot:

It's fashionable to say when famous people die that it's the end of an era. In the case of Jim Nash, it would be more appropriate to say that with his arrival in Chicago seventeen years ago an era began and even his death is unlikely to still its growth.

The cofounder of the Wax Trax record label and record store thrived as a behind-the-scenes player, happy to watch his stable of pranksters, misfits, leather boys, computer hackers, and a lone 300-pound female impersonator named Divine get all the glory.

But when Nash, 47, died Tuesday of AIDS, he left behind a legacy larger than the 200 records he put out on the label he co-founded with his friend Dannie Flesher, larger than the aggressive electronic dance music known as industrial with which he was long associated.

But when Nash and Flesher arrived on Lincoln Avenue to open the Wax Trax record store in 1978, Chicago's music scene became hip again. Today Chicago bands are celebrated worldwide for their cutting-edge cool, a renaissance that began when Nash and Flesher blew in from Denver 17 years ago.

"I remember hearing about this wild record store that was coming to town," says Frankie Nardiello of the sublimely garish electrodance band My Life With the Thrill Kill Cult, which debuted on Wax Trax Records in the '80s. "Lets face it, this town was not that hip. Then Jim and Dannie got here."

It was the record store that brought cutting-edge English acts such as Bauhaus to Chicago, and a place where punks, gays, college students and celebrities like Robert Plant came to buy the latest import singles by Joy Division and Throbbing Gristle.

The owners also brought a friendliness and adventurousness to music making unusual for an increasingly corporate record industry. Many of the record store's patrons and employees became the Wax Trax label's artistic backbone, including Al Jourgenson and Nardiello.

"I cleaned house, worked in their store and ran errands for them," Nardiello says. "They were more like parents to me than anything else."

Giving their friends total freedom to create chaos, or whatever else came to mind, in the recording studio, Nash and Flesher fostered a family-of-misfits atmosphere.

"Whatever Al Jourgenson wanted to do, we did," Nash recalled in an interview last winter. "If he wanted to spend $15,000 in the studio making a single for one of his side projects, I was his yes guy."

Although Wax Trax's music was never overtly political, it was fervently anti-establishment, frequently in bad taste, and quite often done with tongue firmly wedged in cheek. Many of its hard-edged discs were released as a reaction to the conservative bent of the Reagan-Bush '80s.

"When you have a real right-wing shift in society, you have a much more entrenched underground," Jourgenson once said in an interview. "The more right wing things get, the more people get ticked off. When you get ticked off, who ya gonna call? Wax Trax Records."

Wax Trax became almost a brand name for a certain attitude. It was this virtue that led TVT Records to bail out Wax Trax when it was forced into chapter 11 bankruptcy in 1993.

"They were one of the few labels that grew up with a singular identity, a spirit that was all their own," says TVT President Steve Gottlieb. "People would buy their records simply because they trusted the Wax Trax label to put out something they would like."

It was music initially dismissed by the mainstream as migraine-inducing noise, but by the '90s the Wax Trax sound pioneered by Jourgenson, Front 242 and Laibach had become commercial gold. Industrial bands such as Jourgenson's Ministry, Nine Inch Nails and Filter had best-selling records. Even Wax Trax was flourishing at the time of Nash's death, with three bands on the Top-10 soundtrack for the *Mortal Kombat* movie and its best selling album ever KMFDM's *Nihil.*

But Nash was no longer the only game in town. The Wax Trax store moved several years ago to a less expensive location on Damen Avenue, and was competing with a host of cutting-edge outlets that had arisen in recent years. The label also had become one of a dozen in Chicago that specialized in underground music.

But the audacity of Nash's original vision remains an inspiration. Impish and garrulous, Nash doted on his grandchild, his artists and his customers, and laughed at those that didn't understand his frequently outlandish records. When he started a folder on the Internet to help communicate with his fellow HIV-positive patients, he did so without fanfare or self-pity. Before slipping into a coma last weekend, he was still cracking jokes and putting people at ease. Like his records, Nash was going full throttle to the end.

## STANZAS FROM *STREETWISE, THE POEMS OF THE POOR*

*StreetWise,* "the newspaper sold by and for the homeless of Chicago," has regularly included poetry. The verses, many written by people who live on the streets, show distinctive and emotional individuals who defy any attempt we might make at stereotyping them. A booklet of these poems from the newspaper, entitled *from hard time to hope,* was sold by street vendors along with the paper. Richard Longworth, one of its editors, decribed the verses as having an "unblinking authenticity, a drive and spirit and true grit that you don't get in poetry anywhere else."

The following three poems are from the booklet:

1990s

## Only for now

by j.b., vendor #2137

Don't call me bro;
Don't call me dude
It's only sir or mister, please
Or, preferably, by my Christian name

I've earned all three titles by
being a survivor
of bruising loss and derivation
for now I don't have money but
    only for now
Anyways, dollars cannot calibrate
    a person's worth
Money is transitory, spiritual resolve
is forever

I'm going to make it!
It's going to get better; my life will heal
For now, I am surviving without
    money but
        only for now
Rather calibrate that I have endured
an assault and battery to my soul
then measured the span of my wings,
how high I aspire to fly

For now, I am expectantly hovering,
but I am
preparing to soar!

## See me!

by chris christmas, vendor #116

Can you see me?

How can you not hear
the cry of my homelessness?
In the wake of the night,
tomorrow's voices are so unclear.

Can you see me?

Some look through me
clear to the wall.
Am I invisible or am I
just so small?

Can you see me?
I've followed the sun
and the sun follows me.
Each homeless night
feels like an eternity.

Can you see me?

I'm the old lady picking
through the garbage,
that old man smashing
the cans,
ours a skid row marriage hoping for a happy
harvest,
and many outreaching
hands.

*Chaos, Creativity, and Culture*

# Chris

by chris christmas, vendor #116

Like the phoenix I've taken the plunge into
the urban wilderness of the streets, with
the hope of becoming a renewed or
restored man while suffering through the
calamity of homelessness. Braking down
to break through, changing the process
instead of just change, for only I can
change me.

There is a song of Chicago, of Bears, Bulls,
Sox and Cubs, of city streets, and lights of elegant night clubs, of Christmas in Chicago.
This is always hard for me, because
Christmas is my name you see. There is a
song of Chicago and these are the Chicago songs for the likes of me.

## TWO CHINESE-AMERICAN CHICAGO POETS
### Li-Young Lee

Li-Young Lee, a resident of the Uptown neighborhood, understands the power of metaphor in poetry and has won the honors that help write his name above almost all the rest.

Among the awards bestowed on him have been a $20,000 fellowship from the National Endowment for the Arts; New York University's Delmore Schwartz Poetry Award for *Rose*, his first book of poetry; the Lamont Poetry Selection of the Academy of American Poets for his second book, *the city in which i love you;* a $25,000 award from the Whiting Foundation; and the $50,000 Lannan Literary Award.

Appropriately, in introducing him, much is usually said about his childhood. He was born of Chinese parents in Jakarta, Indonesia. His father, a for-

mer personal physician in China to Mao Tse-tung, had fled there. He was, however, jailed in Indonesia for his outspoken opinions. He then escaped with his family and traveled throughout the Far East, earning a reputation as a powerful and popular Presbyterian preacher.

The family emigrated to the United States, and Li-Young continued his studies at the University of Pittsburgh and several other universities. He then took up teaching at Northwestern University and the University of Iowa.

His poetry and autobiographical memoir, *The Winged Seed,* both have seen life and its meaning in metaphors and recounted them in a romantic style that uses pauses effectively to let the reader into the poet's thought and feeling processes. His poems and prose are often connected with the memories of his father, as in the following from *the city in which i love you:*

# A Story

Sad is the man who is asked for a story
and can't come up with one.

His five-year-old son waits on his lap.
*Not the same story, Baba. A new one.*
The man rubs his chin, scratches his ear.

In a room full of books in a world
of stories, he can recall
not one, and soon, he thinks, the boy
will give up on his father.

Already the man lives far ahead, he sees
the day this boy will go. *Don't go!*
*Hear the alligator story! The angel story once more!*
*You love the spider story. You laugh at the spider.*
*Let me tell it!*

But the boy is packing his shirts,
he is looking for his keys. *Are you a god,*
*the man screams; that I sit mute before you?*
*Am I a god that I should never disappoint?*

But the boy is here. *Please, Baba, a story?*
It is an emotional rather than logical equation,
an earthly rather than heavenly one,
which posits that a boy's supplications
and a father's love add up to silence.

An article about him by past Illinois State Poetry Society president Glenna Holloway points out that Marr has translated Carl Sandburg, Li-Young Lee, Emily Dickinson, and other American poets into Chinese.

Li-Young Lee said of him, "Bill's poetry is of a certain school—there's a plainness, but there's also a twist in language and perception that he is good at."

## THE NEW CHICAGO WRITERS

Some 10,000 literary scholars attended the Modern Language Association conference in Chicago in the last week of 1995. One of those who received considerable attention was a Columbia College professor, Fred Gardaphè, who presented a paper titled "A Literary Tour of New Chicago."

In the following excerpts from his paper, Professor Gardaphè speaks of the Chicago literary scene:

Behind the Old Chicago facade there is a new Chicago that has yet to be mapped and experienced. One of the better critical discussions of contemporary Chicago literature is James Hurt's *Writing Illinois*. In a section entitled "Writing Chicago" Hurt fills forty pages by reviewing the renaissance, deconstructing archaic archetypes such as Sandburg's "tall bold slugger" and Algren's Uncle Johnson—an ignorant fighter who never wins, who is the victim of a scam or a fixed deal—and Studs Terkel's working class stiffs. Hurt's presentation of alternative Chicago deconstructs the naturalist myth through an analysis of the fiction of Cyrus Colter, Maxine Chernoff, Stuart Dybek, and Paul Hoover. These authors, he writes, "offer powerful counter examples to the naturalistic, white, male tradition described so often in our literary histories." But then he ends his section with a twenty-page discussion of the

**Fred Gardaphè**

**William Wei-Yi Marr**

Chicago world travelers often report being met with the ratatatat sound of a machine gun when it is learned where they are from. Today, in Taiwan, China, or in Southeast Asia, a person might possibly be greeted with the words and verses of William Wei-Yi Marr, retired Argonne National Laboratory engineer and resident of suburban Downers Grove. He has written ten books, nine of them in Chinese, including one entitled *In the Windy City*. They have gone through several editions, and he is studied in literature classes in Taiwan. His volume in English is *Autumn Window*.

canonically correct Saul Bellow, whose monologism he admits to and writing has overshadowed nearly every attempt to be literary in Chicago.

In 1990 Patrick Comiskey, a journalist for the weekly *New City*, called for writers to move beyond realism and begin working in other forms: "To be a writer in Chicago," he wrote, "means to come to terms with a stubborn and increasingly obsolete literary legacy that finds is roots in the city's image itself. For at least to some extent, a true Chicago writer is not only someone who populates his fictions with this place and its people, but someone who has adopted the city's big shoulders mentality as an aesthetic. It's time to let these myths die."

In "Beyond the Realist Aesthetic," Comiskey argues for writing that "is rigorous enough or subtle enough to engage [the] reader's participation," writing that challenges the reader to "think past what he already knows." Such writing comes from the influx of "global literary developments that [set] out to inform our experience of this city. Cultures keep careening forward—does Chicago care to keep up?"

In the scheme of national publishing and book selling, it is as though New York has invaded the Windy City and colonized Chicago literature. Just this year, one of the oldest local bookstore chains surrendered to the East Coast competition. Kroch's and Brentano's, often, but perhaps not often enough, a strong supporter of the local literary scene, retreated from the onslaught of New York City based chain stores who now dictate what books are available to Chicagoans. Barbara's Bookstore, the only local to have survived the invasion, is joined only by smaller stores such as Women and Children First, and Unabridged Books, as the last sanctions for local writers.

The major newspapers such as *Chicago Tribune, Sun-Times,* and journals and magazines such as *The Chicago Review*—the latest issue does make an effort to bring attention to Chicago writers—and *Chicago Magazine,* are of little help, and in fact, act as though they were outpost offices of the occupation forces, evidenced by their ignorance of anything local that has not first "made it" in New York, and the lack of consistent publishing of contemporary fiction and poetry produced by Chicago writers.

## A CHALLENGE FOR THE (NEW) MUSEUM OF CONTEMPORARY ART

Localism in the arts need not mean parochialism. A city's culture does not have to be narrow and confining, but rather can have as its hallmark a respect for a civilization rooted in a particular time and place. An artistic approach that is elitist, one that is imposed, no matter how rich its background, can stifle all around it. The authentic creative spirit

**The Museum of Contemporary Art**

**Stairway at the Museum of Contemporary Art**

## 1990s

malism, post-minimalism, and conceptualism (to name but a few).

The MCA, as it's known, does find room for art created in Chicago and has published a significant catalog, *Art in Chicago: 1945–1995,* a representative look at Chicago artists and schools of art.

Its new building, with five times the space of the one that housed it before 1996 on East Ontario Street, was designed by Josef Paul Kleihues. It is warm, functional, and imaginative in the Chicago tradition. For example, the architect deliberately chose materials that would age with time and let the building change with the face of the city and with our own. Steel spikes have been left uncovered to emphasize rather than to hide the processes of construction. And the "grand staircase" with thirty-two wide stairs that spiral upward, works to create a drama one can have a right to expect fully to find in the exhibits throughout the building.

The challenge for the museum in the coming century is to identify more with its locale, with the rich prairie flowers of Chicago culture, with the indigenous art and expression of its city. The visitor needs a sense—a richer one—that the Museum of Contemporary Art is not in Chicago by accident. Perhaps adding the same two words to its name that the Art Institute has could be the beginning of just such a powerful cultural message.

### ARLENE MARKS

The cornucopia of exciting artists encouraged and inspired by the Chicago Imagists and other inventive and creative people on the art scene in the city includes many who have created their own distinct brand of painting. One of these has been Arlene Marks, whose works often illustrate individuals and their contributions to Chicago's culture.

Marks's "Graceland Series" paintings are based on tombstones and monuments in Chicago's most famous cemetery. The subject matter shows a pattern that can be seen throughout her

comes from inside us. It needs to be nurtured by the soil in which it is planted.

Chicago's cultural institutions uniquely understand this, even if some art museums, opera houses, and symphony orchestras elsewhere do not. In Chicago, the symphony orchestra and the Lyric Opera both proudly carry the city's name as part of their own. The Art Institute of Chicago would very much like people—including local residents—to use the last two words of its name. The Museum of Contemporary Art does not add "of Chicago."

A new structure a block east of the Water Tower—completed in 1996—houses this home for such varied styles of art as modern, postmodern, mini-

*Chaos, Creativity, and Culture*

work, as she has done a panoramic mural on the Chicago Cubs' ballpark, *Wrigley Field in the Round,* and another on the now thirty-years-gone Riverview amusement park. She has also applied her unique style to portraits of noted Chicago characters, as in the one used in this book for columnist Mike Royko.

Her brand, her style, follows the surreal path carved by members of the Chicago School, including Ed Paschke, her former teacher. Her technique employs what she calls "dottism," which has been described as "a kind of pointillism borrowed from the French Impressionists and adapted to her particular Chicago purpose."

Her Graceland Cemetery series toys with humor—one illustration has Elvis Presley in it and is called *Sorry, Elvis— Wrong Graceland.* Mainly, however, the art shows a pride in the real achievements and mysteries of Chicago. Each painting, meanwhile, has a permanent purple glow with which the artist recalls the cemetery's ultimate purpose of housing the dead. She is, one is reminded, a Chicago artist.

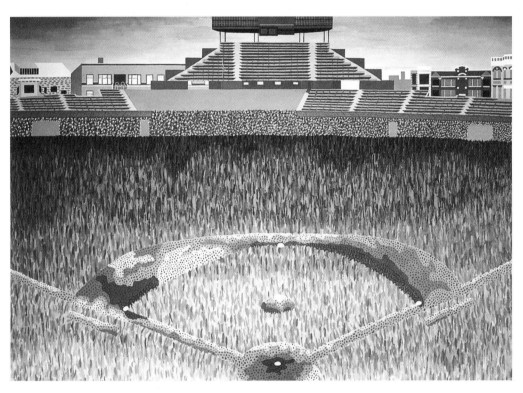

**A panel of *Wrigley Field in the Round,* by Arlene Marks**

# Photographic Credits

The Chicago Arts & Crafts Society Catalogue—Ellen Gates Starr Collection, Special Collection, the University Library, the University of Illinois at Chicago; "Fountain of Time" postcard, Herman Kogan photograph, "Dearborn and Randolph 1909" and "Michigan Avenue, 1923," photographs, and that of the Transportation Building from the World Columbian Exhibition are all from the author's private collection; Hull House Theater logo and photograph of the production of *Alice in Wonderland* and the photograph of Benny Goodman—photographs both from Jane Addams Memorial Collection, special collection of the University Library, the University of Illinois at Chicago. Harriet Monroe, Theodore Dreiser, Hamlin Garland, Henry B. Fuller, Edna Ferber, and Willa Cather, illustrations are all by Scott Holingue from *Creative Chicago,* by Henry Regnery (Chicago Historical Bookworks, 1993); Al Capone, Mary Garden, Ring Lardner, Louis Armstrong, Ben Hecht, Clarence Darrow, Louis Sullivan, William Hale Thompson, Robert Maynard Hutchins, Mary Borden, Maria Callas (photograph by John Austad), Bill Veeck, Katherine Dunham, Gwendolyn Brooks, Richard J. Daley, Hugh Hefner, Claudia Cassidy, Ann Barzel, and Harold Washington photographs are all courtesy the *Chicago Tribune;* The photograph of Anders Zorn's painting of Bertha Palmer, and the *American Gothic* photograph are all courtesy of The Art Institute of Chicago; Gospel singer Robert Anderson performing in *Jubilee Showcase,* 1972, *Stella Dallas* soap opera (courtesy of National Broadcasting Company), and *WLS Barn Dance,* 1944, all courtesy of Chuck Schaden Radio Collection; the Ardis Krainik photograph is courtesy of the Lyric Opera of Chicago; the Polka King album covers courtesy of Jay Jay Records; Frank Lloyd Wright and Carl Sandburg photograph is © Archie Lieberman; Second City early performers photograph courtesy of Second City; Wendy's "Where's the Beef" advertisement is courtesy of Joe Sedelmaier; Nelson Algren's photograph and 1950s street scene are © courtesy of Art Shay; photograph of children playing © courtesy of Ovie Carter; Chicago skyline and Boy and Fireplug © courtesy David R. Phillips; Ruth Page photograph courtesy of Ruth Page Foundation; Mike Royko and Wrigley Field paintings by Arlene Marks courtesy of the artist; "The Wall of Respect," photograph © courtesy of Robert Sengstacke; Carlos Cortez photograph courtesy Carlos Cortez; Larry Heinemann and Fred Gardaphè photographs courtesy of Columbia College; "Shadows of Auschwitz" photograph courtesy Pearl Hirshfield; Siskel and Ebert photograph courtesy of © Buena Vista Television, used with permission.

**Chicago skyline, photograph by David R. Phillips**

*Chaos, Creativity, and Culture*

# Index